NEW MEDIA A
PUBLIC ACTIV

Neoliberalism, the state and radical protest in the public sphere

John Michael Roberts

First published in Great Britain in 2014 by

Policy Press
University of Bristol
6th Floor
Howard House
Queen's Avenue
Clifton
Bristol BS8 1SD
UK
Tel +44 (0)117 331 5020
Fax +44 (0)117 331 5367
e-mail tpp-info@bristol.ac.uk
www.policypress.co.uk

North American office:
Policy Press
c/o The University of Chicago Press
1427 East 60th Street
Chicago, IL 60637, USA
t: +1 773 702 7700
f: +1 773-702-9756
e:sales@press.uchicago.edu
www.press.uchicago.edu

© Policy Press 2014

British Library Cataloguing in Publication Data
A catalogue record for this book is available from the British Library

Library of Congress Cataloging-in-Publication Data
A catalog record for this book has been requested

ISBN 978 1 44730 821 8 paperback
ISBN 978 1 44730 822 5 hardcover

Cover design by Andrew Corbett
Front cover: image supplied by istock
Printed and bound in Great Britain by CPI Group (UK) Ltd,
Croydon, CR0 4YY
The Policy Press uses environmentally responsible print partners

Contents

Acknowledgements

I would like to thank my colleagues in Sociology and Communications at Brunel University, Monica Degen, Sharon Lockyer, Sarita Malik, Sanjay Sharma and Peter Wilkin, for letting me constantly pop into their offices to chat and often laugh about everyday events. I would also like to thank Jonathan Joseph in the Department of Politics at Sheffield University for sending extremely constructive feedback on a preliminary draft of the book. Joseph Ibrahim at Leeds Metropolitan University has been a constant source of friendship and I am grateful for his comradeship and support.

In addition, I have been extremely fortunate to receive support in writing the book by a great team at Policy Press that includes Susannah Emery, Jo Morton, Laura Vickers and Emily Watt, and Judith Oppenheimer, the freelance copy editor. I really appreciate all of their help and feedback, which has been invaluable.

Brunel University allowed me to go on research leave for one term to write some of the chapters for the book, and I am grateful for this time away from normal administrative and teaching duties.

I have used material from a previously published journal article, 'Public spaces of dissent', from *Sociology Compass*, vol 2, no 2 (2008), in different parts of the book. I am grateful to John Wiley and Sons for permission to use this material.

My mother and sister have as always provided me with loads of encouragement throughout the writing process. Extra special thanks go to Lucy for heaps of love and support. I dedicate this book to her.

List of abbreviations

EU	European Union
GSM	global social movement
ICT	information and communication technology
IP	Internet Protocol
NHS	National Health Service
NPM	New Public Management
OECD	Organisation for Economic Co-operation and Development
PFI	Private Finance Initiative
PPP	public-private partnership
SNS	social networking site
UGC	user-generated content

ONE

Introducing new media and public activism

Introduction

For some time there has been a debate about the extent to which people feel disaffected from formal political structures. In the 2001 UK general election, for example, 59.4% of the electorate voted, but this was the lowest turnout since 1918. In subsequent general elections in 2005 and 2010 the turnouts increased to 61.4% and 65.1%, respectively, but this was still below turnouts of between 70% and 80% in previous post-1945 elections (McGuinness et al, 2012, p 13). A survey conducted of 2,273 UK citizens in 2003 by the polling organisation YouGov found that a large number of people (76%) said they felt 'disconnected' from normal parliamentary politics and that more people felt connected with their local GP and local clergyman than they did with their local MP (Coleman, 2005, pp 201–2). Many respondents also considered their elected representatives to be distant from them in the sense that local politicians were not physically 'seen' in their communities engaging with constituents. In addition, MPs were often thought to be untrustworthy, arrogant and even irrelevant.

Under these circumstances, political and social analysts have turned their attention to other possible means to get people connected once again to the political process. Two solutions have regularly been put forward to tackle the perceived decline in formal democratic processes. First, there have been numerous attempts to establish deliberative mechanisms in communities so that ordinary people can gain greater opportunities to have a real say into how their local services and governments operate. From 1997 until 2010, the UK's Labour government introduced a series of initiatives – devolution, the election of city mayors, district assemblies, new ways of voting and so on – with the overall aim of creating more avenues and possibilities for grassroots democratic participation among citizens. One other reason for introducing these schemes was to get ordinary people to engage with representatives from public, private and voluntary bodies in deliberative forums so that they might all discuss local issues that concerned them.

Second, digital technology has been seen by some as a means to get more people involved in democratic processes. Indeed, according to Hands (2011, pp 89–90), the infrastructure of new media is particularly well suited to this task. After all, the network formation of the internet encourages communication between people. What this also entails, according to Goode (2005, p 110), is that digital media involves an endless mediation of information that reinforces, problematises or simply makes us think in different ways about our everyday beliefs, all of which is conducive to a communicative and deliberative way of engaging in democratic practices with one another. Digital technology, moreover, provides a way to improve public service delivery by connecting service providers, officials and ordinary people in a more cohesive manner. Social media in particular is frequently championed as a means to develop these potential benefits. The Haiti earthquake in 2010 was the first time that rescue agencies from the US employed social media to coordinate their activities with other external agencies and also share knowledge about the best way to proceed to alleviate the disaster situation. For example:

> The Centers of Disease Control and Prevention in the U.S. used Twitter to disseminate information about the spread of disease, and found that people passing along the message through the Twitter network amplified the spread of the information. Furthermore, people passed along their own information, which made its way back to CDCP, which then investigated claims and added new disease outbreaks to their database, eventually sending it back through the Twitter feed. (Magro, 2012, p 154)

As this case demonstrates, Web 2.0 sites have the capability to develop lines of communication rapidly around an issue, with certain networks and websites gaining increased value because of this. As such, these sites represent a dynamic form of participating in social and political issues (Chadwick, 2009, p 33).

For some analysts the rise of deliberative democracy and digital technology therefore presents a fortuitous opportunity to introduce new procedures to get people involved in talking about and becoming involved with grassroots political topics. Ackerly, for example, argues that deliberative democratic practices, digital technology and virtual online communities should be brought together in order to create genuine modes of dialogue between individuals that aim to reach compromise and consensus on matters under discussion. In particular, this deliberative model would aim to bring about:

> (1) exchange of information, (2) understanding of one another's values, (3) compromise rather than stratification when pluralism leads to competing views, and (4) consensus when stratification is a result of inadequate communication, not competing interests. (Ackerly, 2006, pp 121)

One notable illustration of this type of online deliberation in the UK occurred during a four-year period from 1998 to 2002 when Parliament organised ten online consultations. The initiative recruited people with a specialist background in specific policy issues that included stem cell research, the draft of the Communications Bill, domestic violence, long-term care of the elderly, e-democracy and women in science and engineering (Coleman, 2004). The rationale underlying these deliberations was to gather evidence from the public about their expertise on the issues at hand, ensure that their voices and opinions were heard in the public domain, give them the opportunity to learn from one another and encourage legislators to listen and respond to a variety of viewpoints about policy areas under discussion.

Generally, Coleman found from two case studies that online consultations did work remarkably well. By actively promoting participation with ordinary people and with experts in a policy area, voices not normally heard by legislators gained recognition in formal parliamentary considerations. Moreover, participants felt broadly connected and they bonded over the issues discussed. And while some participants were unconvinced as to the extent to which some public officials and legislators actually did listen to them, overall deliberation was of a high quality, maintained by references to external sources for evidence, along with the inclusive nature of a discussion open to all who participated. According to Coleman, the consultations were therefore a type of rational democratic deliberation that moved beyond those peer-generated chat rooms based on 'prejudiced and banal political arguments' (Coleman, 2004, p 6).

But, while new media has brought us many innovative opportunities to galvanise democratic participation in society, others have highlighted an altogether more ominous side to digital technology. Unleashing pioneering surveillance devices in civil society, new media is said to subject us to more precise modes of control. Through digital codes, authorities can now anticipate, calculate and predict patterns of behaviour within distinctive 'populations' and thereby foresee and react to specific 'threats' before they occur (Savat, 2013, p 32). At the same time, so some critics argue, these developments have occurred in parallel with the rise of the privatisation of the public sphere. Nowhere is this clearer than in attacks on the welfare state and the rise of the new deliberative agenda.

It was during the 1980s that the Conservative Party headed by Margaret Thatcher started its push to privatise the public sector. Free markets were to be set loose across society, in the 'neoliberal' belief that such policies represent a rational calculative approach to economic decision making and policy intervention (see also Chapter Three). Indeed, the Conservatives were perceptive enough to realise that one way in which they could gain hegemony for the Thatcherite project was to articulate the supposed benefits of privatisation in civil society by highlighting how the range of options and providers that free markets introduce to public services also 'empower' ordinary people. 'Choice' and 'personalisation' in service delivery are two such buzzwords employed by UK governments in the move to privatise the welfare state. Ministers publicly presented them as a means to enable people to meet their own unique (welfare) needs. Digital technology is said to further this agenda, especially by enabling welfare 'clients' to have some deliberative input into service delivery. Digital media allows them to write complaints directly to their local authorities about their respective services, or to gain information about particular service providers to suit their own personal needs.

More critically, however, an increasing emphasis on deliberation from the 1980s onwards has arguably also been part of a neoliberal agenda in which the state engages in negotiation with different public and private partnerships about how best to privatise civil society at local, national and global levels. But while deliberative principles guide much of this thinking these very same ideals often hide and mystify enduring and newly created inequalities between different 'partners', especially between those in power and those in receipt of welfare. As Hirsch notes:

> The current 'realistic' change to 'competitive state' or 'deliberative' concepts of democracy is ... to be seen against this background. These concepts reduce democracy to processes of negotiation within civil society between extremely unequal actors or simply to participatory mobilization for the international competition of localities. (Hirsch, 2003, p 244)

Given this, it is perhaps unsurprising that the promise of deliberative participation by 'customers' and 'clients' of welfare services has also been undermined by digital technology in various ways. In the first instance, new media can help to impose standardised practices on those working in the public sector. '[T]he autonomy of many human service professionals has been reduced through attempts to codify and categorize the competencies they require to complete their work and to quantify and measure the outcomes of professional intervention' (Dutil et al, 2007, p 83). Digital technology also has the potential to change the very nature of universal welfare entitlements. Recent years have seen the pooling together of database information between different 'partners' concerning populations receiving welfare support. Indeed, many voluntary organisations that have contracts with the government to deal with different 'at risk' groups such as the homeless are already compelled to keep surveillance data on the populations they look after. Unsurprisingly, then, there has been an increase in the consolidation of surveillance information among various 'partnerships' about those in sustained worklessness (Pleace, 2007).

Surveillance data on welfare populations likewise breaks down the needs of certain individuals into statistical information that can also then be used to profile the psychological make-up of each welfare recipient. In turn, this data can be used to transform social issues such as unemployment or homelessness into personal issues of why certain individuals cannot find work or shelter. Digital technology therefore plays its role not just in the monitoring of those on welfare benefits but also to change the very notions of what it means to be homeless, unemployed and so on (Marston, 2006). For example, Willse (2008) shows through his study of how the homeless are dealt with in America that quangos and private organisations are empowered to produce statistics through information collated in databases about how particular populations of homeless people in different localities might improve their level of self-sufficiency. Thus, the statistical numbers dominate the real plight of homeless people, which, in turn, psychologises the plight of homelessness by focusing on personal causes as to why these people are homeless in the first place. According to Willse, therefore, the aim is not so much to eradicate the causes of being homeless as it is to manage the homeless. The democratic potential of new media is subsequently turned on its head in so far that digital technology is employed to control and govern specific populations in line with the marketisation of society.

How, though, are all of these various points related to some of the themes to be covered in this book? The first observation to make is that many of the changes just spoken about are related to the broader and more basic observation that the state is hugely important in building, manoeuvring and maintaining the conditions necessary for social and political projects like neoliberalism. While this rudimentary point will be explored in greater depth throughout the book, for now it is simply worth noting that any comprehensive analysis of new media and public activism must ensure that it takes account of wider institutional and socioeconomic practices that are formed through broader capitalist dynamics and processes. And by examining specific communication and media objects of enquiry through the totality of capitalist dynamics we thus have a firmer basis to avoid presenting a one-sided and decontextualised explanation of the democratic possibilities of new media (see also Mosco, 2009, chapter 1).

This brings us to the second related point. The state does not act in an ideological vacuum but, rather, acts through specific political and social projects in civil society and the public sphere in order to gain support from some sections in society. Since the mid-1970s, the state has been used to push forward a neoliberal political and social project in society. Transforming welfare entitlements into a more means-tested workfare version has long been a crucial element to this neoliberal, state-led project. Neoliberal hegemony has thus been gained, in part, by politicians presenting free markets as a way for some individuals to better themselves by moving out from the perceived 'authoritarianism' of the welfare state so that they might embrace the entrepreneurial freedoms offered up by the free markets. Once this much is acknowledged it is easier to appreciate and understand the more general point that the dogged pursuit of free markets and the slow erosion of the public welfare sector requires the backing and support of a strong state.

Third, the discussion so far indicates that states and other political mechanisms can and do implement a neoliberal agenda through digital surveillance systems. As noted, much of the information about the welfare needs of distinct populations is now generated through digital technology, and yet this can actually have the opposite effect to that of deepening and extending democracy in society. Pleace (2007) observes that those welfare recipients subject to these new forms of surveillance often know very well that their civil rights are being eroded, as unaccountable information is being accumulated about them. Through his own research project, Pleace further discovered that service users felt they lacked democratic input over the agencies collecting the information on them. Users were also unsure about whether this information was accurate, how it was being catalogued and interpreted and how they, as users, were being socially constructed by

6

different types of surveillance data (Pleace, 2007, pp 948–53). Far from 'empowering' welfare users through deliberative mechanisms, digital technology regularly adds to feelings of disempowerment for those on benefits. While digital technology thus has the potential to extend the parameters of democracy, it also enjoys the capacity to regulate the behaviour of those in society through new modes of surveillance mediated by state projects.

While deliberative ideals and new media therefore appear as exciting opportunities to establish new democratic capabilities and mechanisms in society, other evidence suggests that they can also have problematic tendencies. More precisely, they are contradictory. On the one hand, they promise greater democratic input and personal freedoms. On the other hand, they seek to govern specific populations in new ways that constrain genuine democratic participation. This is no accident. Neoliberalism is a *contradictory state project* and so it is hardly surprising that these contradictions are reproduced in changing welfare provision and elsewhere throughout society. This, then, is the fourth point we can take from the discussion so far and that will guide the analysis through the book: state projects attempt to govern and regulate specific contradictions in society but will do so in part through discourses of enhancing democracy and through new technologies.

A fifth point concerns the changing nature of the public sphere. Privatising the welfare state has demonstrably altered the public sector. Neoliberalism radically modifies the nature of 'publicness' in civil society. For instance, local authorities in the UK are nowadays legally mandated to work with a number of private bodies in relation to issues around welfare, whether this is related to hospitals or to schools. This in turn transforms at least part of the public sector into a profit-oriented zone for private companies to exploit. Soon, a new public ethos is created in which universal needs are carved up into distinctive segments for the accumulation of capital. The welfare state illustrates this changing ethos remarkably well. Decent welfare provision should be a universal right met through the rational allocation of resources. Yet the extensive privatisation of welfare has instead meant that social divisions and inequalities have increased (see Chapters Three and Four). Welfare provision is thus currently aligned with the growing dominance of the private sector in the public sphere and is founded on the wider 'common sense' belief that individuals should look after their own well-being. The broader observation to make here is that by articulating such hegemonic projects the capitalist public sphere acts as a sort of propaganda machine, to tell us that certain historically necessary contradictions do not exist or that they are unimportant, or that problems accompanying them are being successfully tackled.

The final point is, hopefully, a more optimistic one. The contradictions that result from neoliberalism are refracted in everyday life at different social levels. In their daily lives people experience these contradictions in a variety of ways, whether in the workplace, trying to find a place to rent, buying clothes, watching the TV or travelling on public transport. In all of these instances the contradictions of neoliberalism are present, albeit in varying degrees and in different refracted forms. In this respect, Mikhail Bakhtin is correct when he says that contradictions facilitate a critical and reflexive attitude towards the world. In real life they give rise to 'contradictory opinions, points of view and value judgements' (Bakhtin, 1981, p 281). Correspondingly, everyday beliefs and dialogue carry an antagonistic potential because the opportunity to enter into public dialogue about specific contradictions and their related social problems is a very real possibility. However, these alternative and critical public spheres emerge *in spite* of dominant power relations, not because of them. As we will see, oppositional publics arise through struggles in and against economic and state power and their allies. Therefore, it is more realistic to say that while public deliberation between people is obviously present in society, this will takes secondary place to the constant battle for hegemony and power among contending forces in the *capitalist public sphere* (see also the discussion below).

The rest of this introductory chapter will now outline some of these points in more detail. It starts by saying a little bit more about the relationship between dissent, resistance and new media. From here it discusses why the relatively popular theoretical ideas of the public sphere associated respectively with public deliberative and agonistic counterpublics provide us with useful albeit limited understandings of how the capitalist public sphere in fact operates. This then opens up a space to present an alternative outline of the preferred theoretical perspective of the public sphere that will guide the chapters that follow. This alternative perspective highlights the fact that capitalism contains a number of essential and necessary contradictions that can never be eliminated so long as capitalism remains and that will always constrain the full flourishing potential of people. The chapter concludes by outlining the rest of the book.

Dissent, activist resistance and new media

There are of course many definitions of what constitutes the public. For example, governments commonly construct 'public opinion' around some form of dissent by distinguishing between *the* public and *a* public. The former is constructed as the more 'rational' non-dissenting public, while the latter is constructed as a group of dissenting troublemakers of some sort or another (Warner, 2002, pp 65–6). In making this distinction governments attempt to assemble a 'public sphere' of discussion about certain issues at hand so that they might influence the direction that public opinion takes on specific matters. In turn, others in civil society will read about this debate through different media – newspapers, the internet and so on – and will discuss it with friends, family, acquaintances and strangers. Discussion of this sort can be sociable, but it can also be passionate because it invariably touches on issues around the 'common good' and 'public interest' as well as ideals and values like fairness and justice (see Weintraub, 1997; Roberts and Crossley, 2004). More broadly, these different ways of defining 'the public' lead to disagreements between individuals, groups and politicians about what can be legitimately discussed in the public sphere. As a result, the public sphere also provides a forum for individuals and groups to link certain debates to a wider politics of dissent.

'To dissent' is usually taken to mean to differ in opinion, to disagree with a majority or to take an opposing view to, say, a specific government policy. Dissent thus has a more extensive meaning than resistance. While resistance can be thought of as a type of dissent, not all dissent can be conceptualised as being embroiled in activism or resistance. We can begin to appreciate the difference between the two if we think of the common-sense use of the word 'resistance'. 'To resist' can mean to struggle against, to withstand a force or to refrain from something such as temptation. 'Resistance' thus points towards an *act* of resisting. It can also highlight an active stand against structural sources of power (for example structural forms of inequality) or strategic sources of power (such as a specific policy adopted by a particular government), usually through types of organised political and social activism. Those who hold power, for instance government ministers, also frequently see resistance as a challenge to their own authority, to various degrees (see also below for a further discussion of state power, as well Chapter Three). This being the case, activism, as a moment of resistance, is more often than not conscious of its political and social aims and goals. It can therefore be defined as a politically and socially conscious form of dissent. In other words, there is a conscious *intention* by an individual or a group to engage in acts of resistance through organised activism. Such individuals are therefore *activists* for a specific economic, political or social cause that they believe is worth fighting for in society.

Obviously, this definition of resistance is contrary to many other theories of resistance. Some would argue that in everyday life individuals and groups engage in resistance without necessarily being aware of taking part in it as such. If this is the case, then these individuals and groups are *unintentionally* engaged in resistance. Some people, for example, identify with a particular musical genre and as such adopt specific styles of dress associated with that genre that transgress conventional dress codes. Even though this social group might not consciously believe its acts constitute resistance against formal dress codes, some external observers – academics, journalists, social commentators and the like – might nevertheless interpret its acts as moments of resistance to more conventional habits of dressing in public (Hollander and Einwohner, 2004).

Naturally, the perennial dilemma with claiming that such acts are ones of resistance is that, without a level of intentionality on the part of those thought to be engaged in resistance, such acts must be inferred by the external observer or social investigator in question as constituting resistance. This being the case, a large and diverse range of acts might be said to constitute resistance, making the very concept of resistance a somewhat 'unspecified practice' (Rose, 2002, p 387). 'Dissent' is a useful conceptual tool in this respect because it helps to overcome these problems. It focuses our attention on less political, less organised and less conscious acts of defiance against perceived grievances. And perceived grievances do not have to be directed against *dominant* sources of power to count as dissent, but can be directed at more local causes of frustration, such as disagreeing with fellow school board governors about how a school should be managed (see also Mitchell and Staeheli, 2005).

Dissent, then, relates to on-going, everyday micro-struggles within specific locales in which ordinary people employ resources at hand to make small 'tactical' raids upon the different ways in which our lives are governed (de Certeau, 1984, chapter 3). Dissent belongs to popular lived experience and popular culture because it is embedded within the protracted and drawn-out politics associated with factors such as leisure, voluntarism, friendship networks, family life and 'helping out' in the community. Unlike overt forms of activism in the shape of resistance, dissent consequently blurs the boundaries between everyday life and politics. For example, it is sometimes difficult to assess whether 'helping out' in a community through voluntary activity assumes the guise of dissent or whether it is leisure activity or a combination of both. Looking at dissent in this way is also advantageous because it prompts us to try to ascertain how dissent becomes politically and socially organised, that is to say, how dissent is transformed into intentional resistance. In addition, this approach provokes us to see how resistance moves back to everyday dissent. Often, the boundary between everyday dissent and activism and resistance is a fuzzy and blurred one (as is the division between acceptance of a status quo and dissent against and resistance to it). This is to be expected, because resistance is a form of dissent.

New media has quickly become associated with policies designed to get more people active in voicing their dissent, as well as generating a feeling of being connected with formal political apparatuses. Numerous online chat forums are testimony to this development. Indeed, new media seems to be well suited to giving opportunities for ordinary people to voice their dissent in various ways. First, though, we need to define new media. Flew (2008, pp 1–4) usefully suggests that new media is comprised by three elements: computing and information technology; communications networks; and digitised media and information content in the shape of fibre-optic cables, satellites and so on. One key factor of new media, then, is that it involves a move away from analogue technology to digital technology. A simple recording device illustrates the difference between the two. An analogue recording device translates audio signals – let us say a human voice – into electronic pulses. The recording device therefore produces a sound that is analogous to the original human voice. A digital recorder, on the other hand ,will break a signal down – again, let us say a human voice – into a binary format, or code, based on a series of 0s and 1s. This code is then passed to another place, for example a laptop computer. Once it is at the computer the code can be reassembled into the original signal, namely the human voice. Digital technology thus makes it relatively easy for different media formats and different media materials to converge with one another (Jenkins, 2006). Think of mobile phones. They can read images, take videos, swap pictures with other users, as well as acting as an 'old fashioned' telephone.

As many commentators have noted, new media represents excellent outlets for modes of activism, dissent and resistance. And it does this by opening up public spaces in society for individuals to personalise their grievances. Twitter, for example, grants a platform to ordinary people to express themselves about specific political issues on an emotional level as well as on a governmental level. Hence, in a relatively short space of time new media has nurtured spaces of dissent that are intimately tied up with popular culture and everyday emotional experiences. But, if it is the case that new media does indeed encourage people to reflect on their everyday lives and surroundings we need to move away from a definition that simply equates 'new media' with new technologies. Instead, we need to ask how new media becomes embedded into current social practices and how this creates new social practices. In other words, we need to be aware of the social arrangements and organisations that mediate technology with its specific uses (Sassen, 2002). This is true for any piece of technology and can be demonstrated through a simple illustration. Globally distributed information and communication technologies (ICTs) help financial markets on a daily basis to make highly complex decisions, but it is equally true to say that financial markets also rely on physically located traders and banks situated in specific organisations that operate under and through a number of social norms, rules, resources and so on. In other words, financial markets are reliant on distinctive social arrangements and practices if they are to function with any modicum of success.

The arrival of new media has therefore obviously changed the appearance and shape of the public sphere. It has ensured that the public sphere is truly global in scope and it encourages individuals to speak about their everyday lives on an emotional as well as social level. For many this is an inherent good in its own right. After all, numerous politicians have at least since the 1990s told us how lucky we are to be living in the times of a technological digital revolution that will not just set us 'free' but will also empower us to make decisions about how we are governed. Digital media has therefore become entwined with ideas around participatory democracy. To what extent, though, is it really the case that new media enhance democratic processes in society?

During the 1970s participatory democracy was regularly associated with ideas about ordinary people having political power in workplaces based on a type of economic democracy in which politics and economics would finally be dissolved into one another. Trade unions were often thought to play a key role in helping to foster this type of participatory democracy by empowering the rights of employees and workers in the workplace (see Pateman, 1970). Today, however, people are encouraged to sit back and talk to one another through local community deliberative forums, or to sit in front of their computers to debate on chat forums or to become involved in other similar online activity. We are told that, through this kind of on-going deliberative endeavour, we can simultaneously learn competent skills to help us succeed in civic life. To 'participate' is therefore to 'become' a good, competent subject who learns to the rules for how to engage in public deliberation in civil society but not necessarily in one's workplace (cf. Barney, 2008, pp 99–100). An older belief that participation should include democratic decision making in the workplace alongside other forms of democracy seems quaint and old fashioned in our digital era. At the same time, however, widespread discussions about deeply entrenched contradictions of capitalism and how these might be solved through radical and socialist policies have been side-lined in favour of considerations about how to design deliberative forums that enable groups of people to engage in the liberal ideals of respecting one another's opinions about matters of concern.

Then again, maybe these observations are too pessimistic about the democratic opportunities offered up by ICTs. After all, numerous innovative critical theories have been developed since the 1970s to help us to think about how to reinvigorate democratic opportunities. Perhaps modern-day critical theorists can point us in the right progressive direction with their respective theories about democracy and the public sphere. To gain some answers we briefly turn our attention to two influential current theories of democracy and participation, which are those of deliberation and agonism. While both provide novel and useful theoretical viewpoints about how to reignite democratic possibilities in the contemporary world, we will also see that in their own respective ways both deliberative and agonist theorists tend to repeat a mantra that has taken grip in society of late that implores us to enter into democratic debate with others. It is almost as if we have to participate in the public sphere in order to be seen by others as being good, competent citizens. They cannot therefore but help to construct conceptual devices to make us feel like we should be involved in on-going debate and discussion, and that we should be content and happy when we do so.

Beyond public deliberation and agonistic counterpublics: spatial state regulation of systemic contradictions

One leading theory of the public sphere is an approach known variously as deliberative democracy, discursive democracy and public deliberation. According to the most well-known proponent of this approach, Jürgen Habermas, the public sphere

> can best be described as a network for communicating information and points of view (i.e. opinions expressing affirmative of negative attitudes); the streams of communication are, in the process, filtered and synthesized in such a way that they coalesce into bundles of topically specified opinions. (Habermas, 1996, p 360)

For Habermas, deliberation among individuals on economic social and political issues is a public democratic good because it brings different people, civil society groups, policy makers and politicians together to talk through problems and issues that affect them so that they might then reach a consensus on how to tackle these issues. Naturally, there are areas of disagreement among deliberative theorists over some of the characteristics of a workable public sphere. Some, for example, think that Habermas over-emphasises the correct procedures required for deliberation to occur. For these sympathetic critics, deliberative procedures by themselves will not guarantee that some participants will be able to ascertain outcomes that resolve problematic situations (Bohman, 1996, p 33). In other words, the sort of procedural mechanisms highlighted by Habermas cannot be justified on their own terms but can be so justified only through application in further deliberation. Merely following a procedure, no matter how fair it is, will not influence the quality of the agreement reached between participants or the reasons why they support it (Bohman, 1996, p 51).

Other theorists reject the deliberative perspective because they believe it endorses a liberal perspective that constructs the public sphere in ways that are too homogenous, general and restrictive. Deliberative theory, so the argument continues, tends to bunch different people together in one 'deliberative public'. For some this is problematic because it fails to fully account for the fact that people have different identities based on gender, race, sexuality and so on, which cannot be accounted for in general definitions of 'the public'. Similarly, the deliberative ideal that political activism should be based on, or at least strive for, consensus between relevant individuals involved in a dispute belies the fact that 'consensus' is more often than not a fiction, a construction, that serves to govern, regulate and suppress on-going manifestations and causes of dissent, struggle and contestation (Little, 2007). Think, for a moment, about how notions of the 'public' are tied up with 'public opinion'. Often employed by governments, 'public opinion' is frequently socially constructed and invoked as a means to criticise the political activism and dissent of a group or assembly of persons. A strike or popular protest might be deemed as 'irrational' and/or 'ill-advised' by a government when judged next to what ministers and public officials believe is 'rational' public opinion (Lewis, 2001, p 26). This then opens up the possibility for the state to intervene in a dispute or demonstration in order to curtail and restrict what can be spoken about in society. Overall, therefore, 'consensus in a liberal-democratic society is – and will always be – the expression of a hegemony and the crystallization of power relations' (Mouffe, 2000, p 49).

For these reasons, other theorists have developed alternative frameworks to take account of competing identities, voices and power relations in the public sphere. In this respect some argue that the concept of 'counterpublic spheres' better captures the reality of democratic deliberation. Counterpublics arise 'where members of subordinated social groups invent and circulate counter-discourses to formulate oppositional interpretations of their identities, interests, and needs' (Fraser, 1992, p 123) against dominant mechanisms of governance. Indeed, oppositional identities in different spaces are often formed through and are emergent from counterpublics (Asen and Brouwer, 2001). This leads some to argue further that we need to strive to implement agonistic public spheres.

According to Mouffe (2005), 'agonism' should be contrasted to antagonism. In a situation predicated on antagonism at least two separate individuals or groups see the other as an enemy to be excluded and eliminated from the democratic process. Antagonism is thus based on a 'friend/enemy' distinction in which no common ground can be found between the two (Mouffe, 2005, p 20). By way of contrast, agonism is predicated on the idea that we confront adversaries in the democratic arena, rather than enemies. Unlike enemies, adversaries welcome those democratic apparatuses that encourage a clash of legitimate opinions and democratic political positions. In other words, agonism celebrates pluralism and the right to dissent from deliberative consensus (Mouffe, 2005, p 30). Besides, the very nature of agonism encourages oppositional viewpoints between adversaries. This then sets the stage for real confrontations in civil society and implies that power relations will be confronted and changed if necessary, leading to the institutionalisation of new hegemonic relations in society (Mouffe, 2005, p 53).

Theories of agonistic counterpublics undoubtedly manage to highlight some shortcomings of deliberative theories of the public sphere. However, they are not without their own problems. To begin with, the agonistic model is still reliant on an ideal space of agreement between adversaries, which indeed sounds very familiar to the deliberative ideal of consensus. Mouffe observes, for example, that while adversaries are in conflict with one another they still nevertheless 'see themselves as belonging to the same political association, as sharing a common symbolic space within which the conflict takes place' (Mouffe, 2005, p 20). Like deliberative democrats, then, agonists argue that real social relations of antagonism between different social forces in society need to be 'tamed' through the institutions of civil society, through a 'common symbolic space' (Mouffe, 2005, pp 20–1). This common symbolic space thus acts like a consensus, or a 'conflictual consensus' to use Mouffe's preferred term (Mouffe, 2005, p 52), in so far that inherent antagonistic social relations in society are subjugated under democratic mechanisms. For Mouffe, these democratic mechanisms are legitimate to the extent that adversaries have already agreed upon their form (Mouffe, 2005, p 21). How they have been agreed upon is, however, never entirely clear in her account. Nevertheless, while adversaries engage in a 'conflictual consensus', agonists still maintain that each adversary must recognise the 'legitimate' right of the other adversary to engage in dialogue about their interests.

Problematically, though, while this position might be slightly different to deliberative ideals, it is still based in a liberal perspective in the sense that it retains the classic liberal belief that civil society is a realm of rational dialogue between different individuals. Mouffe after all rejects the Marxist idea that there needs to be a revolutionary break from the existing ideological form of democratic institutions (Mouffe, 2005, p 53). With deliberative thinkers, agonist theorists ultimately hold the belief that different opinions can be reconciled in capitalist society. What they therefore disavow is any notion that capitalist societies are built on necessary and inescapable *contradictions* which will constantly disrupt everyday social relations in various ways. These contradictions can certainly be regulated for specific periods of time but they will nevertheless always remain a constant feature of capitalist societies. The capital–labour relationship for instance is a social relationship of exploitation that structures social life under capitalism. Everyone *must* work for a wage in order to survive and so everyone *must* transform himself or herself into a commodity to be exploited by capital. Through exploited labour, capital accumulates surplus value and generates profit for itself (see Chapter Two for a further discussion about surplus value). This represents a necessary exploitative relationship in capitalism, and without it capitalism as a system would cease to exist. The capital–labour relationship is therefore also an essential and necessary contradiction of capitalism in so far that it can never be extinguished as long as capitalism remains active as a system (for a range of other necessary contradictions embedded in the capital relation, see the list in Jessop, 2002, p 20).

Bhaskar claims the capital–labour relationship in fact denotes a *dialectical* contradiction in which at least one element is '*opposed*, in the sense that (at least) one of their aspects negates (at least) one of the other's, or their common ground or the whole, and perhaps vice versa, so that they are *tendentially mutually exclusive*, and potentially or actually tendentially transformative' (Bhaskar, 1993, p 58; original emphasis). This 'generative contradiction' takes on new guises as it is reproduced into other forms of life – the capitalist state, education, religion, public spheres and so on (Bakhtin and Medvedev, 1978, p 14). '[T]rue individuality and specificity' is thus arrived at 'precisely in living interaction with other phenomena' (Bakhtin and Medvedev, 1978, p 28; see also Bakhtin, 1984, p 28). Contradictions are subsequently not merely discursive constructions but the very material stuff of life and gain an 'objective' existence in concrete social forms, including everyday public spheres (Bakhtin, 1984, p 27).

Four additional points need to be made here in order to avoid any unnecessary confusion about what is being argued. First, nothing in what has been said so far further implies that such contradictions operate, and therefore can be regulated, at a purely abstract level. In this respect, Mouffe is correct to point out that some contradictions are experienced at a concrete level as agonism, as conflicting everyday points of view. But she goes on to argue that these everyday conflicts have the potential to be reconciled with one another. However, from the position put forward by Bakhtin and dialectical theorists of a similar persuasion it is also true to say that agonistic viewpoints will always be underpinned by essential structural contradictions that remain opposed to one another and will never be reconciled.

Second, deeply embedded and necessary contradictions of capitalism are also reproduced at more concrete levels in numerous institutional and organisational strategic forms. After all, while structural contradictions are palpable in the capital relation they nevertheless 'assume different forms and different weights in different contexts' (Jessop, 2002, p 21). Distinctive accumulation and political strategies emerge to govern, order and regulate the different configurations that these contradictions take during specific periods in time and in particular spatial confines. These strategies secure law and order by winning hegemony from sections of the population. Some degree of stability can then also be achieved for fractions of capitalist social relations – for example, financial capital – to operate across society and accomplish certain goals. Hegemonic strategies thereby have the potential to momentarily suspend the more negative effects of a particular set of contradictions for a period of time.

Third, institutional and organisational hegemonic strategies can therefore be conceptualised as being a condensation of different power relations that work through the likes of competing belief systems, compromises, ideologies, groups, rules, social identities, surveillance, ways and means that those in charge administer and manage behaviour, and so on. A person or social group might experience these conflicts as being a series of strategic dilemmas that need resolution in some way or another. Naturally, a hegemonic strategy can attempt to provide such a resolution. Yet, strategic dilemmas might nevertheless still result in the formation of public spheres in institutions and organisations which then go on to open up a space for a range of individuals to engage in critical debate, discussion and dissent. Some of these public spheres could develop to provide a challenge of sorts to a dominant hegemonic strategy. In their everyday lives, people therefore experience underlying contradictions in a number of ways, some of which are mundane, others more spectacular. And by experiencing different contradictions in a multitude of ways people will enter into dialogue about them (Bakhtin, 1981, p 291; see also Voloshinov, 1973).

Fourth, if it is the case that 'abstract' contradictions are reproduced and regulated at a concrete, strategic everyday level, then it follows that one way in which crisis tendencies attached to these contradictions are ordered and suspended lies with *state power*. Indeed, the exemplary strategic regulatory mechanism is that of the capitalist state, which achieves political unity through a condensation and ensemble of social forces and political projects. Poulantzas's description of the capitalist state is useful in this respect. He suggests:

> In locating the State as the material condensation of a relationship of forces, we must grasp it as a *strategic field and process* of intersecting power networks, which both articulate and exhibit mutual contradictions and displacements. (Poulantzas, 2000, p 136; original emphasis)

As a condensation of strategic power relations, the capitalist state also refracts power relations and mutual contradictions at play inside different spatial contexts. For, as we now know, capitalism operates through specific concrete *state projects*, which will attempt to gain hegemony in public spheres located in actual spaces. As a result, the state will also attempt to regulate specific contradictions evident in society by articulating hegemonic strategies in actual public spheres. At the same time, however, while the state might be able to displace some contradictions in certain everyday places, new ones might reassert themselves in other public spaces through a politics of dissent by ordinary people.

Consider the significance of monuments. Many monuments are built in public spaces to embody dominant representations of society. Nelson's Column in Trafalgar Square, London, for example, was originally unveiled in 1844 to celebrate the naval military commander Admiral Horatio Nelson. By constructing this monument through public subscription, the British elite, with support from the state, sought to articulate one of many other spatial strategies during this time to celebrate Britain's imperialist identity in major cities (Watson, 2006, p 131). Indeed, at an imposing 51.6 metres, Nelson's Column helps to anchor and connect together the nearby surrounding spaces in central London through its imperialist and military symbolic markers (see also the excellent discussion by Mace 1976 on this architectural history).

Nevertheless, monuments also regularly act as anchors for alternative public spaces of dissent to emerge in cities. Indeed, they have the potential to make connections with other identities that enter a monument's public space. After all, a single monument is *acted* upon by a plethora of individuals, groups, objects, symbols, utterances and so on, which can alter its material form into a people's history of protest.

> Monumental space permits a continual back-and-forth between the private speech of ordinary conversations and the public speech of discourses, lectures, sermons, rallying-cries, and all theatrical forms of utterance. (Lefebvre, 1991, p 224)

If this occurs, then the popular culture of ordinary people begins to merge into monumental public space. If constructed successfully, such popular public space will condense state strategies into a focal point of dissent by acting as metonymy. 'Trafalgar Square', for example, is both a tourist attraction and a narrative about Britain's imperialist history. Since the early twentieth century, however, many radical social and political groups have appropriated Trafalgar Square in order to stage demonstrations within its spatial confines. By so doing they have subverted its earlier imperialist identity by making it into a public place for protest. 'Trafalgar Square' is, in other words, a dialogical space, a concrete public sphere for debate and discussion, that sometimes offers up a place for individuals to express antagonism towards original and current state strategies to govern this space. In this instance, Trafalgar Square internalises a number of contradictions in its concrete spatial surrounding and reproduces them in unique ways.

For Lefebvre public space is therefore immersed in contradictions and provides potential for ordinary people to author and re-accent their urban surroundings and bring it back into their history, a people's history, at some distance from dominant and state-based narratives. Contradictions in fact open up new opportunities for a politics of dissent to emerge in city places. As Harvey observes: 'Intensifying contradictions within a rapidly accelerating and often uncontrolled urbanization process create all sorts of interstitial spaces in which all sorts of liberatory and emancipatory possibilities can flourish' (Harvey, 1996, p 420). Urban spaces of dissent thus constitute a dialectical unity of dominant and oppositional forces that remain in flux (see Howell, 1993; Mitchell, 1995; Goheen, 1998). Both dialectically fuse into a dialogical struggle with one another.

This dialectical relationship is also at play in new media public spheres. Digital technology both empowers capitalist ideology and destabilises it to some degree. To focus on one at the expense of the other is therefore questionable. More importantly, we cannot assume that the public sphere is automatically a realm that promotes participatory discussion in society, as perhaps some deliberative theorists assume. In many respects, the opposite is in fact often the case. Clearly, the capitalist public sphere is regularly employed as a communication tool for the rich and powerful to try to get us to be good, cultivated and, especially today, competent citizens. They do this by using the public sphere to encourage us to work harder, to respect and accept the rule of law, no matter how unconvincing or repugnant it may sometimes seem to be, and to legitimise appallingly unfair and unequal relationships in society. Naturally, in making these claims I will no doubt be accused of articulating a rather depressing picture of how modern capitalist societies operate in entrapping us in webs of power. Surely when somebody goes on Twitter to complain about a politician they are not merely reproducing existing relationships of power? Of course, I would be rather foolish to claim that ordinary people can never see through or beyond relationships of power. In fact, I do not argue this. My point is, rather, that the public sphere in capitalism is not necessarily orientated in the first instance towards democratic inclusion. That people do however create and use public spheres to advance democratic claims is a consequence of the fact that capitalist societies are contradictory and thereby unstable socioeconomic systems. As a result, they cannot but help to open up spaces for oppositional voices to be heard in the public sphere.

Conclusion: outline of chapters

New media is part of the battle for hegemony in and around political and social projects and has certainly altered the terrain through which this battle is fought. At the same time, new media has to operate through on-going capitalist contradictions that have been with us for years and will always remain with us as long as capitalism is the dominant socioeconomic system. The next chapter starts to think through what this means for an analysis of new media and public activism today. In particular, the chapter critically explores some of the main arguments that claim we now live in a new informational global economy in which 'older' contradictions of 'industrial capitalism' have been transcended. By recourse to some of the ideas of Marx, we will see that it is wrong to make this claim. These 'older' contradictions are in fact still very much with us today even if they have assumed new guises. The chapter thereby argues that Marx's key contribution to critical theory, namely that labour is exploited through the expropriation of surplus value, is still found to be convincing. From here, an alternative Marxist vision of capitalism in the digital and financial era is developed and outlined.

Chapter Three continues this line of thinking in relation to how the contemporary state serves to govern and regulate society in order to secure modes of profit amenable to the financialised form of capitalist accumulation. Neoliberalism is a state project that has helped to open up new places in civil society for financial capital to exploit. In particular, and as the chapter shows, neoliberalism has sought to penetrate the public sector and reorder the public sphere. One customary way the neoliberal state accomplishes these actions is to off-load welfare responsibilities to 'public-private partnerships' (PPPs) in civil society. A typical illustration is the payment by a local authority to a private constructor to build a new hospital. What was once a public welfare initiative – building hospitals by the public sector – is thereby transferred over to the private sector. Without doubt, many PPP schemes often consult local residents about their plans through a community forum of some sort. Key individuals steering the PPP can, however, use the community forum as an opportunity to convince local residents of the benefits to be gained for the public sector by inviting the private sector to take over part of the running of welfare services. Neoliberal ideology is thereby disseminated to public spheres in civil society. At all times the state steers and monitors these activities through a host of governance mechanisms to ensure that neoliberalism does indeed gain and retain hegemony in society.

The chapter goes on to show that the administrative mechanisms of the neoliberal state have also been reorganised by the practical ideology of New Public Management (NPM), which has sought to 'modernise' the way in which government operates. For example, NPM is said by its advocates to have generated greater efficiency and cost savings for local authorities. The ideological themes entrenched in NPM are also important because they help to reorganise the internal administrative mechanisms of the welfare state in ways favourable to neoliberalism and to establish what will be termed as the competent public sphere. Competence is the belief that competitive advantage for an organisation lies in identifying combinations of resources that, when brought together, can accomplish a required outcome. However, these resources need not only be 'hard' resources but can also be 'soft' resources such as knowledge and intellect, affective skills like emotions, values, motivations, or personality traits like faith in one's abilities, and social skills such as a knack for communication. These ideological themes are well matched with a neoliberal agenda to the extent that neoliberalism stresses the benefits to *individuals* if they draw on their own hard and soft skills in creative ways. In this respect, competence is an appropriate ideology for our so-called informational times. In fact, it is now possible to talk of a competent public sphere becoming increasingly dominant in civil society. Nevertheless, the chapter also demonstrates how the competent public sphere reproduces the contradictions of neoliberalism in new qualitative forms. As a result, it is far from being a stable and self-sustaining mode of governance in society.

In Chapter Four, these points are developed and extended to look at e-democracy and public deliberation in the competent public sphere. In particular, the chapter shows that the contradictions evident in neoliberalism and the competent public sphere serve to have negative effects over attempts to build participative public spheres through new media. Given this, the chapter shows that deliberative theorists will always be disappointed by the potential of new media to facilitate opportunities for e-democracy in society. Indeed, given the fact that experiments in and around e-democracy are invariably operationalised within a neoliberal environment, it is almost inevitable that the conditions for 'good' online deliberation between participants on a level of presumed equality will never be successfully realised.

Maybe, though, social media provides a better prospect for democracy and participation. Chapter Five explores this issue and finds that in one respect social media instils a neoliberal subjectivity into people. For example, it encourages individual users to create a brand for themselves based on their 'affectual' traits, as well as social media harvesting this 'affectual' information in order to sell consumer goods to users. This represents a powerful ideological mode of subjectivity. Some studies, for example, show that while users of social media are aware that they are freely giving information of their 'brand' tastes and consumption habits to big media habits, they simply do not care that they are doing so. In this case, then, neoliberal ideology operates through a critical awareness by users.

Certainly, ideology is incredibly important in how neoliberalism operates in civil society, but so too are other material practices. Chapters Six and Seven therefore investigate the relationship between new media and the changing nature of public space. Chapter Six deals with how new modes of digital surveillance alongside conventional police zoning practices have shaped ordinary people's predisposition to become involved in public activism. Chapter Seven continues this investigation by turning to issues around community publics and how they are shaped by the likes of urban regeneration schemes and new gentrified spaces in cities and towns. The chapter also looks at how the monitoring of these spaces by closed-circuit television (CCTV) cameras reproduces social and spatial divisions that hinder the formation and democratic potential of community publics. Both chapters show that state power is at the forefront of the redevelopment and redesign of public space by, for instance, making cities and towns clean and safe for neoliberal investments to take root.

In Chapter Eight, the focus shifts to the role that global social movements (GSMs) have played in expanding and widening the terrain of public activism through new media. Arguably, in fact, GSMs appear to represent *the* archetypal groups that seek to employ new media to push forward social and political campaigns. Their celebrated practice of creating decentralised and horizontal networks of activism seems to fit well with the globally networked character of new media. Through a number of examples that include the Arab Spring, the chapter highlights some positive features to this relatively new type of political and public activism. At the same time, the chapter notes several weaknesses with it too.

This leads to the final chapter. Through the case study of the Occupy Movement, Chapter Nine argues that one positive avenue open for a reinvigorated public activism is for campaign groups to adopt some of the tactics employed by GSMs, while remaining embedded in 'ordinary' local communities. Movements for change must similarly forge links with other established campaign groups in society such as trade unions. In fact, trade unions can focus an activist's mind on the need to combat the exploitative tendencies of capitalism that ordinary people face in their everyday working lives. However, activist movements also need to develop an alternative hegemonic project to that of neoliberalism. Any genuine movement for equality and justice must, simultaneously, be prepared to critique the very source of capitalist power that resides in the exploitation of labour. For this to occur, then, public activists must be ready to articulate a socialist politics in their respective campaigns.

TWO

Creative digital capitalism? Exploitation, information and finance

Introduction

In a speech delivered to the World Economic Forum on 24 January 2008, Bill Gates told his audience that while capitalism had made life better for the world, he was increasingly impatient at the speed of progress. Capitalism is good at harnessing self-interest to generate innovations in the economy, Gates remarked, but often only for those who pay to enjoy the fruits of these innovations. Measures are therefore required to ensure that those who cannot pay can nevertheless gain access to goods and the inventive actions of business. 'Creative' capitalism, according to Gates, is just such a system that has the potential to promote both self-interest *and* caring for others.

> Creative capitalism takes this interest in the fortunes of others and ties it to our interest in our own fortunes – in ways that help advance both. This hybrid engine of self-interest and concern for others serves a much wider circle of people than can be reached by self-interest or caring alone. (Gates, 2009, p 11)

Capitalism can be profit driven and compassionate. We can have our capitalist cake and eat a portion of it but then share the rest to others less fortunate.

In this socioeconomic model 'creativity' is naturally seen to emerge from market incentives provided to 'individuals' so that they can then exploit profitable opportunities that become available. But Gates also alleged that market incentives can be employed to initiate a move towards caring capitalism. How is this so? Ordinary consumers often like to see companies acting in a compassionate manner. They will, therefore, reciprocate by acting positively towards those companies. 'As such', reflected Gates, 'recognition triggers market-based reward for good behaviour' (Gates, 2009, p 10). Free market capitalism can be used to help the less fortunate. Profit maximisation is in everyone's interests.

Gates was, and indeed is, in good company in championing a type of 'creative capitalism'. After all, the concept of 'creativity' is one that has been used by governments for some time now to persuade people that it makes good sense to foster a creative, knowledge-based society. In 1998, for example, Tony Blair's Creative Industries Task Force defined creative industries as:

> Those industries which have their origin in individual creativity, skill and talent and which have a potential for wealth and job creation through the generation and exploitation of intellectual property. This includes advertising, architecture, the art and antiques market, crafts, design, designer fashion, film and video, interactive leisure software, music, the performing arts, publishing software and computer games, television and radio. (Cited in Deuze, 2007, p 55)

'Creative industries' are thus considered to be progressive because they create wealth and jobs, and are thought to be integrally related to knowledge-based activities.

In many respects, New Labour's attempt to fashion creative communities and to give these a thoroughly positive spin was part of an agenda about the advantages and benefits of knowledge-based economies that had already been carved out by other global institutions. For instance, in 1995 the Organisation for Economic Co-operation and Development (OECD) circulated policy documents that set out the gains of knowledge-based economies over traditional manufacturing sectors (Godin, 2006, pp 19–20). Then, at the European summit in March 2000 attended by a number of politicians and policy advisors a statement read:

> The shift to a digital, knowledge-based economy, prompted by new goods and services, will be a powerful engine for growth, competitiveness and jobs. In addition, it will be capable of improving citizens' quality of life and the environment. (Cited in Leydesdorff, 2006, p 15)

A year later the OECD once again claimed that 'symbolic' production – the financial sector, service sector and the ICT industry – had surpassed that of 'physical' production (Warhurst, 2008, pp 73–5).

Some academics too supported, and indeed still support, the idea that advanced economies had made a transition to a new informational and creative capitalism. Manuel Castells (2000) and Richard Florida (2002) are both prominent advocates of this viewpoint. They argue that capitalism has moved away from its industrial Fordist past, towards being a creative 'informational' and 'knowledge-intensive' global economy structured around 'post-bureaucratic' organisational business enterprises and 'learning regions'.

Since the 1990s, then, it seems that a consensus of sorts has been consolidated across sections of the academic, business and political communities. This has been based in part on the idea that industrial capitalism, however defined, is part of a bygone era, of a time that has now been surpassed by informational global capitalism powered by innovative creative clusters that stretch across different spatial scales of the local, national, regional and global. But to what extent are these claims true? Do they present a realistic picture of contemporary capitalism, or are some of them overstated?

The aim of this chapter is to begin to unpack some of the main themes evident in the various arguments put forward that insist that we live in a new informational global economy. What will soon become apparent in the chapter is that an overriding narrative that connects them together is the idea that we are no longer dominated by the social traits of industrial societies. It is for this reason that many of the ideas associated with social theorists related to the industrial age are similarly thought of as having little relevance in our contemporary age. Marx is usually thrown in as a thinker of industrial capitalism, ensuring in the process that his fate is sealed. The most one can say is that Marx has some interesting thoughts about industrial capitalism, but that the main thrust of what he says is inadequate in grasping how capitalism now operates. What, on balance, can Marx really tell us about how people actively create content on social media sites? However, we will see, first, that many claims about the supposed transition from industrial capitalism to informational capitalism are overstated, which then, second, opens the way to re-evaluate some of Marx's core ideas about how capitalism functions. In particular, Marx's key argument, that labour is exploited through the appropriation of surplus value, is shown to be convincing. This, then, further shows the way for an alternative, Marxist-inspired description of capitalism to be presented.

Digital, informational, networked capitalism

In essence, so some argue, what we have witnessed in the last few decades is a move away from the industrial Fordist factories of the past to something more fluid, less structured and inherently global. Populist managerial gurus Ridderstråle and Nordström (2008) argue that such global fluidity has obliterated the divisions between local and global, confirming that capitalism now operates through an array of concrete actors coming together in different interconnected spatial scales.

> There are megastates, such as the EU, APEC, NAFTA; multinational firms that are legally local, but operatively global; global products such as Coca-Cola and the Big-Mac; global super-specialists; and a host of global musicians, consultants, chefs, researchers, actors, and many more. (Ridderstråle and Nordström, 2008, p 92)

Many contemporary theorists agree with this basic premise. Globalisation has demolished spatial scales to such an extent that it is no longer possible to look for underlying causes or structures that give rise to visible events. Instead, we are told that we live in a 'flat' world dominated by the global movement of everyday 'things' – images, the internet, finance, people and so forth. These 'flows' connect, break apart and reconnect through a whole variety of different configurations that are often hard to predict (Latour 2005: 16).

One way in which these processes are bound together is through global communication networks. Indeed, many social theorists today suggest that we live in a 'network' age of 'complexity' and 'fluidity' where social relations express a degree of 'mobility' because they become detached from the constraints of time and space. Castells (2000; 2009), for example, argues that we live in a knowledge-based economy that at the same time has a global reach. At the forefront of the new network society are microelectronic and digitally processed ICTs. Indeed, Castells is adamant that ICTs are the main contributory factor that 'separates, in size, speed and complexity, the current process of globalization from previous forms of globalization in earlier historical periods' (Castells, 2009, p 25). He thus insists that what separates the current form of capitalism from previous forms is that major capitalist players today arrange and manage their businesses by 'maximizing knowledge-based productivity through the development and diffusion of information technologies, and by fulfilling the prerequisites for their utilization (primary human resources and communications infrastructure)' (Castells, 2000, pp 219–20; see also Castells, 2001, p 67).

In their celebrated business manifesto, *Wikinomics*, Tapscott and Williams, like Castells, similarly view knowledge capitalism as opening up new possibilities for decentralised and horizontal firms to prosper. Accordingly, a 'truly global firm' is one that 'breaks down national silos, deploys resources and capabilities globally, and creatively harnesses the power of human capital across borders and organizational boundaries' (Tapscott and Williams, 2008, p 306). McKeown (2009, p 7) claims that this new network economy is comprised of three characteristics: computers, connectivity and knowledge. Computers keep track of stocks and portfolios, while connectivity speeds up the circulation of data across the world. New digital communications transform data more easily into meaningful knowledge for business organisations (McKeown, 2009, pp 12–15). In a similar vein, the business advisor Burton-Jones (1999) suggests that a globally competitive world demands that businesses must transform data and information into usable knowledge through the channels of creation, learning and innovation. Practically, this means that a business organisation must tap into and develop its intellectual capital in its workforce or in the demands and preferences of its customers (Burton-Jones 1999, pp 5–6). Businesses can achieve this goal if they codify knowledge into specific meanings for commercial purposes. Codified knowledge is advantageous in this respect because it enables one to anticipate contingent and uncertain circumstances by constructing representations of possible futures (Leydesdorff, 2006, p 17).

Intangible assets like desires, excitement and passion are also said to be essential components for this type of economic success. As the creative industries guru John Howkins observes, physical goods are undoubtedly crucial for competitive advantage in business, but so too are ideas. Creative industries operate in part through the production of 'possible ideas and people's genius for using those ideas to generate new products and transactions' (Howkins, 2007, p 131). Florida similarly says that creativity shuns bureaucratic organisational behaviour for the belief that economic growth depends on good ideas; economic value originates in the creative ideas that people hold (Florida, 2002, pp 36–7). Creative organisations thus no longer rely only on their physical resources to expand, but instead increasingly draw on both their tangible and intangible capabilities and resources to open up new opportunities.

The idea that intangible resources are critical resources for today's global economy is one that figures strongly in respect of selling products. Lash and Urry, for example, argue that economic life 'is itself becoming cultural and aestheticized' (Lash and Urry, 1994, pp 131–4). As Sennett (2006) points out, standard consumer objects stand out in the marketplace to the extent that they magnify small differences between themselves and similar products. Different cars, for example, have roughly 90% of their 'industrial DNA' in common. Car manufacturers therefore concentrate on marketing the other 10% in order to justify the prices at which their cars are sold (Sennett, 2006, pp 144–5). In other words, it is the brand image that becomes all-important to the marketing of very similar objects.

Some analysts further argue that high-tech expansion of the economy shows that capital can now delink itself from corporeal 'real-life' workplace experiences and instead invest directly in knowledge work, irrespective of where it is materially located. 'Communication support systems – codes, languages, shared meanings – allow knowledge to circulate on its own, independently of fixed capital and legal ownership' (Marazzi, 2008, p 50). However, this also throws up interesting questions about the nature of work today and the changing relationship between digital media, labour and exploitation. It is to this issue we now turn.

Informational capitalism and co-creative 'free' labour

In an informational and networked world, the nature of the capitalist labour process is said to have been fundamentally altered. One key element of this new configuration concerns the changing relationship between production and consumption. Digital media has made it possible for peer-to-peer communities to grow in and around objects of consumption and to evaluate and co-create these objects through their 'affective' investments, like desires and passions. This co-creative labour is seen as a key factor in the rise of the creative industries and informational economies (cf Florida, 2002, p 55).

One illustration is that of Massively Multi-Player Online Games (MMOGs). MMOGs are different to other virtual games to the extent they are an on-going activity that connects together different players across the world. This means that players located around the world can go offline whenever they wish and then return to continue playing the game. In addition, MMOGs require a certain amount of 'affectual' investment from users over how the game in question is constructed. Users and players are, for instance, normally allowed to co-create their own online characters for a particular game within the end user licence agreement and terms of service drawn up by the owners. Users will therefore invest their passions and desires in co-creating their online characters. But, as Herman et al (2006, p 192) indicate, this active on-going involvement between consumers and producers also means that players evaluate MMOGs to the extent that they are allocated some sort of value, often in terms of intellectual property rights, over their input in co-creating and modifying a game. Terms such as 'prosumption' or 'produsage' thereby capture what is unique about these modes of collaboration. Digital networks make it possible for a community of users to employ a collaborative logic among them to design and develop content for a digital product, which they can then all consume (Bruns, 2008, p 19). As Potts et al (2008) observe, creative industries in particular flourish through 'word of mouth, taste, cultures, and popularity, so that individual choices are dominated by information feedback over social networks rather than innate preferences and price signals' (Potts et al, 2008, pp 169–70).

Such examples also point towards new modes of conflict opening up between those that own and control digital media companies and those that unfortunately do not. To understand this let us return to MMOGs. Grimes (2006) documents how players of the MMOG fantasy role-playing game *EverQuest* started to sell their virtual characters, weaponry, magic wands and so forth on eBay. Eventually, this market grew into a $5 million real-profit market. Sony Entertainment, who owned *EverQuest*, took umbrage and in 2000 cooperated with Yahoo and eBay to stop players from buying and selling these virtual goods. Grimes suggests that one reason why Sony took this legal action was not only to enforce its intellectual property rights over this particular game, but also because it wanted to ensure that players still had to take part in the *whole EverQuest* game experience, in order to prolong individual player consumption. By simply buying virtual characters, players could in effect short-circuit the various levels that users have to pass through on *EverQuest* – a practice Sony wished to halt. Of course, the players felt it was entirely legitimate to sell their characters and so on, because they had partly created them. Such examples move Cover (2004) to argue that digital games demonstrate a conflict between the author-industry and audience-user of media texts. The interactivity of digital games empowers audience-users and helps to challenge the narrative of media texts created by the author-industry; game users (implicitly) question the 'voice' of the 'author' of electronic games. According to Cover, this is one reason why digital games are increasingly opening up a field of democratic possibilities for users.

Other theorists go further, arguing that prosumers are illustrative of new modes of exploitation that are increasingly becoming hegemonic in society. In this vein of thinking Fisher suggests that social media presents capital with different outlets for accumulation, 'particularly the production of information through communication and sociability' (Fisher, 2012, p 179). This is a unique form of exploitation. Users willingly give their free labour to co-create social media sites and products but at the same time feel they are in control of what they help to create. After all, users have some influence over their own personal social media web page, feel like they are part of a community and can utilise social media for a whole array of cultural, economic, political or social relationships. Alienation and objectification of activity no longer seems to be present on social media sites, which of course makes it more difficult to detect (see also Chapter Five).

Some post-Marxists espouse a similar view and further argue that prosumption and the like imply that people seem to freely and voluntarily channel their aspirations, desires, narratives and wishes directly into the production of goods (Terranova, 2004). As a result, exploitation occurs through the exploitation of 'immaterial labour'; those personable traits such as 'feelings of ease, well-being, satisfaction, excitement or passion' (Hardt and Negri, 2000, p 293). This might be said to be a total theory of exploitation, to the extent that exploitation is thought to reach into every corner of society. Accordingly, so some insist, what is crucial for capital in our digital world is not the exploitation of productive units of labour from workers as such, but rather a 'multiplicity of factors characterising a social and regional space that transcends the single worker and allows her to create wealth by being *a member of a community*' (Marazzi, 2011, p 95, original emphasis; see also Fuchs, 2010).

Without doubt, all of these perspectives do indeed capture something 'new' about the way in which capitalism operates. Yet, at the same time, many also overstate the degree to which the changes they describe have surpassed 'older' capitalist processes. Normally these accounts juxtapose industrial production, with its repetitive standardised work tasks, to newer, glossy, and digitally augmented work. Contrasting two somewhat static models of capitalism – the old industrial model and the new informational network model – makes it easier to place well-known critical theorists inside one of these models. The most obvious illustration of this move lies with old Marx. Apparently, because Marx developed his main critique of capitalism via his labour theory of value during what is commonly known as industrial capitalism, some contemporary theorists then castigate him as a scholar of an industrial age. For example, Arvidsson and Colleoni claim that Marx could develop his theory of labour exploitation only during industrial capitalism. With arrival of Fordist factories labour was finally 'subdivided into discrete units that lend themselves to be measured and controlled in terms of the productivity of the time deployed' (Arvidsson and Colleoni, 2012, p 139). Such changes opened up the possibility for Marx to devise a measurable theory of exploitation in the workplace. As industrial capitalism has now been transcended by creative informational capitalism, so is it the case that Marx's labour theory of value has finally become obsolete. But is this really the case? We now turn our attention to this question.

Marxist value theory and the question of labour

Certainly, Marx's labour theory of value is one of the most misinterpreted elements of his general oeuvre. Often, this misunderstanding is founded on the belief that Marx works with a concrete theory of labour that can be more properly termed as an embodied theory of value. Arvidsson and Colleoni, for example, unquestionably ascribe this theory to Marx. But what the critics fail to note is that Marx himself sets out to critique this particular labour theory of value. Why does he do this? Normally, an embodied theory of value suggests that the value of a commodity is decided by the quantity of concrete physiological labour needed to produce goods with the knowledge and techniques to hand. A general average of labour-time to produce the good in question is then derived (Saad-Filho, 1997, p 463; 2002, p 10; see also Bonefeld, 2011). For Marx, however, the *historical* peculiarity of capitalism is not that embodied labour constitutes value and profits in society through its physiological characteristics, *but that labour becomes value for others* and is reduced to the status of being a 'thing' in the form of a commodity (Clarke, 1991, p 101).

Unlike the case of an embodied theory of value, Marx is therefore not troubled by the *individual* time each actual labourer works to produce a commodity. His focus instead lies with the *socially necessary labour time*, or abstract labour, taken as a whole to produce commodities. Marx thus argues that what sets capitalism apart from past historical systems is the fact that the whole of social life is transformed into a commodity-producing society. As a result, it is through the exchange of commodities that a labourer discovers whether their individual time spent making an object corresponds to the socially necessary labour time that on average it takes to produce the very same commodity. Exchange therefore represents the constitution of abstract labour in capitalism (Kay, 1979; Saad-Filho, 1997; Heinrich, 2004; Bonefeld, 2010).

This deceptively simple idea provides the basis for Marx's theory of exploitation. Under capitalism labour is a commodity to be traded and sold in the market for monetary wages. By buying the labour power of workers, capitalists can thus extract surplus value from them in a workplace. Surplus value in this respect is the greater sum of value created by labour in the production process than is paid out by capitalists in the form of wages and the purchase of new means of production. However, Marx does not believe that all workers create surplus value. He reserves this category for those workers who labour for industrial capital. Marx says that these workers are productive labour primarily because they help to create the source of wealth, namely surplus value, within capitalism (Marx, 1988, pp 1039–41). Other workers who are employed in commercial sectors like accountancy or retail, or employed in financial sectors like banking, certainly spawn profits for capitalists, but they do not create surplus value.

Marx further argues that while abstract labour, and ultimately human labour, is the source of profits, this detail is mystified in capitalism because wealth is seen to magically spring from commodities and not from labour. As the first sentence of *Capital* reads: 'The wealth of societies in which the capitalist mode of production prevails appears as an "immense collection of commodities"' (Marx, 1988, p 125). Human beings are also transformed into commodities, and for Marx this represents the social basis of power within capitalism. A daily indirect coercion compels each person to convert themselves into commodities by selling their labour power to capital. But this occurs in the first instance without explicitly forcing anyone by violence through state and political apparatuses to become a commodity. Naturally, at the end of the day, if one refuses to sell their labour they will most probably starve or live in rather grim conditions. This 'silent compulsion' of economic relations is part of how capitalism operates, irrespective of individual embodied labour (see Marx, 1988, p 899). Exploitation is therefore embedded in this compulsion. Ellen Wood puts it like this:

> What compels direct producers to produce more than they will themselves consume, and to transfer the surplus to someone else, is the 'economic' necessity which makes their own subsistence inseparable from that transfer of surplus labour. Thus, wage-labourers in capitalism, lacking the means to carry on their own labour, only require them by entering into an exploitative relation with capital. (Wood, 1989, p 53)

Labour's fundamental importance in the capitalist economy fades even further into the background when money is taken into account.

This is because money acts as a universal medium through which commodities exchange with one another. Money therefore appears, albeit misleadingly, to inaugurate exchange without the need of labour. Still, once money is generalised across society as a whole then the absurd nature of capitalism becomes more readily apparent. Capitalism is grounded in a social compulsion, a structural imperative, based on the formula M–C–M1 – money creating a commodity to make more money and so on. This social compulsion is important for capitalism because it ensures that the need to generate profit will always trump the satisfaction of human needs and human values. Scaling back the amount of necessary labour we do, making sure there is less social oppression, clearing up pollution, taking bad managers to task and so on, take second place to the structural need to increase surplus value by embarking on a quasi-autonomous competitive path to exploit labour more 'efficiently' so that it can accumulate money (Albritton, 2010, pp 44–5). More money implies that a capitalist can then purchase new machines and technology to maintain an ever-expanding production of commodities, which in turn lays the foundations to increase relative surplus value (Smith, 2010, p 155).

At the same time, this is an anarchic and uncoordinated system because commodities are produced without thinking about the limits of the market. Remember, the primary incentive for capital is to increase surplus value and to try to overcome the barriers of the market. A vicious circle thus prevails. The more commodities are produced, the more that a competitive pressure drives capital to conform to the external pressure of realising added surplus value. This pressure becomes such that commodities are produced without regard to the limits of the marketplace. Overproduction is the result and a crisis of capitalism the solution (Clarke, 1990–91).

This contradiction will often manifest itself in the sphere of exchange as a crisis of consumption, as the failure to realise surplus value through purchase and sale. Interest-bearing capital, or M–M1 (money making more money), refers to the borrowing and selling of money-capital in order to accumulate surplus value and can be employed to overcome a crisis of consumption and develop new routes for profits (Fine, 2010, p 110). By lending money to an industrialist, interest is gained by a money-capitalist. Surplus value is thus distributed from an industrial-capitalist to a money-capitalist. A money-capitalist can then build and expand lines of credit and other financial mechanisms across society. Capital's aim is to create the illusion that this contradictory destructive structural imperative is both natural and necessary. But how, exactly, is this theory useful for an analysis of contemporary capitalism? To begin to see how it might be valuable we will now consider the state of global finance and its relationship to present-day forms of knowledge.

Value theory, knowledge and global finance

According to some informational and network theorists, the rise of global finance demonstrates that we now live in new networked times. In *Economies of Signs and Space* Lash and Urry go as far as to argue that global finance has been allowed to grow as a separate circuit from industrial capital. Finance now forms its own financial networks that have enabled it to transport financial material or 'traffic' across the globe (Lash and Urry, 1994, p 292; see also Lash and Urry, 1987, pp 207–8; Castells, 2000, pp 147–62). Langley (2008) goes further and insists that the power of financial networks rests in part on the fact they are enacted through financial models that not only 'describe economies … but are intrinsic to the constitution of that which they purport to describe' (Langley, 2008, p 25). For Arvidsson and Colleoni, financial models help to construct 'calculative frames' of 'convention' in financial markets that enable a 'rational analysis' of finance to take shape amongst financial traders, commentators and policy makers. These calculations and conventions in turn guide interpretations of financial data and lead to financial evaluations of companies and goods that can have real effects in stock market prices (Arvidsson and Colleoni, 2012, p 142).

These perspectives on global finance make many astute observations, not least their aptitude and skill to show that economic financial models are socially constructed entities that also help to construct reality. It is wrong, however, to make hard and fast distinctions between 'industrial' and 'financial' representations of capitalism, as some of them suggest. To begin with, it is simply not true to say finance has detached itself from industry, as they argue. Credit, bank capital, finance and speculation are in fact normal consequences of a fully functioning capitalist economy (Albo et al, 2010, pp 33–4). Money, for example, circulates within the boundaries of a more concrete national currency and it can become part of abstract global flows of international currencies, while wages act as a concrete source of demand and credit while being an abstract factor of production, and so forth (Jessop, 2010, p 175; see also Jessop, 2002).

In addition, the idea that finance has separated itself from industrial capital overlooks the fact that many businesses in the service and financial sectors are locked in with the manufacturing sector. 'One of the champions of service science, IBM, generates some 50% of its revenues from the supply of consulting services to other corporations looking to use ICT for business tasks such as inventory management, component purchasing, personnel records, payroll, and customer relations' (Daniels, 2012, p 634). Some of the major new media companies operating today are also not opposed to drawing on 'old fashioned' work practices of employing low-paid workforces to produce their goods. As McChesney notes, Apple employs only about 60,000 people in the US, while indirectly it employs 700,000 people elsewhere in the world. In 2012, it was reported that some of these people worked in factories in China that operated draconian employment practices: seven-day weeks, little or no union protection, extreme overtime and unsafe working environments (McChesney, 2013, p 32).

Furthermore, if one argues, as is the case once again with some informational theorists, that capitalism operates within 'rational' calculative financial frames of convention, then, as Engelen et al (2012, p 367) observe, one arrives at the conclusion that contemporary financial practices are to some degree *predictable* because certain rules of 'convention' are followed by financial actors. Engelen et al, however, suggest this presents a misleading picture of global finance primarily because it is in fact highly *unpredictable*. Financial strategies do not follow a set pattern or logic but more often than not evolve from a set of contingent and volatile circumstances that prove impossible to foresee. Moreover, such unpredictability is deeply embedded in the global financial architecture. To give one illustration, risks are leveraged in many financial deals and financial mechanisms. Credit default swaps are a case in point because they enable a trader to sell insurance on a security and charge interest payments on the underlying security. Financial traders thus gain access to the risks of securities without having to purchase these outright. This has facilitated a boom in these types of financial trading. According to Engelen et al: 'The notional value of contracts outstanding on ... over-the-counter ... derivative markets increased 950% from $72,134 billion in June 1998 to a peak of $683,814 billion by June 2008, before falling back to $614,673 billion by the end of 2009' (Engelen et al, 2012, p 367).

The volatile and unpredictable nature of finance arises because it is a distinct moment in the reproduction of the contradictions of capitalism as a whole. Since the 1980s, interest-bearing capital through financial markets has proved particularly attractive to many companies, mainly because they are able to gain access to money more flexibly and at lower costs compared to regular banks (Ivanova, 2011; Lapavitsas, 2011). Indeed, the UK corporate sector as a whole has been buying and holding financial assets at an increased rate. 'Between 1987 and 2008, net corporate sector acquisition of financial assets was 20% higher than of fixed assets' (Freeman, 2012, p 176). But these developments have given rise to specific ambiguities and dilemmas. Orhangazi (2011) remarks that the creeping financialisation of society through the likes of pension and investment funds has shifted the balance of power in the workplace from managers to financial markets, leading in many cases to an intensification of work practices (see also Chapter Three). For these reasons workers in the US, the UK and elsewhere have experienced steady declines in wages, incomes and wealth in recent decades. To give one illustration, the share of income going to workers has dropped significantly, while the share going to segments of the middle class has increased. This intensification of class politics is readily notable by the following figures from the US:

> In 1976 the top 1 percent of households in the United States accounted for 9 percent of income generated in the country; by 2007 this share had risen to 24 percent ... Between 1989 and 2007, the share of total wealth held by the top 5 percent of wealth-holders in the United States rose from 59 percent to 62 percent, far outweighing the wealth of the bottom 95 percent. (Foster and McChesney, 2012, pp 61–2; see also Chapter Three).

To gain access to money, ordinary workers are thus forced into financial markets through the likes of easy credit, pension funds and second mortgages (Froud et al, 2002, p 127). These interest-wage streams – money gained by people through interest paid from financial mechanisms – then became new income streams for financial traders to make money from, especially through collateralised debt obligations in the shape of mortgage-backed securities (Bryan, 2012, p 55). Many people have thus built up unsustainable levels of debt as they save less and spend more of their disposable income on credit or mortgage repayments. In the US the personal sector debt to disposable income ratio increased from 76.2% in 1988 to 138.4% in 2008 (Turner, 2009, p 71). Such levels of debt have adverse effects on consumption, especially in times of economic crisis when creditors want their money back quickly or when interest rates on loans are raised.

The financial processes discussed so far are also rooted in the production of knowledge and technology in various ways. Unleashing new financial devices created new opportunities in technology. During the technology boom of the mid-1990s to 2000s, venture capital made huge gains in its funds. Roughly, 85% to 90% of these profits were invested in ICT projects. In addition, 'at the peak of the boom the technology stocks represented as much as 35% of total market capitalisation, and internet alone almost 10% (more than a quarter of all technology). It was a process of differential asset inflation' (Perez, 2009, p 784). As Perez goes on to show, the value of technology stocks soared by 300% during 1997–2000. By 2000, technology stocks stood at $5 trillion of $15 trillion total market capitalisation (Perez, 2009, p 784; see also Chapter Four).

Knowledge, technology and finance also reinforce 'conventional' work practices. Those who give their labour 'freely' to help create free and open source software, for example, will often do so 'to signal potential employers as to their employment potential' and demonstrate their set of skills (Ross, 2013, p 219). In other words, they work on free and open source software in order to enter the 'normal' labour market. Indeed, if those who perform 'free labour' for a new media company are not rewarded they may very well engage in disruptive activities against the company in question along 'normal' workplace routes. Van den Broek (2010) illustrates this point through the American internet and media company America on Line (AOL). Before 2005, AOL recruited thousands of volunteers to work on various online activities such as monitoring chat rooms and managing online libraries. Volunteers were in turn granted concessions on AOL accounts for their labour. In 1999 two former 'Community Leaders' launched a class action against AOL on the grounds that they should in fact have been compensated in wages. The case rolled on for many years until finally, in 2010, there was a settlement between Community Leaders and AOL totalling $15 million. Importantly, what this case illustrates is that even so-called 'free labour' of 'prosumers' is still mediated by regular and standard capitalist labour processes concerning wage contracts. This being so, observes van den Broek (2010, p 124), capital–labour relationships are at work in digital informational capitalism even if they are often embodied today in more multifaceted arrangements.

Without doubt, some types of knowledge generated by ordinary people using social media might enter the sphere of productive labour and thereby create surplus value. But it is equally true to say that lots of other everyday activity on social media sites is what might be termed as being unproductive labour in so far that it does not contribute to the creation of surplus value. Naturally, this 'free labour' could very well increase the use value of particular types of concrete labour. It is fairly easy to appreciate how one person who educates themselves at home on how to operate different types of digital media might prove useful to an employer later on. However, this does not mean that this person produces surplus value. The new knowledge they gain at home is a potential use value for an employer and it is a different question as to whether this will result in the person becoming productive labour and thus producing surplus value (Carchedi, 2011, p 224). It is most likely that their knowledge will not become surplus value.

Carchedi is therefore surely correct to observe that it is an exaggeration to argue, as some informational theorists do, that the extraction of surplus value is now located in numerous 'non-factory' spheres of social life. This view assumes that exploitation is with us 24 hours a day and occurs inside and outside the workplace, be it in work-based employment or in spaces of leisure when on social media sites. Yet this clearly is an overstatement, if for no other reason than that it assumes exploitation is channelled equally between work and leisure. Such a view underplays the extent to which capitalists still try to extend and increase the hours of the formal working day and get workers to carry out more tasks during those hours. In other words, exploitation in the workplace is still the preferred method for capitalists to extract a surplus from their workforce (Carchedi, 2011, pp 234–5). 'Creative labour' is thus a complex form of work and encompasses both new, conventional and existing socioeconomic dynamics and practices. As Cohen observes:

> The nature of the market economy, regulatory frameworks, state and employer policies, the organization of industries, wages, and access to union protection, for example, influence workers' actions and experiences. For a full understanding of cultural work, research should integrate an understanding of 'enduring features' of cultural work, such as risk and uncertainty, with historical analysis of the political economic context structuring these dynamics. (Cohen, 2012, p 144)

Conclusion

Knowledge has of course always been important to the development of capitalism. At a relatively high level of abstraction, for instance, capitalism functions through a division between intellectual and manual labour (Poulantzas, 2000). Each capitalist must also invest in new technology alongside research and development in order to remain competitive and to continue to extract surplus value. However, and contrary to what Arvidsson and Colleoni (2012) argue, not all knowledge necessarily creates value. In fact, much of the knowledge created in capitalism is valueless exactly because, once created, it can be easily copied. As Carchedi (2011, p 224) notes, the production of information and knowledge does not have to have any relation whatsoever with so-called free labour. Indeed, the opposite is frequently the case. Intellectual property of corporations is monopolised and strengthened, along with the privatisation of other common spaces such as that of urban public space.

How these processes develop in any one locality, country, region or globally is dependent on a number of mediating factors that operate at meso and micro levels. Indeed, capitalism is distinctive in its need for the regulation of the separate spheres of production, circulation and consumption. Hence, the best approaches to political economy are those that are aware of capitalism's need to *institutionalise* economic relations in order to ensure their reproduction and development. This recognises that economic relations are socially embedded and that their reproduction is dependent on successful forms of institutionalisation and regulation. In particular, this approach quite rightly recognises that the state is the key institutional form of regulation in capitalism, even in our free-market neoliberal age. Deeper economic conditions such as tendencies towards overproduction, stagnation and declining rates of profit thus require institutional, and state, intervention. During the current phase of financial neoliberalism, for example, politicians have sought to use state and governance mechanisms in innovative ways to privatise new areas of civil society. Most obviously, social policy and public services have been subject to privatisation agendas that are then frequently transformed into innovative financial assets and mechanisms to be sold and traded on financial markets (Whitfield, 2012).

Contrary to the claims of the informational literature, then, the state remains at the centre of these strategies, albeit with a changed, more devolved understanding of its regulatory responsibilities. As Jessop (2013, p 12) observes, the contradictions and strategic dilemmas embedded in the very identity of capitalism imply that it will always require agents and groups to gain hegemony in order to pursue and promote economic and political projects and thus to prioritise certain policies over others. Regulation of socioeconomic relations also occurs through cultural, discursive and semiotic material. Politicians and policy makers strategically bring all these together to create representations of the global economy to help to win consent and hegemony for modes of capitalist accumulation.

The next chapter starts to look more closely at how the state is still an indispensable mechanism for the regulation of finance, knowledge and technology. In particular, the chapter will show that the state seeks to justify ideologically and legitimise deep-rooted contradictions and relations of exploitation of financial capitalism through neoliberal and workfare political and social projects. This ideological justification is achieved, in part, through what will be termed as the competent public sphere and its relationship to the workfare state.

THREE

Neoliberalism and new public management: the rise of the competent public sphere

Introduction

This chapter starts to develop and extend the points in the previous chapter so as to move beyond a network approach in order to flesh out a state-centred analysis of the public sphere. In spite of recent communication and technological advances, capitalism is still a system that relies on the state for regulatory assistance to ensure that its inherent crisis tendencies are kept in check. This can be achieved in part through specific state projects that aim to win hearts and minds in civil society for accumulation strategies and for distinctive policy objectives and ideologies. As the chapter shows, one state project that has gained and retained hegemony across the globe at least since the 1980s is that of neoliberalism. According to Harvey (2006), neoliberalism refers to the 'maximisation of entrepreneurial freedoms within an institutional framework characterised by private property rights, individual liberty, free markets and free trade' (Harvey, 2006, p 145). Notwithstanding its advocacy of free markets, neoliberalism is nevertheless equally distinguished by its penchant for a strong state in terms of robust law and order programmes in areas such as crime and welfare (Bonefeld, 2012). Indeed, and as this chapter and other chapters will show, neoliberalism relies on a strong interventionist state to initiate and continue the marketisation of society.

Neoliberalism is also contradictory, and so it always contains a number of ambiguities and strategic dilemmas in the concrete forms it assumes. Take for example the case of the regulation of the media in the UK. The Office of Communications (Ofcom) was formed through the Communications Act 2003. Uniting five regulators under one organisation, Ofcom's remit is to maintain and develop a common approach to broadcasting and telecommunications. As part of this agenda, Ofcom has followed the customary neoliberal policy of nurturing public-private partnerships with relevant bodies and interests in order to 'democratise' the way in which decisions are made for and about the media in Britain. Ofcom thus sees its role as facilitating links and connections between the marketplace and civil society so that the two can work in a harmonious relationship with one another. Yet, as Livingstone and Lunt (2007) note, this throws up various ambiguities and dilemmas. For instance, Ofcom sometimes equates the term 'citizen' with the term 'consumer', ensuring that 'consumer interests' associated with the likes of wants, choice, private benefits, deregulation, are implicated with 'citizen interests' related to the likes of needs, society, rights, the public interest and the correction of market failure. Perhaps it should come as little surprise that the word 'citizen-consumer' has been used by Ofcom to bridge the gap between the two (Livingstone and Lunt, 2007). Civil society groups like the Campaign for Press and Broadcasting Freedom that aim to make corporate media interests more accountable to the public must operate through this neoliberal agenda.

Due to its contradictory nature, neoliberalism requires not only a number of political strategies to try to offset the worse vestiges of these contradictions but also a certain amount of ideological legitimacy and justification to gain hegemony from state administrators and from groups in society. One particular ideology that has been created to win support for neoliberalism within the state is that of NPM. Supporting market-based policies introduced into the state and public sector since the 1980s, NPM claims that it has helped to modernise the way that government operates, especially in respect of greater efficiency and cost savings. The ideological themes entrenched in NPM are also important because they contribute towards the reorganisation of the internal administrative mechanisms of the welfare state in ways favourable to neoliberalism. Importantly, this reorganisation also constructs a novel public sphere in civil society that articulates neoliberal themes to different groups and populations. This public sphere can be termed as the competent public sphere.

The competent public sphere is compatible with the neoliberal state project for a number of reasons. First, it positions a person as being an 'individual' rather than as somebody belonging to a social class or social group with specific needs. This follows neoliberalism's belief in the sanctity of individual self-interests in guiding society. Second, the competent public sphere conveys to people that they need to tap into their own tangible and intangible core competences in order to be successful in society. As well as educational and practical skills, core competences might include using one's emotions creatively to achieve certain goals and cultivate the talent to work well in a team, or the ability to communicate effectively with others. Again, all of this is fairly compatible with a neoliberal agenda to the extent that neoliberalism underlines the importance of people drawing on their own individual skills in creative ways – in the words of that dreadful phrase, 'to think outside the box'– in order to take advantage of opportunities thrown up by contingent market forces. Third, the competent public sphere shuns the welfare state, in the belief that people should look after themselves through honest hard work. This is based in the belief that deregulated labour markets and privatised public and welfare services are a social good and that those who find themselves on welfare require moral discipline and welfare sanctions in order to get them back to work (Wahl, 2011, pp 9–10). Finally, the competent public sphere legitimises the move towards governing and regulating the public sphere in civil society through the likes of public–private partnerships rather than through universal welfare state mechanisms.

The chapter concludes by highlighting some contradictions inherent to the competent workfare public sphere. This will then provide a basis not only to move on to the subject of e-democracy in Chapter Four, but also to examine how the contradictions of neoliberalism and the competent public sphere come to be refracted in experiments to construct digital democracy in civil society. We begin the discussion in the current chapter, though, by first presenting a brief and critical exploration of network approaches to governance and civil society so that an alternative, state-centred analysis can be presented. This will then guide subsequent analysis in the rest of the chapter.

Beyond a network approach to politics: the case for a state-centred analysis

Some claim that networks have spread across society as a whole and in the process have fundamentally changed the way we live, how we experience our environment and how we identify with ourselves and with others. In these networked times 'normal' boundaries in 'modern' societies have become blurred and liquid-like. Numerous people now both work in the 'normal' 9-to-5 linear working day and also check work e-mails and go online for job reasons at different points in the continual non-linear 168-hour week. Through digital technology we can also sit in a physical place to do some work and then leave that place, travel somewhere else and start working again. Freed from spatial ties, digital networks and nodes bring to life new spatial relations in other places and so on (Laguerre, 2004; Sheller, 2004; Hannam et al, 2006).

For Castells, a network society establishes a new type of sociability called 'networked individualism', wherein people 'build their networks, on-line and off-line, on the basis of their interests, values, affinities, and projects' (Castells, 2001, p 131). Rainie and Wellman (2012) similarly suggest that the 'triple revolution' of social networks, the internet and mobile communications has profoundly reshaped society. 'The hallmark of networked individualism is that people function more as connected individuals and less as embedded group members' (Rainie and Wellman, 2012, p 12). Person-to-person interaction is becoming the norm. Mobile phones are a case in point because they allow one individual to talk with another individual almost anywhere in the world. As a result, 'each person has become a communication and information switchboard connecting persons, networks, and institutions' across different spatial scales from the local to the global and from person to person (Rainie and Wellman, 2012, p 55). Performing different expressive identities across multiple spaces, the networked self therefore demonstrates how new technologies have rendered communities more complex – different spheres like work and leisure become increasingly blurred – and yet we all seem more connected with one another in both global and personal terms (Papacharissi, 2011, p 317).

Others follow a network perspective and use some of its key ideas to claim that a new 'decentred' political formation has emerged in many societies based around 'conflicting meanings and beliefs, competing traditions, and varied dilemmas' (Bevir and Rhodes, 2010, p 92). Accordingly, the so-called rise of a network society has reconfigured state capacities around a new policy agenda. For instance Bang and Esmark (2009), influenced by the work of Castells, suggest that 'thick sociability' found in close-knit communities and regulated by nation-states has been replaced by 'thin sociability' centred in a reflexive networked individualism. New public spheres materialise in this network constellation and comprise the likes of grassroots organisations, local institutions, cultural events, expressive identities and political organisations, which all come together in novel network formations (Bang and Esmark, 2009, p 17). Larner and Walters (2004) similarly declare that the state and politics have become more globally networked. Specifically, different 'assemblages' in distinctive locales bring together heterogeneous networks of objects, partnerships, groups and so on, which become contingently enrolled together through discourses, narratives and governance mechanisms. We saw this in Chapter One in relation to the homeless in America, who have recently been assembled as a specific networked population through the likes of digital technology and other public-private partnerships. Once constructed, these socially assembled populations can then be governed by the authorities through specific policy issues and through more precise regulatory mechanisms (Larner and Walters, 2004, pp 508–9).

Without doubt, such perspectives provide valuable insights on the nature of state and governance mechanisms operating today in a new policy landscape. However, they also tend to overstate the changes they describe, or they emphasise some changes at the expense of other, equally important social factors. As Marsh (2011) observes, governance mechanisms are nevertheless located in and attached to *centres* of power that encapsulate but also move beyond local assemblages, networks and webs of beliefs and meanings. More precisely, the state is still a crucial mode of enquiry when governance networks are being explored and investigated. But, if this is the case then we require more knowledge, first, about the historical specificity of the *capitalist* state. We need to ask the question: 'what is peculiar about the social relations of capitalism that gives rise to the rigidification (or particularisation) of social relations in the form of the state?' (Holloway, 1995, p 120).

As we know from the discussion in Chapter Two, the real drive of capital is to increase surplus value through the production of goods, irrespective of the limits of the market. Indeed, such limits are external constraints that capital seeks to overcome. Ever-increasing production certainly leads to innovation as different capitals seek to remain competitive, but this in turn constructs competitive pressure between *and* within workplaces (Gough, 2003). Importantly, these pressures are not merely local occurrences based in concrete networks, mechanisms, narratives or webs of beliefs, but are also embedded in the very foundations of capitalism. In other words, they are structurally inscribed into how capitalism works and reproduces itself as a distinctive historical system and they give rise to strategic policy dilemmas in more empirical contexts.

The state emerges as a political mechanism to regulate these various structural contradictions and strategic dilemmas.

> The conditions under which definite productive forces can be applied are the conditions of the rule of a definite class of society, whose social power, deriving from its property, has its *practical*-idealistic expression in each case in the form of the State … (Marx and Engels, 1994, p 52, original emphasis)

At an abstract level the state achieves its power of practical regulation through its objective separation from civil society and its ability to reconcile the contradiction between competition among particular capitals and capital-in-general (see Clarke, 1988). Ideologically, the power of the capitalist state lies in its capacity to sustain an illusionary community that proclaims that *particular* interests of capital are in fact the *universal* interests of everyone (Bonefeld, 1993, p 48). Both practical and ideological components of the capitalist state come together in its 'legitimate' *administrative* power to govern a nation. In this respect, the state presents itself externally to other states as a distinctive body with a specific culture, nationality and means of regulating socioeconomic activity, and internally to its own population as a complex array of bureaucratic apparatuses, mechanisms and national identity. Taken as a whole, the capitalist state is thus a bureaucratic entity whose power is enshrined in law and order *and* in its capacity to regulate global flows of private credit money, national currency and international money with and against other nation-states and economies (de Brunhoff, 1978, p 41; Bonefeld, 1993, p 101).

It was in the mid-nineteenth century that, observes Picciotto (1991), the modern international state system started to come of age. For example, the Paris Convention for the Protection of Industrial Property (1883) helped to establish an institutional framework for corporate capitalism. In particular, it modernised, harmonised and enforced the global intellectual property rights of corporate capital. Nation-states have therefore always been willing to establish global political and governance mechanisms in order to regulate global relations of production and compete with one other for a share of total global capitalist production and total global surplus value (Corrigan et al, 1980; Holloway, 1995). Far from representing a functional mode of regulation for the economy, the capitalist state is in fact engaged in a permanent offensive of resolving and offsetting the inevitability of crises in the various stages of the circuit of capital. Rising inflation, for instance, is always a real problem that confronts the state, especially if governments purchase means of production and labour power that then negatively affect the balance of payments. Governments, moreover, have to control the flow of money within and between countries so that money capital is converted into productive capital and then back to money capital. But this circuit can always be disturbed by capitalists hoarding money, which causes yet more problems for the state. A state also has to ensure that its workforce remains both competitive and healthy vis-à-vis the populations of other nation-states, hence the requirement of welfare policies. Welfare policies are, though, expensive and might in fact serve to take resources away from maintaining a competitive economy (Burnham, 2006, pp 77–9).

For it to succeed in regulating these contradictions, dilemmas and problems, as well as to win legitimacy from sections of the population for the reproduction of capital, the state will aim to build specific political projects embedded in certain cultural and moral ideals that appeal to targeted sections of a nation's inhabitants. In this respect state projects aim to influence everyday common-sense understandings of the world held by some in society. This can be a particularly difficult task for a state to undertake, especially once it is realised that common sense 'is not something rigid and immobile, but is continually transforming itself, enriching itself with scientific ideas and with philosophical opinions which have entered ordinary life' (Gramsci, 1986, p 326). In order to overcome the conflicts and contradictions inherent in everyday life, and in order to articulate a social and political project that resonates with ordinary lived experience, the state relies on a set of 'organic intellectuals' in civil society that will disperse a hegemonic agenda to different social classes and social groups (cf Poulantzas, 2000, p 32). Organic intellectuals are those individuals, groups and institutions attached to aims and ideals of a specific state project and that try to win enough support within civil society to enable a state project to become hegemonic and thereby assume power. Key individual thinkers, public figures, politicians, religious leaders, think-tanks, public forums and public bodies, and the media, are just some illustrations of organic intellectuals.

A state project is thereby a relatively unified ensemble of different social forces and strategies 'organised around (or at least involved in) making collectively binding decisions for an imagined political community' (Jessop, 2002, p 40). But, as a hegemonic force, state projects are simultaneously 'strategically selective' entities that have different effects upon 'the ability of various political forces to pursue particular interests and strategies in specific spatio-temporal contexts through their access to and/or control over given state capacities' (Jessop, 2002, p 40). Strategic selectivity is dependent on a number of factors. Some important ones include the scope of change that a state undergoes at any one moment in time, the direction of change and whether regularities can be detected as a state is transformed from one regime into another, the tempo of change and whether a state regime evolves over a number of years or whether the transition is more abrupt, and whether change in this instance occurs because of external or internal sources (Buller and Flinders, 2005, pp 530–1). In other words, the nation-state operates within specific institutional arrangements that affect its capacities and capabilities (Lacher, 2003; Chorev, 2005).

Now that the case for a state-centred analysis has been broadly sketched we will begin to explore more closely the state project which has come to dominate the social and political landscape since the late 1970s. Commonly known as neoliberalism, this state project is closely associated with the rise of Thatcherism and Reaganism and their adherence to free markets and a strong, coercive state. An important aim of neoliberalism has subsequently been the rolling back of the Keynesian welfare state through policies such as privatising the public sector, attacking universal welfare payments and boosting consumer demand by prioritising finance over industry (Peck and Tickell, 2002; Jessop, 2003). The next section begins to outline this neoliberal state project in more depth. It does this first by describing some of the more abstract characteristics of the neoliberal project and then highlights a number of its inherent contradictions. Following this, the chapter then shows how neoliberalism has endeavoured to change the public sphere through the workfare state.

Neoliberalism as a contradictory state project

Neoliberal policies have been adapted to suit different contexts, from the neoliberal shock therapy in Russia during the collapse of the Soviet Union, to Atlantic neoliberalism in the UK and US, to privatisation schemes in developing countries, and finally to Nordic neoliberalism (Jessop, 2010, pp 172–4; see also Kiely, 2005). Even so, two broad themes guide much neoliberal thinking: that people interact through their ego and self-interest and that free markets lead to spontaneous order which in turn resolves economic crises and social problems (Birch and Mykhnenko, 2010, p 3). Successive politicians and policy makers have developed these two basic themes into a set of distinctive socioeconomic strategies. Trade barriers need to be lowered, say those besotted by free markets, so that the liberalisation of economic and financial markets can proceed unfettered by excessive global regulation, while anti-inflationary measures must be put in place to avoid wage–price spirals and overloaded governments (Cerny, 2008, pp 18–20). States have thus been made to be ever more dependent on capital investment, which is why so many of them across the globe have given corporations tax breaks, reduced labour and wage costs and minimised regulations on the business community (Farnsworth, 2006, p 80).

To ensure that these conditions are maintained, those who implement neoliberalism are prepared to see some living standards decline and unemployment rise. Indeed, in one respect growing unemployment has been advantageous for free markets because it has weakened trade union influence both in government circles and in the workplace, while it also helped to establish a degree of flexibility in labour markets. Just as importantly, unemployment introduced a certain amount of fear among groups of workers that they might be made superfluous to market requirements. '[J]oblessness and the fear of joblessness became key instruments in the struggle to raise profitability' (O'Connor, 2010, p 698; see also Gough, 2002; Doogan, 2009). Neoliberalism is thereby consistent with a strong state bent on regulating the behaviour of those who are seen to fall outside of the neoliberal project (see also below).

Neoliberalism is of course also compatible with financialisation. In fact, the two work off one another. Neoliberal projects across the world have prepared the way for and have promoted the interests of finance-led accumulation strategies. Deregulating and privatising huge chunks of the UK's public sector, neoliberalism paves the way for private investors to buy and repackage public services for financial markets and investors. These state strategies have thus 'benefited highly leveraged, hypermobile financial capital, rewarding "financial innovation", reinforcing its share of total profits and boosting its ability to displace and defer problems onto other economic actors and interests, other systems and the natural environment' (Jessop, 2012, p 31).

For many years, sections of the media have acted as organic intellectuals in similarly championing the virtues of neoliberal ideals. Indeed, as far back as the early 1970s well-known financial magazines were supporting key neoliberal motifs. Financial responsibility lies at the feet of individuals, the popular magazine *Money* suggested in 1972, but not with bankers or insurance companies. Just as neoliberalism started to gain hegemony during the 1980s, so was it the case that these publications experienced a surge in sales.

> Beginning in the 1980s, most notably, there commenced an extraordinary global expansion of business and financial news coverage of stocks, mutual funds, commodities and other products aimed at individual investors. Investors Business Daily was established in 1984. CNBC launched in 1989 in Englewood Cliffs, NJ; by 2008, it claimed to reach 340 million households worldwide with multilingual channels and sites spanning the globe. Bloomberg News started in 1990; by 2008 it was broadcasting in seven languages and its print news wire reports went to 400 publications in 70 countries; Bloomberg acquired the faltering Business Week in fall 2009. (Chakravartty and Schiller, 2010, p 678)

Through the years, these magazines would continue to support neoliberalism and the financialisation of everyday life. Self-reliance, managing risks and gaining control over one's personal finances are now all understood by various media to be highly positive character traits (Davidson, 2012, pp 11–13).

Even after the 2008 financial crisis these themes remain dominant. In fact, they have been strengthened through new moral beliefs. Some financial companies, for instance, have sought to rebrand their image by stressing their honest virtues that bring them a degree of stability in the financial markets. Such media narratives then allow these companies to distance themselves from recent uncertain excesses of financial capitalism (De Cock et al, 2011). Reality TV likewise has many examples of programmes that articulate neoliberal themes. *The Apprentice* is arguably one of the most obvious illustrations of this, emphasising as it does the need for 'successful' employees to manifest certain individualistic character traits in the workplace, being dismissed if performance is poor, passion, taking calculated risks and a willingness to indulge in expensive consumption if deemed to be a success (Couldry and Littler, 2011).

Some academics nevertheless balk at the idea that neoliberalism is a coherent and pervasive discourse that seeps into our subjectivities (see Barnett et al, 2008; Clarke, 2010). Yet a degree of caution about the coherence and stability of neoliberalism is also found in Marxism, for the simple reason that Marxists see neoliberalism as an inherently contradictory social and political project. On this score alone the belief that neoliberalism is 'coherent' is found wanting. Indeed, for Marxists, neoliberalism is a political manifestation of the system of capitalism, the latter of which is defined by a number of internal and necessary contradictions. Neoliberalism is therefore dialectically connected to the system of capitalism and, at the same time, reproduces the contradictions of capitalism in a new form. Some of these contradictions are now fleshed out in more detail.

- Neoliberals support a strong state that regulates the behaviour of 'irresponsible' workers and trade unions who struggle in and against free market ideology (Bonefeld, 2012). Ultimately, then, neoliberals seek to *depoliticise* democracy in the realm of the economy, believing instead that economic markets guarantee social rights by themselves without the need for a welfare state to guarantee these rights (Glinavos, 2008, p 1097; see also Cramer, 2002; Gough, 2003; Korf, 2006). Minimum state intervention in certain areas of civil society is, however, contradicted by the need to develop interventionist multinational governance to contain, manage and regulate the negative effects of global free trade (see Harmes, 2006; see also other chapters dealing with state regulation). Furthermore, state intervention always runs the risk of *politicising* the incursion of the marketplace in the public sphere, which further contradicts the neoliberal need to depoliticise economic decision making.

- Neoliberal capitalism encourages individuals to finance their own consumption. In practice, though, more people are forced to rely on credit and debt to finance payments for consumer goods (Migone, 2007, p 191). These matters are not helped by successive government attacks on wages. In the 1950s, 1960s and late 1970s the share of national output going on wages in the UK lingered around 58% to 60%. In the 1980s, when Thatcherism took grip on British society, this started to decline, so that by 2008 it stood at 53%; a figure that resembled labour's share in the latter half of the nineteenth century (Lansley, 2012, p 41). These policies contradict the neoliberal injunction that individuals should consume goods.

- If a key refrain of neoliberalism is that people in communities should come together and 'empower' themselves, rather than look to a welfare state for assistance, then the processes noted above will inexorably have negative effects on these practices. For example, neoliberalism privatises essential public services such as that of housing, which in turn institutes levels of competition and segregation among residents for access to these public amenities (McCulloch et al, 2012, pp 1143–5; see also Gough, 2002; Roberts, 2004). In addition, neoliberalism intensifies work practices (see Green, 2006), but this again has detrimental effects on community cohesion because people have got less time outside of work to be involved in community activities.

- Pursuit of free markets invariably strengthens the corporate power of those companies that already dominate particular marketplaces. For example, the revenue of the top 200 corporations in the US has increased, from about 21% of total business revenue in 1950 to around 30% in 2008 (Foster and McChesney, 2012, p 71; see also Tabb, 2005). But this contradicts the idea that markets should be free, and not dominated by a few corporate entities.

- Neoliberalism pushes companies to engage in short-term speculative activity, as witnessed in the 2008 financial crash (see Hassan, 2011). However, this cancels the obligation placed on businesses to build 'partnership' networks with a number of public, private and voluntary organisations rather than rely on the welfare state. This also contradicts the neoliberal directive to encourage businesses to develop networks that draw on extra-economic resources like communities of learning, social capital and trust in order to maintain a high-skilled economy (Jessop, 2000, pp 65–70). To overcome this problem local, and national, governments will often engage in 'fast policy transfer' that imports 'off-the-shelf' solutions in place of incremental policy development (Peck and Tickell, 2002, p 398), which of course contains its own problems, not least its inability to engage in long-term policy considerations.

Since neoliberalism is a contradictory state project, it needs to gain legitimacy in civil society at least from some sections of the population, as well as gaining legitimacy in its own state administrative structure. Neoliberals have tried to gain hegemony in a number of ways, but one in particular stands out. In parallel with the rise of neoliberalism there has been a concerted effort to change the culture and ideology of the administrative structure of the state. After all, if neoliberalism was to become an effective state project it had to reorient the strategic rationale of state mechanisms and departments towards a neoliberal ethos. NPM became the ideological weapon to achieve this ethos in the welfare state.

NPM emerged from rubble of Keynesian demand management. Stagflation had hit major capitalist economies in the 1970s and this led some politicians and policy makers, particularly those susceptible to neoliberal ideals, to raise doubts over a skills-based model of economic development tied to what was seen by some to be an overly cumbersome and bureaucratic welfare state apparatus (Leicht et al, 2009, pp 584–5). Indeed, NPM has become one important way for neoliberals to regulate and mask the contradictions inherent in the neoliberal project and help to prepare the way for a new public sphere. NPM also facilitates the restructuring and reorganisation of the administrative mechanisms of the state in ways favourable to neoliberalism. Before we map out the contours of a new competent public sphere in civil society we therefore need first to give a little more detail about the ideological and practical significance of NPM.

New public management: the ideological and practical reorganisation of state administrative mechanisms

Hood (1991, p 3) claims that NPM is associated with four 'megatrends' that have gained importance in the public sector at least since the 1970s: a reversal of and a decrease in government spending on the public sector; a move towards the privatisation or semi-privatisation of government institutions and the marketisation of public service delivery; increasing use of new digital technology in public service delivery; and promoting a global agenda on public sector management that facilitates inter-governmental cooperation between nation-states.

As these four points indicate, a key ideological theme of NPM is its belief that the boundaries between business and government should be dissolved in order to build an 'enterprise culture' across the public sector. In practice this has meant implementing market-based policies in public services that include cost-cutting, establishing discrete 'enterprise' entities in order to abolish what are seen as bureaucratic conventions, implementing performance-related systems, decentralising structures, contracting out services, and introducing 'customer-focused quality improvement systems' (Box et al, 2001, p 612). A strong managerial current is also evident in the sense that those who champion NPM do so by promoting a vision of management as representing a higher source of knowledge about how to solve problems. Through this knowledge, management can build greater success in service delivery than other professional groups working in the public sector, such as doctors in the UK's National Health Service (NHS) (Lapsley, 2008, p 79). Lapsley further notes that another trait of NPM is the constant necessity to engage in structural reform of public services to help create market-based environment. Even though these reforms are often seen to fail, they nevertheless succeed in placing new performance measures on particular services and help to engineer a competitive environment in different sectors. Audit cultures grow that start to expose public services to new accountancy mechanisms such as pre-arranged targets and value-for-money exercises (Lapsley, 2008, p 88).

But while NPM seemed to offer a panacea for the tribulations affecting the public sector, its advocates also pushed forward a variety of theories as to how best to implement its core principles. NPM is based in rational choice models that suggest that government reforms can be used to get individuals in the public sector to accept market-based principles into their own self-interests in the workplace (Haque, 2007, p 180). Others argued that managers had to be liberated from bureaucratic red tape by decentralising and streamlining decision-making powers. Another group of policy tacticians recommended that the best way forward was to subject public officials to business and market-based principles. Competition became the new mantra for those supporting this latter perspective, not least the idea that markets are wholly efficient mechanisms for allocating resources among populations, so that creating internal markets inside public services makes perfect sense (Terry, 2005, pp 430–1).

A range of organic intellectuals sought to articulate these new ideas in civil society so as to gain hegemony at both national and global levels.

New Right think-tanks in the UK like the Adam Smith Institute were, by the 1980s, arguing that the British public sector should be subject to new business and market-based ideas. 'Competitive advantage', based on Michael Porter's (1985) idea that to remain competitive firms should first gain and then exploit a value that their competitors lacked, was one influential strategy they pushed forward. In particular, they were drawn to Porter's belief that constant innovation was at the heart of creating competitive advantage for organisations and the public sector. Releasing a competitive ethos into the public sector therefore came to be seen as a positive way to improve efficiency in the delivery of public services (Osborne and Brown, 2011, p 1337). New Labour took forward these ideals in various policy documents. The *Modernising Government* White Paper in 1999, for example, stressed that public services need to embark on a journey of continuous flexible innovation. Four years later, new economy guru Geoff Mulgan was advising the Blair government that innovation and the ceaseless striving for new ideas should underpin government activity and policy (Osborne and Brown, 2011, pp 1338–9).

At a global level, NPM thinking started to emerge in international policy statements dating back as far as 1979. During this time a major international conference in Madrid – Managing Change in Public Administration – placed the idea that there was a crisis in public management on the agenda for developing nations. Organised under the auspices of the OECD, the conference in part explored and debated President Carter's Civil Service Reform Act (1979). This Act had underlined the importance of establishing management flexibility in the public sector. It also offered monetary incentives as rewards for efficient public management performance (Salskov-Iversen et al, 2000, pp 194–6). The OECD then launched a number of NPM initiatives in order to promote its version of 'good governance' across the globe and this helped to make significant steps in NPM's becoming accepted in major capitalist states. Indeed, by 1994 the OECD was heralding NPM as a way to make the public sector 'lean and more competitive while, at the same time, trying to make public administration more responsive to citizens' needs by offering value for money, choice flexibility, and transparency' (cited in Groot and Budding, 2008, p 2). In 2005, the OECD endorsed these policies once again.

Some suggest, however, that NPM has now had its day. Governments prefer to employ digital-era governance, so it is argued, to ensure a holistic approach to policy among state departments rather than the fractured and bureaucratic policy networks associated with NPM (see Dunleavy et al, 2005). Yet, such is the embedded nature of NPM governance networks that even explicit attempts to curb its extensive bureaucratic tentacles have been difficult. Nowhere is this clearer than in the UK. David Cameron's Coalition government announced in 2010 that of the 900 or so quangos, 192 would be abolished while many others would be downsized, merged or reformed (Flinders and Skelcher, 2012). Most of the quangos pencilled in for removal were relatively insignificant advisory bodies that had spent little or no money during 2009–10. Moreover, while the government had claimed that the transition costs for abolishing quangos would be £425 million, the National Audit Office put the figure at £830 million, stating in the process that the government had drastically underestimated costs involved (Flinders and Skelcher, 2012, p 332). Even a concerted effort then to get rid of the huge amount of 'decentralised' networks, which have been rooted in British society through NPM, has so far failed. In this respect alone it is fanciful to argue that we live in a 'post-NPM' regime (see also Chapter Four). But, as we will now see, this restructuring process has also created a new public sphere in society congruent with a neoliberal policy agenda.

Workfare and the competent public sphere

According to Jessop (2002), a workfare state seeks to encourage innovation in open economies with the intention to strengthen the structural competiveness of the national economy. Workfarism also strives to promote the global competitiveness of a national economy by bringing on board foreign agents and institutions to develop and implement workfare policy ideas and policy design. Indeed, under the patronage of neoliberalism new intellectual labour has proliferated in the guise of 'experts' who steer policy provision and whose knowledge is believed to transcend historic-geographical boundaries. Supply-side economics becomes a key feature of policy making in this respect and is bolstered by the desire of governments to hold down wages and promote labour market flexibility so as to attract business investment. Workfarism therefore guarantees that a supply of potential labour will be available by depressing wages.

Jessop is clear that the workfare state assumes a number of forms depending upon specific institutional arrangements and different path dependencies. While liberal strategies pursued by the US and UK governments might be said to be the most well-known workfare strategy, there also exist neo-corporatist strategies (based upon, for instance, high taxation for social investment), neo-statist strategies (based upon, for instance, state-regulated competition and state auditing of public-private sectors) and neo-communitarian strategies (based, for instance, upon the empowerment of voluntary organisations, fair trade and social cohesion) (Jessop, 2002, pp 259–67). In many cases, and as we will see in other chapters, these different forms exist and work together in specific spaces and locales.

A common way in which neoliberalism and the workfare state has altered the public sphere is by generating formal and informal networks of information, communication and cooperation between local authorities, community groups, voluntary organisations and a variety of private bodies to solve and provide remedies for local, global and translocal problems and policy provisions. These 'public-private partnerships' (PPPs) are formed on the basis that, through contracts with the state, the private sector can deliver public services and capital projects. PPPs are therefore usually justified by claiming that they enhance cooperation between different 'partners' in delivering services, that they spread risks more efficiently among 'partners' in building new public infrastructure, that they lead to creative and flexible responses to the complexities involved in building new public infrastructure and that they provide better value for money by contracting out services to other businesses and agencies (Lindsay et al, 2008; Steijn et al, 2011; Smith, 2012). More critically, one might say that, given the form and content of how PPPs operate, they can be seen to act as organic intellectuals for the workfare state, even if some people operating within PPPs networks are hostile towards workfarism.

In the UK, PPPs have been around since 1992 and at least two different models are evident. An alliance model is based on the principle that the government will be directly involved in distinct phases of a PPP scheme. The Private Finance Initiative (PFI) probably comes closest to this model. PFIs try to attract private sector companies into the public sector. Unlike the contracting-out of public sector facilities to private companies, however, PFIs insist that the private sector stumps up outlays of capital for a particular public service as well as providing the services in question. A concession PPP model, on the other hand, sees the government selling the long-term rights to exploit a PPP to a business for a one-off large payment. The Public Interest Company (PIC) probably comes closest to this model. PICs are characterised by their legal independence from government and by their remit to deliver public services. While PICs can borrow necessary funds from sources of private finance, this is scrutinised by the government. One aim of PICs is to create 'stakeholders' for respective PIC boards, and this can be achieved by ensuring that some board members are elected from the local community (Flinders, 2005, pp 219–20; Sager, 2011, pp 163–4).

In parallel with the rise of NPM and the workfare state, 'competence' has also emerged in the public sector and in business organisations. Materialising during the late 1980s in areas of management thinking, competence is the belief that competitive advantage for an organisation lies in identifying a number of factors that are integral to how it operates. According to Prahalad and Hamel (1990, p 82), core competencies 'are the collective learning in the organisation, especially how to coordinate diverse production skills and integrate multiple streams of technologies'. Tarafdar and Gordon similarly note: 'Competencies are a firm's distinctive abilities, developed as a result of the deployment of combinations of individual resources in unique ways and through specific organizational routine' (Tarafdar and Gordon, 2007, p 355). Competencies come into being, then, when combinations of resources are brought together to accomplish a required outcome.

By employing core competencies, an organisation can decide to focus its energies on a number of core products. For example, one core competency of Sony is its ability to mobilise skills and technologies in order to create miniaturisations of its products. A core competency of the 3M corporation, on the other hand, is to create core products in the guise of different types of sticky tape. A core competency of Honda is its aptitude to build different types of engine. Once core products have been decided upon and designed an organisation can then produce a final product. In the case of Sony this might be a digital recorder that is small enough to place in one's pocket, or in the case of 3M, its famous Post-It notes, whereas with Honda end products include different brands of cars, lawn mowers, motorbikes and so on (Prahalad and Hamel, 1990, p 85).

One of the main ways in which competence has infiltrated the organisational form of the welfare state and public sector has been by means of Human Resource (HR) experts, principally through two main lines of thinking. First, some HR experts started to follow psychological theories that aimed to locate those behavioural attitudes in individuals that 'distinguished excellent from merely adequate performance, and which were independent of technical knowledge or skill' (Lodge and Hood, 2005, p 782). Second, some in HR were less concerned with psychological and behavioural traits and concentrated instead upon the concrete requirements for successful competence, like the acquisition of particular vocational qualifications (Lodge and Hood, 2005, p 783). Different countries have strategically adopted these approaches over time for their own ends. The psychological approach has arguably found a home in the US to a greater degree than in other western countries, primarily because the American government has tended to place more emphasis on *individual* competencies and capabilities that different people and individual firms possess (Horton, 2000). In the UK, however, the second route to competency has been more prevalent. For example, the competency movement gained public recognition during the 1980s, when Margaret Thatcher's government established Industry Lead Bodies to develop new training standards (Horton, 2000). Consequently, the UK government tends to assess competency at a macro level rather than through a psychological and behavioural attributes at micro and meso levels (Garavan and McGuire, 2001; Moore et al, 2002).

Crucially, what both the US and the UK point towards is the importance that competence has played in the move towards implementing a new skills agenda in the public sector and other sectors in society that is at the same time congruent with NPM thinking. These are not merely 'hard' skills but also represent a softer, touchy-feely form of management in the style of a more 'humane' neoliberalism that has become so prevalent in the workfare state. The need to implement PPPs through 'intangible' traits such as 'trust' between different 'partners' has forced those working in the public sector to draw on and apply other intangible core competences in their policy agendas. 'Customer satisfaction', 'image', 'care', 'effectiveness' and 'efficiency' are the sorts of measurable intangible resources that public officials increasingly employ today when devising their policies (Cina et al, 2003). As Macauley and Lawton (2006) discovered in their study of local monitoring officers who promote ethical principles in English local government, the boundaries between competence and intangible attributes such as 'virtue' are now often blurred in the public sector. For instance, some respondents in the study claimed that competence-based skills such as gaining legal expertise are clearly important in their job, whereas the same respondents would also highlight the importance of virtue-based skills such as personal resilience, perseverance, along with the character trait of empathy. Personal intangible ethics thus become blurred with public sector skills (Macauley and Lawton, 2006, pp 708–9). More broadly, in an era of NPM in which consultants with their 'expert knowledge' are given contracts to enact policy objectives with a variety of 'partners', competent intangible assets like trust are seen by some as crucial elements for the successful contract completion of policy objectives (see Noordegraaf, 2000; Virtanen, 2000; Woolthuis et al, 2005).

Competence is also important in forging a new public sphere in civil society that at the same time is compatible with a workfare agenda. One key theme of competence is its focus on the capacity of an individual to tap into their human capital in order to complete a task. These might be perceptual motor skills, cognitive skills in the form of knowledge and intellect, affective skills such as emotions, values, motivations, or personality traits like faith in one's abilities, and social skills such as a knack for communication (Ellström and Kock, 2008, p 6). Crucially, such personal competencies are seen as part of a *learning* process to *acquire* the requisite skills to succeed in work and in society.

The workfare state promotes this ideology in the public sphere by declaring that those who cannot find work will be given new training prospects and sustainable welfare benefits so that they can become competent workers once more. One common strategy at the workfare state's disposal to implement this agenda is the re-commodification of labour in order to make workers act in a more competent, efficient and responsible manner in the labour market. Employability is key in this respect, in so far that the workfare state is willing to grant workers more employment opportunities as long as they are willing to make themselves attractive to employers. A series of supply-side policies delivered by the state places responsibility for employability on the shoulders of individual workers. Workfarism thus categorises welfare recipients as *individual* users of state services and benefits. Moreover, as consumers of welfare services, they have to 'pay back' their welfare dues by making themselves attractive for the job market (see Fitzpatrick, 2001; McKnight, 2005; Whitfield, 2012).

Workfarism therefore ditches any residual claim to redistribute resources on an equitable footing. Instead it favours the redistribution of opportunities on the assumption that this will ensure that people take an *active* participative role in society in order to become competent by bettering themselves. This will then provide a basis for well-being in society (for more in-depth discussions of this point see Lister, 2004; McLaughlin and Baker, 2007; Newman and Clarke, 2009). At the time of writing, for example, the Coalition government in the UK is extending and redeveloping the workfare state through its Work Programme, which aims to get private contractors to put the workless and those on benefits into paid employment and ensure that they remain there for at least a year. One way it is seeking to accomplish this task is to review 1.5 million people currently on incapacity benefits by assessing their eligibility through new medical examinations in order to increase the number of people on the Work Programme (Newman, 2011, p 92).

The workfare state subsequently positions itself as an 'enabling state'. In a globally competitive world individuals are encouraged and coerced to reflect upon, realise and actualise the possibilities for work and self-advancement that globalisation brings (Fudge and Williams, 2006). In accordance with the 'intangible' attributes of competence at the heart of NPM, the workfare state has therefore increasingly tried to blur the boundaries between public and private spheres. It encourages those in receipt of welfare benefits to draw on their emotional and psychological character traits in order to become employable in the long term, thereby making them competent for the labour market. In particular, they are urged to draw on a range of their core competences of 'soft skills' to become employable; skills such as motivations, commitment and social status, along with a more 'flexible' attitude towards gaining employment (see Daguerre, 2004).

Arguably, one of the most noticeable features of the competent workfare public sphere is indeed its anticipatory nature. In an age where welfare is now calculated along supply-side lines, it becomes imperative to calculate the costs of welfare in radically new ways. Risks associated with levels of welfare are estimated in order to govern specific populations in receipt of benefits, limit welfare opportunities to these populations and provide disincentives to apply for state welfare. Means-tested benefits are just one disincentive strategy. The state therefore tries to constantly anticipate problems in civil society in order to pass legislation to regulate them. Such welfare 'problems' in need to regulation – the homeless and poor, for example – are thus defined and mapped out in advance.

It is worth reiterating, however, that the processes described above do not represent a coherent and stable set of policies. Instead, they refract the contradictions and dilemmas evident in neoliberalism, but do so in their own unique way. Some these contradictions include the following:

- NPM and the workfare state insist that private business can deliver and manage public services. But to manage costs a private company will seek to 'rationalise' the employment conditions and working environment of the public service it manages by in part implementing work-related targets for its employees. However, this often leads to a demoralised workforce in the public sector, which hampers issues of quality in service delivery.
- Moreover, many private companies will deliberately underestimate their initial costs in managing a PPP scheme in order to win a government contract, only then for a local authority to pay extravagant interest rates to a private company over the ensuing years as stipulated by a contract between both parties (Funnell et al, 2009; Smith, 2012; Whitfield 2012). As a result, PPPs in the form of PFIs can actually be more expensive over time than public ownership.

- Proponents of workfare argue that neoliberalism and financialisation will generate wealth that will eventually 'trickle' down to other social classes and groups in society. Unfortunately, the opposite has been the case. For example, workfarism dictates that spending per unit of public service delivery has also been held down in many areas, with the savings made going to encourage businesses to invest in localities (Gough et al, 2006). These and other policies have, however, helped to generate significant increases in poverty and inequality. In the UK, for instance, the richest 1% of the population during the early 1970s earned 5.7 times the average income, but by 2008 this had risen to 17.7 times. And in the world today just 1% of the population hold 90% of all of the world's wealth (Dorling, 2012, p 73 and p 113). Indeed, evidence suggests that the more neoliberal and workfarist the country, the more its population will suffer from ill-health associated with the likes of work-related stress (Bambra, 2011, p 746).
- The competent workfare public sphere tries to persuade people that partnership networks will in fact bring together different groups and organisations in a locality to solve common problems. This, then, is an empowering agenda. Once again, however, reality regrettably intervenes in this ideological justification of the neoliberal workfare agenda. Often, for example, different 'partners' – charities, community groups, business and so on – come together with different ambitions and assumptions concerning the remit of specific partnerships that actually conflict with one another (Newman and Clarke, 2009, p 61). Communication between 'partners' can then start to break down (see also Milbourne and Cushman, 2013).
- The greater the number of policy networks that are generated, the more bureaucracy takes hold in society. Somewhat ironically, the number of quangos in the UK soared during the 1980s just at a time when Thatcherism was taking hold in British society (Thiel, 2012). But this form of mass bureaucracy and centralisation of policy decision making contradicts the neoliberal requirement to cut back on bureaucracy so as to ensure that markets work to their potential, unfettered by what is seen to be government interference. Besides, diluting rules and modes of governance by stretching them across a large number of policy networks is not an effective or efficient way to govern society and uphold the common good (Terry, 2005).

Conclusion

Asbjørn Wahl (2011, pp 84–5) rightly argues against those who claim that NPM is no longer a guiding policy in the public sector. Indeed, he maintains that NPM is fundamental for the restructuring of the welfare state along neoliberal lines. He gives two main reasons for claiming this. First, NPM seeks to privatise the public sector where possible, or at least make it business friendly. It is then easier for businesses to take over public and nationalised amenities, break them up where necessary and run them in the hope of making massive profits. Second, NPM has also brought with it new accountancy mechanisms that favour private business practices for the public sector. They thus justify neoliberal practices such as the outsourcing of particular public sector roles and responsibilities to the private sector. Wahl is also correct to note that NPM has been a hugely important ideology that has given legitimacy to the restructuring of the state from a welfare model to a workfare model.

The competent workfare public sphere is part of the NPM agenda and openly declares that people on welfare benefits choose not to work and that high benefits deter people from finding work. Competence demands that individuals *develop* certain character traits so that they will flourish in the workplace and in the marketplace. At all times, though, the emphasis is placed on individuals to help themselves, albeit with guidance from 'experts' regulated and mandated by the state.

Such assumptions about individuals becoming competent are, however, contradicted by the complexities of reality. At a minimum, we can say that capitalism is founded on uneven socioeconomic development at national, regional and global levels. As Wright (2012) observes, some localities will inevitably experience low employment opportunities but high levels of jobseekers. That is to say, 'welfare-to-work' programmes are dependent upon the contingencies of local labour markets (Wright, 2012, pp 320–1; see also Newman, 2011, pp 95–6). Under these circumstances one might very well acquire competent personality traits to make oneself attractive to employers but then discover that few job opportunities are actually available.

But competence and its relationship to workfarism also establishes a pre-emptive agenda through various partnership networks in which different organisations – government departments, charities, voluntary groups, quangos, the private sector – exchange information between one another in order to tackle social issues and problems. As Garrett (2005) notes, the new workfare agenda is based in part on joined-up government and the coming together of the public and private sectors in and around policy issues. Private ICT companies, in particular, gain opportunities to sell their latest gadgets to the public sector while at the same time being co-opted into government partnership networks in and around particular social policies. Garrett discusses the example of Connexions Service in the UK, an ICT company that in 2001 won a government contract in partnership with the Department of Trade and Industry to provide a Connexions Card for young people aged between 13 and 19 years. The card monitored a young person's educational activity by giving them 'reward points' for regular attendance at school that they could then redeem for consumer items like cinema tickets. While the scheme was abandoned in 2006, being deemed a failure, we can nevertheless appreciate how in this instance a private company utilised digital technology to take over the running of a particular welfare service in order to make a profit for itself.

To what extent can similar processes and practices be noted in relation to digital democracy in civil society? Does the competent public sphere have a role to play in experiments around e-democracy in civil society? If so, does this lead to new contradictions and dilemmas in and around digital democracy? The next chapter continues the discussion of the competent public sphere and its relationship to digital technology by looking at government policies in and around digital democracy and e-democracy. We will indeed see that the contradictions mapped out in relation to neoliberalism and the competent public sphere are refracted in specific ways in government programmes to establish and then implement digital democracy. These contradictions thus hamper the full potential of e-democracy in civil society.

FOUR

E-democracy and public deliberation in the competent public sphere

Introduction

E-government refers to the use of ICTs to deliver public services and related public service activity. ICTs facilitate new ways for governments to join up and deliver their services, as well as complementing existing service delivery. Moreover, e-government initiatives can be employed to transform services for the good of citizens, business, the public sector and voluntary sector. To give one illustration, e-government holds the potential to make public service delivery more accountable and transparent to its users. The reverse is also said to hold. Greater online activity has the potential to stimulate people to take part in formal democratic activity. One study found that participation in online discussion forums increased the likelihood of voting in an upcoming general election (Grant and Chau, 2006, pp 74–5; Yildiz, 2007, pp 650–1; Boulianne, 2009, p 203; Gauld, 2009, pp 105–6).

Yet, while e-government should therefore provide great opportunities for the promotion of a deliberative version of e-democracy, evidence suggests that the uptake of e-government has in fact been rather slow. One European study found that user participation has been sluggish and that satisfaction levels with existing e-government websites have been relatively low (Capgemini et al, 2009). Kotamraju and van der Geest (2012, p 271) discovered that users of government websites in fact frequently hold different and conflicting viewpoints of what e-government should promote. Some users want their own specialised interests catered for on an e-government website, while governments recognise the need to cater for both specialist *and* universal needs. In addition, governments wish to create rapport with their citizens by building up data and information about the specific needs of citizens. Many people, however, are generally more cautious in their approach to e-government sites, often wishing instead to remain anonymous before they divulge information. In this respect, users might favour a less direct and less intimate relationship with their local government even when using e-government (Kotamraju and van der Geest, 2012, p 271).

So, what is going on here? If digital and deliberative democracy is so good, why has it not been more successful in getting an increasing number of people to believe in and practise its ideals? This chapter builds on the previous chapters by looking critically at the application of deliberative democracy in relation to e-government and e-democracy. We will see that while deliberative democracy holds some great possibilities for citizens it is also beset by a number of contradictions that it refracts from NPM and the competent workfare public sphere. As a result, the deliberative ideal is constantly undermined by the contradictions and dilemmas that these throw up for digital democracy. The discussion begins, though, by briefly defining e-government and e-democracy in a little more depth.

E-government and e-democracy

E-government came of age in the 1990s and offered a new way for citizens to 'get connected' with their elected representatives and for elected representatives to try to connect once again with their constituents (Anderson et al, 2010). In the UK, e-government arrived in 1996 with the Conservative government's publication of *Government Direct* (cited in Coleman, 2004), which argued that new technology had great potential to save costs and to be more efficient than some existing delivery mechanisms. A parliamentary website was established soon afterwards to further some of these aims (Coleman, 2004). E-government in the US started life in 1993 with the introduction of the National Performance Review. Primarily employed for reasons of efficiency, the National Performance Review followed a managerial line at the outset by employing new technology to save staffing costs in the public sector and to minimise expenditure on normal outgoings (Gauld, 2009, p 116). The Obama government went further. The Open Government Initiative, established on 21 January 2008, was an attempt by the White House to ensure that federal government and executive agencies opened up their participative structures to the public and other stakeholders (Stromer-Galley et al, 2012).

Of course, since the 1990s technology has progressed in new directions. Wireless and mobile communications are increasingly seen by many public officials as a way of personalising services as well as of ensuring that they are networked up to a 24/7 timeline (see Bannister and Wilson, 2011, pp 68–9), while social media is starting to be used as a means to coordinate service delivery more efficiently (Magro, 2012, p 154). Given these perceived benefits, it should come as no real surprise that e-government is often linked to other social and economic advantages. In 2002 the European Commission released the *eEurope 2005 Action Plan* (cited in Walterova and Tveit, 2012), with the stated aim of giving everyone living in Europe an opportunity to take an active part in the bourgeoning global information society. Such policies were especially important to the European Union (EU) because policy makers recognised that European economies were increasingly reliant on the information sector. By 2009, the EU estimated that the ICT sector contributed about 5% to the overall GDP of EU member states and 25% to GDP growth. Harnessing e-government would therefore unlock more potential benefits for socioeconomic development (Walterova and Tveit, 2012, pp 346–7).

Debates around e-democracy emerged in parallel debates about e-government. According to Chadwick (2003, p 448), there are two principle themes on e-democracy. First, e-democracy presents new ways for government to enhance consultation with the public. It is able to promote online questionnaires, create websites with information posted up on them for local residents, help to maintain partnership networks in a community and reduce costs in gathering information (Anderson et al, 2010). Moreover, e-democracy reproduces conventional democratic mechanisms into the virtual world. E-petitions are a well-known illustration, which many governments welcome (Panagiotopoulos et al, 2011).

The second theme is an offshoot from e-democracy but lies specifically in enhancing democracy through deliberation. Conventional liberal ideals like free speech and the free circulation of information can of course be catered for and extended through new media. But it is also true to say that many expect more of new digital media. At a minimum they expect, or at least hope, that new media open up new channels for 'self-determination, participation, voice, and autonomy' (Hague and Loader, 1999, p 7). For some, deliberative democracy offers up this possibility. Indeed, it has quickly become the norm to co-opt some new media sites into social and political campaigns (Chadwick, 2009, p 33; Evans–Cowley and Hollander, 2010).

Deliberative approaches are therefore thought to have great prospects in encouraging ordinary people to exercise their democratic rights. To understand the intricacies of the deliberative model of democracy we will first briefly explore some of its main principles. Once this has been accomplished we will have a basis to appreciate not only why many find deliberative democracy attractive but also why it is frequently applied to make sense of, and to stimulate, e-democracy.

Deliberative digital democracy

According to Chambers:

> [W]e can say that deliberation is debate and discussion aimed at producing reasonable, well-informed opinions in which participants are willing to revise preferences in light of discussion, new information, and claims made by fellow participants. Although consensus need not be the ultimate aim of deliberation, and participants are expected to pursue their interests, an overarching interest in the legitimacy of outcomes (understood as justification to all affected) ideally characterizes deliberation. (Chambers, 2003, p 309)

For Gutmann and Thompson, deliberative democracy is:

> [A] form of government in which free and equal citizens (and their representatives), justify decisions in a process in which they give one another reasons that are mutually acceptable and generally accessible, with the aim of reaching conclusions that are binding in the present on all citizens but open to challenge in the future. (Gutmann and Thompson, 2004, p 7)

In each definition we see that democracy and deliberation is a dynamic process. A key characteristic of deliberative democracy in this respect is the idea that through discursive interactions with one another citizens can be transformed into politically and socially competent members of society. The more information one is prepared to listen to about a specific issue from a range of speakers, the more one is willing to be open to a number of perspectives about the issue in question. In the process one gains a more 'reasonable' position towards an opposing point of view (Polleta et al, 2009).

Dahlberg (2001) argues that deliberative approaches have a number of advantages over two other prominent digital democratic models. A liberal-individualist model is based on a minimum amount of interaction between people on discussion forums and is therefore found wanting from a deliberative perspective. A communitarian model is based on online communities that come together around specific activities, pastimes, pursuits and so on. Often, however, this type of talk reinforces homogeneous interests between tightly knit groups and this leads to a diminished form of critical-rational discourse

(Dahlberg, 2001, p 618). For Dahlberg, a deliberative approach is a superior means to enhance democratic participation. To illustrate its advantages he focuses on Minnesota E-Democracy. Known today as E-Democracy.org, Minnesota E-Democracy was originally established in 1994 to facilitate e-mail-based discussion forums to enable participants to engage in a whole host of debates. It encourages its key members to take responsibility for debates, such as using private e-mails to guide one another on suitable postings. Management teams monitor the rules of the forum and ensures that users post topics only about Minnesota. As a result, the forum attracts sincere and honest posters who respect the viewpoints of others. During his study Dahlberg discovered that abuse was kept to a minimum and, because the subjects discussed relate to everyday local issues, people have a sense of ownership of and commitment to what is being discussed.

Deliberative democracy is therefore attractive for many because it encourages 'rational' arguments based on reasonable critical claims that are continually being reflected on by participants. In one respect, it seems almost intuitive to think that new media cannot cater for this stringent test of 'good' deliberation. Yet, advocates claim the opposite. Online deliberations have the potential to be more democratic than face-to-face encounters because the social identity of participants – social class, ethnicity, gender and so on – does not have the immediate impact on deliberation that it would, no doubt, enjoy in 'real life' encounters. In addition, visible emotional cues that are on show during face-to-face encounters are similarly bracketed by online interactions, which again allows participants to concentrate on the discursive issues at hand and build rational-critical arguments (Min, 2007; see also Coleman and Moss, 2012; Freelon, 2010). And contrary to what many might also think, online deliberations do not necessarily lead to abusive posts. If designed to ensure maximum deliberation, and if supervised by moderators, then insulting posts can be tackled by other online participants that then bring a discussion back to its reasoned content (Albrecht, 2006, p 73).

Some empirical findings certainly confirm that deliberative e-democracy can at least in some cases encourage citizens to engage with one another through online forums, irrespective of 'physical' and 'visible' characteristics like age and gender. Evidence suggests too that people are willing to utilise Web 2.0 applications like YouTube to deliberate in a rational manner about candidates who put themselves up for public office (McNeal et al, 2008). This is true for not only government-sponsored forums but also forums associated with popular entertainment. In his analysis of season six of the UK version of

Celebrity Big Brother, T. Graham (2010) found that people were prepared to use online chat and discussion forums to engage in rational-critical and reflexive discussion about the show. He discovered that 72% of the people involved in online discussions did engage in reasoned discussion (providing reasoning with a claim), while 42% engaged in critical reflection (arguments that directly challenged or contradicted another claim) (T. Graham, 2010, p 31). Just as importantly, Graham discovered a number of 'expressives' in how people engaged in discussion, not least the use of humour and banter to create social bonds between discussants, or sarcasm to support a political point being made.

Another important element for a deliberative approach lies in its ability to facilitate a critically reflexive attitude during deliberations. The point of deliberative democracy is not merely to get people to participate in decision making by voicing their concerns, but also to encourage them to do so in a more active reflexive manner during discussions with others. This requires investment by participants in listening to the arguments of others in a balanced and fair way, reading materials around an issue being debated and ensuring equality and respect for all reasonable opinions being aired. Institutional arrangements targeted towards achieving these aims are therefore crucial in encouraging a deliberative approach among a group of citizens during a consultative exercise by public officials (Åström and Grönlund 2012, pp 90–2). Digital culture is particularly well suited to this type of reflexivity. It is, after all, an on-going process of becoming. Web pages are continuously being developed and updated, while mobile phones access and reproduce data beyond any set timeline. Constituents can therefore interact with their MP from the security of their own home and work lifestyle (Coleman, 2005).

Transparency is a further crucial ingredient of deliberative theory. Just as new media initiates a new kind of directness between elected politicians and their constituents, social media can potentially empower ordinary people and lead to a new kind of transparency in politics. User-generated content and media sharing through the likes of YouTube, Facebook, Flickr, Twitter and Vimeo, encourage citizens to report about local, regional and national issues that might normally be ignored in the mainstream media, or to share media content about public officials in order to hold them to account about a policy issue. Some government websites have also experimented with social media in making themselves more accountable to local populations. Many government agency websites in the US have blogs that the public can use. In an effort to promote openness, officials will then use these blogs to answer concerns and queries from the public (Bertot et al,

2012, pp 82–4). Wikipedia also follows a type of transparency in how it operates that can be said to work within a deliberative ideal. On each Wikipedia page, for instance, a 'Discussion' link is evident that allows contributors to follow a history of discussion between different people about the changes made about a particular subject. Wikipedia's very design therefore conforms at least in part to the deliberative principle of transparency through openness (Hansen et al, 2009, p 52).

Some studies, which apply deliberative theory to analyse government websites, are more critical as to the effectiveness of public deliberation and its relationship to digital democracy. A case in point is the study by Wikland (2005), which explored the deliberative potential of the ICT-enabled services of all 289 Swedish municipalities (lower-level local governments) from data gathered in 2002. The scope for online deliberations is particularly good in Sweden, especially when one realises that at the time of the research 80% of the Swedish population had access to the internet at home, at work or through an educational institute. The results of the study, however, were decidedly mixed. For example, one key element of public deliberation is that of universalism – the principle that all those affected by a political decision have a right to be included in deliberations about the rights and wrongs of the decision before it is made law. In the case of Sweden, though, Wikland discovered that those in higher socioeconomic groups were more likely to visit a municipality website, and yet public officials showed little interest in trying to get other socioeconomic groups involved. Another deliberative ideal is that of the impartial point of view, which rests on the principle that only the force of the better argument should affect the outcome of deliberations. To ensure that the impartial point of view holds, it is important to regulate the power embedded in administrative services during actual deliberations. In the case of Swedish municipalities, notes Wikland, it is uncertain as to whether their power is indeed kept in check. For instance, it is up to an individual municipality whether or not they wish to establish a website, but it was not clear at the time of the study what information they had the right to post.

What might we conclude from this particular study? Without doubt, many advantages accrue to local public officials by using digital technologies in service delivery. They carry the promise of making services more efficient, they save time and money, integrate services, ensure resources are employed on a more equitable basis, provide personalised feedback to individuals, assist with planning and so on. Yet, these advantages are often negated by different systemic contradictions and strategic dilemmas. As we have seen in other chapters, these contradictions and dilemmas are mediated by the workfare public sphere, which is itself internally related to neoliberalism. Just as the public sector has been subject to a relentless attack by financialisation and neoliberalism, so has e-democracy been subject to a host of contradictory pressures that are reproduced in how the virtual public sphere is formed in local government settings. Therefore, we now turn our attention to some of these contradictions and dilemmas and begin by noting how media corporations have increased their grip on digital technology, and from there move on to discuss how competence and NPM affect e-democracy.

Corporate power, neoliberalism and e-democracy

Media corporate power has grown immensely over the years. Google, as McChesney (2013, p 131) notes, holds almost 70% of the search engine market, while Microsoft's Windows is used on 90% of all computers. Through iTunes, Apple dominates about 87% market share in digital downloads. McChesney goes on to observe:

> The monopolistic firms that have capitalized on the digital revolution have grown to world-historical proportions. In 2012, four of the ten largest US corporations in terms of market valuations, including number one and number three, were Internet giants Apple, Microsoft, Google, and AT&T. Add IBM and that is five of the top ten. (McChesney 2013, p 131)

Disney sits in the top 30 of this list and it provides an interesting case study of how major media companies conquer markets. Wayne (2003, pp 73–8) nicely maps out Disney's strategy in this respect. He observes that by the 1980s Disney had seen its fortunes decline somewhat and was no longer the media player it once was. Then, in 1984 Michael Eisner was made chief executive officer and brought with him a new management ethos based on decentralisation, diversification and a massive global expansion. By 1996 Disney had bought Capital Cities, the parent company of the ABC TV and radio network, for $19 billion. Disney also began to enter other media markets, such as the sports media market, and this entailed doing media deals in other parts of the world such as in Asia and Latin America. Disney then started to diversify its film markets through a process of horizontal integration. For instance, a number of film production companies were created to cater for different movie tastes. These include: Walt Disney Pictures, which caters for children's films, for example, *The Lion King*; Pixar Films, which produces innovative animation films, for example, *Toy Story*; Touchstone Pictures, which makes big-budget films, for example, *The Sixth Sense*; Miramax Films, which concentrates on independent films, for example, *The Talented Mr Ripley*; and Dimension Films, which focuses on teen films, for example, *The Faculty*. As the horizontal integration of different film companies under the Disney umbrella was under way there was also a degree of vertical integration of Disney films through, for example, the distribution network of Buena Vista International.

Disney is therefore a useful illustration through which to highlight how media conglomerates have increased their power in the media world in recent years. They gain control over 'production, distribution, and exhibition' as well as hardware and software products and 'by taking advantage of an international division of labour that makes possible the flexible and cost-effective use of labour, capital, research, and development' (Mosco, 2009, pp 161–2). Monopolisation also considerably strengthens their influence. Media corporations spend millions in protecting their copyrights and acquiring new patents. Google spent $12.5 billion alone to acquire Motorola Mobility in 2011 and this was mostly to obtain 17,000 patents that came with Motorola. In 2012 Google then paid $5 million to lobby Washington politicians about its interests. In turn, politicians have more or less supported the ambitions of these companies (McChesney, 2013, pp 134 and 144).

Some no doubt would argue that what is sketched out above insinuates that capitalists represent a broadly unified class, and with a coherent set of interests. In addition, it might be said that it also paints an unduly pessimistic picture of media production and consumption. After all, decentralised network formations of the sort established by global media corporations might throw up interesting opportunities for such companies to encourage their targeted audiences to be more active in creating user content for particular products like a popular book, movie or TV show. And as part of this process users might deliberate with one another around the product in question.

To take the first point, Sparks (2006) is correct to say that capitalists generally, and media capitalists specifically, are far from being a coherent and unified group. Naturally, there are some common interests among diverse capitalist groups such as the right to own and control property and the right to hire workers for a wage. Beyond these common interests, however, the capitalist class is more often than not divided among itself over various issues. Think of media organisations that produce newspapers. Owners of national newspapers invariably reflect different political beliefs. At this simple level, then, some news media capitalists will be divided over certain political and social convictions. Different management and employee relations are also evident in media workplaces. Some contractual working conditions reduce news media employees to the status of poorly paid labour, while other employees working in the same media organisation will enjoy better and more secure working conditions. For their part, several managers might follow the biased organisational news agenda of the owners, while others will be committed to impartial reporting that conflicts with whatever political agenda the company wants to construct (Sparks, 2006).

Moreover, and as Sparks further observes, the media industry in many capitalist countries is fragmented in so far that a number of small independent TV production companies vie with one another to win contracts to produce TV shows. But this in turn generates its own set of social divisions. For instance, if a contract is won to produce a TV show, then the person who owns the company in question will become a capitalist by hiring others to work on the production for a period of time. Yet, at other times this very same person will probably be temporarily unemployed themselves at some point and will therefore have to work for another company to make a living (Sparks, 2006, pp 117–29). Subsequently, it should always be borne in mind that the capitalist class refracts contradictions at play in capitalism, which is one reason why the state is required to regulate their behaviour through specific socioeconomic projects. Other chapters have already dealt with some of these issues.

In respect of the second point, in an age of increasing social divisions in and around financial corporate power and neoliberal hegemony, to what extent is deliberative democracy really a viable option? Certainly one general and rather blunt point to make is that deliberative ideals are usually not something that the private owners and controllers of media corporations are particularly worried about or concerned to include in their content. In the main, the furthest they will go to is to limit user involvement to posting and creating items around popular culture and personal lifestyle features. Newspapers in the UK, for example, enable readers to post comments about news stories in their online editions, or to write blogs around news items. What is less visible is direct user involvement in actual newsgathering or news production (Örnebring, 2008).

If material conditions associated with the likes of neoliberalism and corporate power are indeed crucial ingredients in trying to understand the relationship between deliberative digital democracy, states and ordinary people, then we also need to understand some of the ideological attributes of digital policies enacted by the state. For, as we established in the previous chapter, both state ideology and state coercion are hugely important levers to gain hegemony in society for socioeconomic projects. To this extent, we established that NPM had become a key ideological device for governments to employ in order to restructure state administrative mechanisms in a manner that was amenable towards neoliberalism. We will now see how NPM is also related to attempts to reshape some of the key characteristics of e-democracy.

New public management and e-democracy

Without doubt, NPM is connected with moves to implement e-government in the public sector. New media has opened up more channels for the public sector to carry out its main business objectives. Not only can local government officials employ digital technology to make it easier for residents to gain information about specific local services and to make any necessary payments to their local authority, but digital technology also creates new ways of making public officials accountable to their constituents. Placing reports on a local government website, for example, facilitates quick and relatively easy access for people to gain information about the activities of their local officials. Teicher et al (2002, p 387) therefore claim that e-government has the potential to support three main characteristics of NPM's quality agenda: that the public sector is customer-driven; that it is empowering for communities, workers and customers; and that the public sector is effective and efficient.

Naturally, some dispute the relevance of NPM in today's contemporary public sector and local government. Dunleavy et al (2005) argue that NPM has had its day. They claim that many policy makers no longer take it seriously, and some of its themes have stalled while a few others have fallen by the wayside. Competition, which was such a characteristic feature of NPM, is still with us but it is being implemented at a slower pace in the public services of many countries like the UK, while splitting up public services into smaller, flexible units and 'flattened', horizontal networks is no longer in vogue. Dunleavy et al therefore assert that 'digital-era governance' has now surpassed NPM. Digital-era governance brings together a number of changes that are nevertheless dominated by ICTs. New media reverses the NPM trend of fragmenting public services because it encourages a holistic approach to policy agendas by linking together and reintegrating different components and units. It also opens up opportunities to take back some activities and ventures into the public sector that had initially been privatised. The re-nationalisation of the UK's Railtrack infrastructure in 2000 is just one illustration (Dunleavy et al, 2005, p 488). Public service customers can also more easily access information through digital-era governance and this again demonstrates how a holistic public management can move forward in ways that overcome the fragmentation inherent in NPM. As a result, digital-era governance 'add[s] a new impetus for a more agile and customer-centered approach, opening up a prospect for citizens or businesses to easily track and self-monitor the processing of their applications or cases' (Dunleavy et al, 2005, p 488).

While Dunleavy et al's argument might prove seductive it nevertheless contains a number of problems. Maybe it is true that a competitive ethos has stalled in the public sector, but it is equally true to say that in other areas of major public service delivery competition has been drastically extended. In fact, in the UK it has open the gates for corporate power to take advantage of the increasing prevalence of neoliberalism in the public sector. Take the UK's NHS. Leys and Player (2011, p 73) point out there are five big private companies that tower over the marketisation of the NHS: Netcare, Spire, Nuffield Health, Ramsay and HCA. In 2006, just a year after the publication of Dunleavy et al's article, Netcare purchased the General Healthcare Group, and through this acquisition it also gained a chain of 60 BMI (private) hospitals. By 2009 this chain was generating an income of £750 million for Netcare, and this included the treatment of NHS patients. No wonder, then, that just before the 2010 general election Netcare was lobbying politicians for more NHS contracts. And, lest we think this is a one-off example of the marketisation of the NHS, by 2009, 106 NHS Private Finance Initiative (PFI) schemes with a total capital value of £11 billion had been signed off. Over the next 30 years or so, these various PFI schemes can expect to receive on-going payments from hospitals that will amount to £58 billion (Leys and Player, 2011, p 72). Concrete examples like these demonstrate that the sort of wholesale qualitative shift from NPM to a digitally sophisticated mode of governance misses crucial continuities in how neoliberal workfarism still exacts a dominant mode of regulation in the public sector. At the very least, it is quite legitimate to argue that many of the structural effects of NPM are still with us (Haque, 2007).

Greater integration of services through digital technology therefore does not signify the end of a workfare ethos in public management. 'Value for money' and 'lean management' still play a prominent role in the public sector, and these are associated with some of the main traits of NPM. In their quantitative and qualitative study of work restructuring at the UK's HM Revenue and Customs (HMRC), Carter et al (2011), for example, discovered that the principles of NPM were alive and kicking. Management had embarked on large-scale changes at HMRC that included £5 million in efficiency gains through 16,000 job reductions in the sector (Carter et al, 2011, p 115). HMRC employees subsequently experienced considerable changes in their daily working lives. NPM principles were applied at HMRC that placed more stress on the autonomy of public sector management, introduced free market principles into the sector, sanctioned the hourly monitoring of work activities, created multi-tasking for employees, set performance targets and so on. These practices were bolstered by the £106 million spent on consultants who sought to time the hourly tasks of employees and then devise new performance targets for each hour observed. Managers were also empowered to sanction new accountancy mechanisms that minimised the cost of the workforce but maximised output effort, in line with the new performance targets. This shifted the management focus to 'the collation of statistics and the "cherry-picking" of particular types of work to show success' (Carter et al, 2011, p 118). New performance measures also lead to greater intensification at work and to greater levels of anxiety and stress among the workforce being investigated, while the accumulation of statistics around targets deskills employees by stripping away important levels of discretion.

In this respect, the transition from NPM to what might be termed the post-NMP and digital-era governance environment is far from as smooth as Dunleavy et al appear to suggest. It is truer to say that the transition is blurred and messy, with many elements of NPM firmly embedded in what might be labelled a post-NPM regime (Lodge and Gill, 2011, pp 154–5). This can be seen in respect of the use of digital technology in public service delivery. As Cordella (2007) observes, employing ICTs in the public sector plays a role analogous to that of NPM. For example, ICTs have been used to implement what are said to be flattened-out bureaucratic structures in the public sector based on supposedly accountable and transparent flows of communication between policy units and departments. ICTs have also smoothed the progress of market-based mechanisms in the public sector by developing new modes of coordination for how public procurements might progress, which then of course helps to form the basis of increased competition in public management (Cordella, 2007, p 269). In respect of HMRC, Carter et al observe that the coding of data through new performance targets actually fragments work patterns. For instance, a number of HMRC employees once dealt with a variety of tasks related with one tax return. Through new modes of coding these tasks have been broken down into separate individual tasks, with each separate task now requiring a single employee to carry it out. The whole system thus becomes fragmented, employees are deskilled because their range of tasks is significantly narrowed and the introduction of a new coding system is arguably less efficient than previous coding systems (Carter et al, 2011, pp 117–18).

This mixing of a neoliberal sensibility in the workplace with new media is noticeable at a global institutional level too. In 2004, the EU published its mid-term report for the Lisbon Strategy. Formulated in 2000, the Lisbon Strategy argued that global competition, especially from the US and countries in Asia, meant that European countries had no other option but to nurture new outlets for knowledge economies to prosper. It thus sought to put into practice a European-wide plan to initiate new types of innovation in the economy based on the latest digital technology, learning processes and employment practices and policies. The 2004 mid-term report stressed the continuing need for the EU to press ahead with its programme to develop the required frameworks for information societies to flourish and grow across Europe. Lifelong learning, e-commerce, mobile technologies, training and so on were all highlighted as being key areas for the EU to cultivate in the future. Joseph (2012), however, sees another narrative entwined in the positive account presented about information societies in the 2004 report. Specifically, Joseph argues that the report constructs the information society as an unstoppable global force that societies need to accommodate themselves to in order to gain competitive advantage. One way that leaders can do this is to ensure that their labour markets remain flexible. Only then can business and governments harness information to make employment and production relations competitive. Governments should also introduce 'active' welfare policies that aim to make recipients employable and mobile. Joseph adds that this informational narrative has been a prominent feature of EU policy design at least since the early 1990s. Nonetheless, he further argues that one continuing theme has been a concerted effort on the part of EU policy makers to restructure the relationship between capital and labour in a neoliberal direction. To meet the needs of the information society, for example, the EU says that labour must be flexible enough to face the challenges of a decentralised network society, and that individual employees and workers should be 'empowered' to take part in 'participatory deliberations' and responsible decision making with other 'stakeholders' (Joseph, 2012, pp 195–201). These are all typical neoliberal themes (see also Chapter Seven).

But if deliberation is thought to be a social good in the information society narrative, to what extent can it be used to play a positive role in attempts to build a deliberative approach to policy provision through e-government in civil society? And if NPM is still a prominent feature in the public sector, is this the case with respect to the workfare public sphere? We now turn to these questions.

The competent public sphere and its impact on digital deliberative democracy

Reddick (2011) maps out three models of e-government. First, there is the managerial model in which governments employ ICTs to notify citizens about a particular service, but they do not enable citizens to interact with or change the service in question. Consultative models, on the other hand, do have a more interactive element to the extent that governments employ ICTs to seek advice from a range of stakeholders about specific policies, with the aim of enhancing various policies. Participatory models take this further by using new media to develop the democratic capabilities of local citizens through the likes of e-petitions, e-voting and online town hall meetings (Reddick, 2011, pp 169–71; see also Axford, 2001, p 13).

In reality, however, these models operate together alongside various types of neoliberal governance. For example, David Cameron's Coalition government championed the benefits of self-government through associations *and* the need for hierarchical government administered through elected representatives. This reflects broader strategies by the UK government policy on e-democracy, which has oscillated between centralised cost-driven and standardised approaches to approaches that emphasise local autonomy, cross-boundary communication and horizontal network formations across a range of 'partners' (Kolsaker 2006). Indeed, as we saw in Chapter Three, workfarism is embedded in an NPM regime that highlights how government departments 'learn' to respond to rapidly changing policy environments with different social needs while at the same time trying to impose standardised policy ideals across local contexts (see Chadwick, 2003, p 446).

Under these conditions, power is ever more centralised in the regulatory mechanisms of the workfare state so that the voices of clients then get lost in increasing digital bureaucracy (Bannister and Wilson, 2011). With respect to deliberative democracy, then, a customer-focused orientation to policy might take hold of policy agendas in a digitally enhanced policy environment. In fact, digital deliberative democracy between residents and other 'partners' is in danger of becoming a moribund expression employed by voluntary organisations and private business in their bids to take over the running of particular services from the public sector (Dutil et al, 2007, p 86).

These points are related to another issue concerned with standardisation. Under New Labour, 'continuous innovation' in the public sector became a key buzzword in the late 1990s and early 2000s. The message was simple: local government officials had to ensure continuous improvements in service delivery and should use digital technology to do so. For Osborne and Brown (2011), however, this represents flawed thinking in public service delivery. Continuous improvements imply a rapid turnover in policy without the necessary time for particular policies to embed themselves into a context to see if they actually work. At the same time the speeding up of policy innovation frequently means that citizens do not gain enough information through old and new media about emergent issues in their communities, why these appear in the first place and the rationale behind the policies that are designed to tackle them (Hughes, 2011). Lack of clarity about this use of e-government by local officials then leads to greater levels of distrust among constituents towards e-government websites (Kotamraju and van der Geest, 2012, p 271).

Anyhow, in an age of constantly changing welfare policy directives those working in the public sector often have little time on their hands to try to administer yet more procedures, such as online deliberations. Indeed, they may very well perceive such initiatives as increasing their workloads, which in turn leads them to be sceptical of e-government policies (Stromer-Galley et al, 2012, pp 92–3). One study of local government websites in the US, for example, found little evidence of interactivity, let alone deliberation, on these sites, due to limited financial resources. E-government was in the main used instead to circulate information to local residents. Nevertheless, one positive change reported by local government officials was an increase in customer service through government websites, but this indicates once again a consumer-focused relationship to e-government rather than a deliberative one (Coursey and Norris, 2008). A more recent study of public servants' attitudes to e-democracy in New Zealand discovered similar results. Only a minority (36.7%) of those who took part in the 240 web surveys from six New Zealand core government agencies felt that e-participation facilitated greater participation in decision making. The authors of the study conclude that the most consistent message among public servants is that e-government simply serves as a way to disseminate information to local community members (Baldwin et al, 2012, pp 118–19).

These issues feed into another deliberative matter, concerning transparency in deliberations. If local officials feel overburdened by new constraints from NPM and workfarism, then they may not have the time to outline clearly the rules and regulations about how local citizens can use a government forum. If this is the case, then users may easily become disillusioned with the deliberative potential of the site in question if they think their contributions can be subject to censorship without any clear rationale from the moderators (Wright, 2006; Wright and Street, 2007). But this also raises the question of how a moderator will judge the 'political competence' of users on an online discussion board in the first place. On what grounds can moderators provide further information to a discussion, or on what grounds can they banish or inhibit information sharing that they feel is problematic (Polleta et al, 2009)?

Transparency similarly comes under pressure from another attribute of NPM and the workfare state. This is associated with the penchant to foster 'joined-up' thinking in service delivery with new types of knowledge management. A key resource is the use of digital technology to assist these ends. Digital Identity Management systems are a case in point. They refer to those rules, procedures and technologies that try to exchange and garner digital information about local populations to ensure better access to and delivery of specific public services. In this respect, 'digital identification occurs when an entity compares the identifiers of an individual with a set of identifiers that the entity has previously recorded, and finds a match between the two' (Lips, 2010, p 276; see also Lips et al, 2009). So, a person can be identified through digital identifiers that include their name, what they do, a password they use or a physical object a person possesses like a smartcard. Still, digital identity management systems pose serious problems for the issue of transparency in public deliberation. Often, individuals are not aware of the risk categories assigned to them through digital identification, or how they are being socially constructed in the virtual world. 'Individuals, instead of being treated as fundamentally "all the same", can now be (instantly) graded against a whole range of factors, as belonging to different levels of risk' (Pollitt, 2011, p 385).

'Accountability', another key deliberative ideal, also comes under pressure in this workfare environment. Conventional bureaucracies operating in the state or in local authorities have to adhere to formal rules and regulations that, at least in principle, appear to be inclusive. However, partnership organisations from the private sector function under a different set of rules and regulations. While these commitments must be accountable to the public sector they are also semi-autonomous of them. Indeed, they 'can subscribe to opaque governing norms and all too often these norms reinforce broader patterns of discrimination and power' (Kreiss et al, 2011, p 252; see also Chapters Six and Seven).

Guiding these more private procedures is a logic of market-based individualism that is regularly quite at odds with public norms. It is also true to say, though, that an individualist ethos also permeates other areas of digital democracy and serves to disrupt deliberative ideals in different overlapping ways, as we will now see.

Individualism versus collectivism

There is no doubt that new media has the potential to help to bring people together and encourage or support them to become involved in social and political activism. Theocharis (2012), for instance, studied the 2010 UK student protests against planned cuts to higher education and increased university tuition fees. He found that, far from being an apolitical homogeneous mass, these young people in fact used social networking sites in order to publicise opposition to the cuts and circulate information about the protests and demonstrations as they were actually taking place. A range of people, including fellow students, journalists, politicians and parents, then followed this information.

The competent workfare public sphere nevertheless focuses not on social classes or on other social collectivities but on individuals. It suggests that the best route to an inclusive democracy is arrived at when individuals empower themselves through both their tangible and intangible traits or when they come together to exchange ideas and deliberate with one another in public forums. As part of this individualistic ethos, people are encouraged to take part in digital 'civil' actions (Wilhelm, 2004; Dahlberg, 2011). For example, in their study of the 2000 US presidential election Earl and Schussman (2003) found that digital media inspired a new breed of individual activists to become involved in formal American politics. 'Movement entrepreneurs' were largely responsible for employing and coordinating online tactical voting. Movement entrepreneurs are people who are frustrated by electoral politics and seek to change it where possible through their own skills. In the case of the 2000 election this meant that left-wing activists who were concerned that left-liberal votes might be split between Al Gore of the Democratic Party and Ralph Nader of the Green Party constructed a website that 'linked electorates in swing states with like-minded people in states that would likely go for Bush or Gore. In exchange for somebody in a safe Bush or Gore state voting for Nader, a constituent in a swing state, where every ballot counted, would vote for Gore' (Earl and Schussman 2003, pp 158–9). For Earl and Schussman these websites demonstrate how, through digital media, individual movement entrepreneurs have a large input into conventional politics that at the same time goes beyond formal institutionalised politics.

Some see these developments in highly positive terms as signifying a democratic renewal by providing stimulating grassroots activism, creating more self-directed political campaigns and increasing levels of civic trust (Price and Cappella, 2002; see also Gibson, 2009). However, there are noticeable contradictions and problems entrenched in this form of activism. Earl and Schussman admit that those movement entrepreneurs in charge of the sites studied were not part of an ideological movement or embedded in conventional activist networks. Indeed, many movement entrepreneurs embodied what might be thought of as neoliberal utterances. As Earl and Schussman note: 'The webmasters we studied referred to participants as "users", "traders" and "voters" but did not refer to participants as "members"' (Earl and Schussman, 2003, p 180). Such utterances refract an individualised discourse associated with a corporate and business language in which people are deemed as individual 'users' of digital media. Actually, even when it comes to normal democratic procedures such as voting in a general election it is not at all clear that digital media serves to galvanise the public sphere. Some evidence from the US indicates that people value digital media to the extent that it allows them to vote in the privacy of their home. In other words, new media forms like online voting might actually take people away from being visible in the public sphere (Stromer-Galley, 2003). We will therefore briefly explore this issue in more depth through recent instances of individualised online politics.

One avenue open to those who wish to oppose a particular planning application in their community – for example, if they wish to oppose planning permission being granted to a corporate supermarket store – is to start a Facebook group centred on their opposition. Many other 'users' might join this group through the click of a button. Whether this then translates to actual protest is of course another question. In her study of 34 social networking campaign sites against various planning proposals, Evans-Cowley (2010) found that on average each site attracted just under 300 people signing up to support the protest in question. Few administrators of these sites managed to translate these supporters into 'real' activists involved in the likes of local public meetings around a campaign. Little wonder, then, that such social networking campaigns are more often than not an irrelevance to planning officials when they make their final decision about a planning application. Indeed, Evans-Cowley found that few of the planning officials she spoke to had even heard of a particular online campaign in their planning area.

In their study of 522 Facebook groups linked to 300 unique e-petitions associated with the main UK government website, Number10.gov.uk, Panagiotopoulos et al (2011) similarly found that no necessary relationship was evident between being a member of a Facebook group about a particular social or political cause and signing an e-petition around the cause in question. Specifically, the authors found that 51% (154) of the e-petitions examined were associated with an ineffectual or failing campaign on Facebook. In other words, being a member of a Facebook campaign does not necessarily translate into any basic online activities in and around political campaigning.

Such examples lead Marden (2011) to observe that while social media sites have of course reconfigured public space and the virtual world it does not follow that we now live an enriched civic life full of new political possibilities. In fact, it might be the case that social networking sites simply enhance the connection between individual lifestyle choices and politics. In other words, individuals choose to sign up to sites about social issues that chime well with their own personal interests (Breindl, 2010, p 47; see also the next chapter).

Other practical examples lend support to this thesis. Howard Dean's race for the Democratic Party nomination in the 2004 US election is arguably one of the most cited in this respect. Dean's campaign is especially noteworthy. It was the first times that a politician had attempted to systematically utilise new media resources like blogs in order to gather grassroots support in a political leadership race. In reality, as Kreiss (2011) notes, Dean's campaign emphasised the benefits of *individuals* going online to become part of a decentralised political movement. But problems with this campaign approach surfaced in the state of Iowa. Here, Dean's field-staffers discovered that they did not have a basic campaign to marshal activists on the ground. Held hostage to its 'new media' brand, Dean's left-leaning political message was lost in an individualistic cyber-utopian rhetoric. These dilemmas become even more pronounced when social hierarchies, divisions and inequalities are added to the analytical picture.

The reproduction of social divisions and social hierarchies

For successful deliberation to occur there must be a degree of equality between the participants involved to ensure that social hierarchies do not infringe on deliberative procedures. But equality is a complex subject in the deliberative canon. Knight and Johnson (1999), for example, suggest that deliberative democracy supports an equality of opportunity through deliberation to influence political decision making. Each citizen should, ideally, be allowed to put forward arguments that enjoy an opportunity to convince others of their merit. To foster this kind of equality other stipulations must also be met. For instance, each person must have the capacity to act freely and voluntarily to establish his or her preferences about an issue. Moreover, each must have the requisite degree of cognitive capacities and skills to engage in deliberation, which can be achieved if governments intervene in society to ensure that citizens receive the necessary education to develop these skills. For this to occur, however, governments need to ensure that there is a redistribution of wealth so that citizens receive the necessary income and resources to participate as fully as possible in deliberation (Knight and Johnson, 1999, pp 305–7).

While these are undoubtedly laudable proposals, it is equally true to say that capitalist socioeconomic systems are structured through *essential* and *necessary* inequalities. Capitalism relies for its very existence on the exploitation of labour in order to procure surplus value (see Chapter Two). For this reason alone it is extremely unlikely that the type of social welfare state required by deliberative democrats could exist fully intact. For example, one way to ensure that individuals gain the necessary resources to participate in deliberation is to maintain full employment. In capitalist systems, however, full employment implies that wages should increase relative to productivity gains. Yet, if this does indeed occur it will possibly lead to higher inflation. Higher inflation, though, proves to be an incentive for capital to uproot to places with lower inflation. If this happens, unemployment increases in the place vacated by capital (Smith, 2006, p 39). What is more, an equitable distribution of income is usually generated through state revenue in the form of taxes. Nevertheless, we know that excessive claims of government on the tax burdens of big business prompt capitalists to indulge in all sorts of anti-tax schemes to lessen the amount of tax actually paid. Thus, 'the costs associated with the transfer and distribution branches tend to fall on the so-called "middle class" and ordinary workers, as opposed to the corporations and individuals who enjoy both the greatest wealth and the greatest number of effective exit options from the domestic economy' (Smith, 2006, p 42).

The reason for highlighting these points is simply to point out that capitalism's very existence is predicated on systemic relations of exploitation and inequality. While certain social policies can of course be employed to try to diminish some of the worst effects of these relations, systematic inequalities will always remain a fundamental element in the very identity of capitalism, and these will inevitably contradict some of the main principles of deliberative democracy.

Given this, it should come as no surprise that different types of social hierarchies and inequalities are reproduced in e-democracy. For instance, a quantitative study of a relatively prosperous town in south-east England found that those citizens who were already frequent users of online services were more inclined to obtain new knowledge and to get their voice heard than were non-users. In other words, those who considered themselves politically and socially aware were 'more able and likely to express their opinions via the e-government portals' (Kolsaker and Lee-Kelley, 2008, p 733). Similar results are found in the US. Reddick (2011) reports that US citizens tend to access government websites for management activities rather than for participative democratic goals. For Reddick, even this activity mirrors digital divides, with income and education being the main factors that increase citizen interaction. Those with a higher income are thus more likely to interact with government online (Reddick, 2011, p 179). We should not be surprised at these results, especially since, as we have seen in previous chapters, different forms of inequality have increased in the neoliberal age. Such figures are reproduced in the digital environment. For example, in 2009 it was reported that 40% of US homes lack internet access (Jaeger and Bertot, 2010, p 373). Those who lack access will then rely on other institutions such as public libraries to log on to e-government websites. If these public institutions start to lose funds, then internet access is once again limited for those of relatively deprived backgrounds.

Social hierarchies are naturally reproduced in other related ways. One important point about the workfare state is that it has unleashed a new type of elitism into social policy. In the UK, business leaders have been promoted in social policy agendas. This takes different forms, but one common way that it occurs is to have non-elected business specialists sitting on local government committees associated with the likes of education, health and housing (Peck, 1995). This elitism is found in online forums. A number of UK MPs have blogs but, apart from a few celebrity politicians, there is very little evidence that these blogs have much impact in the public sphere. Few people read them or post comments. According to Francoli and Ward, 'blogs so far are mainly about politicians representing themselves to the public rather than vice-versa' (Francoli and Ward, 2008, p 37). In other words, blogs have become a mechanism for politicians to reproduce their elite 'distance' status. This is not, of course, to deny that political blogs and other websites dealing with formal parliamentary politics have encouraged the growth of new horizontal knowledge and information networks in and around Parliament. But it is to say that blogs are used regularly for promotional purposes by MPs.

But what about Twitter, a site that is often held up as an example of new media activism? In reality, few internet users employ Twitter as a means to further political or social deliberation (Larsson and Moe, 2011, p 742). Those that do so often serve to reproduce political elites. One study found that only one in ten MPs actually employed Twitter to interact with the public, although a prominent reason for those that did was impression management and self-promotion (Jackson and Lilleker, 2011). Davis (2010) further argues that digital information often reinforces already existing elite networks of knowledge. Political and media elites read one another's publications and writings, especially when these are written online, and they will cite one another as well.

Many of the so-called 'ordinary' members of the public who are said to read these online news sites are nothing of the sort. Instead, what one often finds is that the rhetoric of 'ordinariness' masks the reality that those who do indeed read these news sites come from a narrow band of people who actively consume parliamentary news. 'Thus, in several respects, new media has contributed to a weakening of the already fragile communicative links that existed between political elites at the centre and ordinary citizens at the periphery' (Davis, 2010, p 756).

In their analysis of the 2010 Swedish election campaign, Larsson and Moe (2011) found that high-end Twitter users constituted the substantial part of tweeting about the campaign, which included those belonging to mainstream political parties, journalists and well-known bloggers. While recognising that Twitter does provide opportunities for minor political parties to gain a voice in the electronic public sphere, Larsson and Moe nevertheless found that the majority of posts on Twitter about the election campaign were designed to disseminate information rather than to engage in real political dialogue (Larsson and Moe, 2011, p 741). Arguably, then, new media might reinforce elitism as people reject pluralistic discourse with others who have different identities to their own and instead opt to connect with like-minded people (Wilhelm, 1999, p 173).

One possible and plausible explanation for this attitude on the part of elites can be found simply in how they work at an everyday level. Local policy officials and policy planners want to ensure that they get their job done. And to do this they often welcome new initiatives that will add benefits to their already established ways of working. This does not mean, though, that they also welcome a communicative or deliberative approach to decision making. E-government, observe Åström and Granberg (2007), therefore becomes a means to further normal work patterns in and around service delivery and/or planning, but not necessarily furthering of deliberative ideals. E-democracy thus holds no intrinsic benefits for some policy officials and will instead be judged on the instrumental merits of costs and benefits for furthering normal work routines (Åström and Granberg, 2007, p 74).

Conclusion

Governments that propagate the belief that the creative information revolution is 'unstoppable' and that the state has no choice but to apply new technologies to welfare service delivery (Hudson, 2003, p 282) belie the fact that states have been extremely active in establishing the creative agenda in the first place. As Hirsch (2003) notes, the shift towards a competitive society requires the mobilisation of huge reserves of knowledge and power found in various public sector networks. States will often appeal to ideas of deliberation to make these changes more palatable for local populations. As a consequence, however, a number of contradictions emerge in this agenda that disrupt and prevent the potential of deliberative digital democracy.

Interestingly, however, there are some who employ the ideas of one of the leading thinkers in deliberative theory – Jürgen Habermas – but do so in a manner that is noticeably different from deliberative democrats. A number of scholars use Habermas's work on instrumental and strategic rationality, especially his point that instrumental rationality on the part of the economy and the state has the potential to 'colonise' and thereby damage the public sphere (Habermas, 1987, p 304). As Fisher (2010, pp 19–20) observes, the basis for this critique centres on an earlier argument of Habermas's that suggests that during the 1960s and 1970s political debate was being swamped by a technological discourse that transformed political and social issues into technical ones about how to solve problems through a functional logic associated with an interventionist welfare state. Arguably, this technological discourse is still with us today but has morphed into a competent workfare public sphere (see also Salter, 2005).

In many respects these perspectives point towards an alternative use of deliberative theory, and one in which corresponds to the theoretical perspective that runs through this book, which is 'to challenge the very requirement of any moral universalism from the particular' (Morris, 2001, p 157). This suggests that universal deliberative norms will always come up against real concrete problems like corporate power, inequalities and neoliberal ideology. While deliberative theorists might try to bracket out these social factors in experimental online forums in much the same way that psychologists set up ideal conditions in laboratories to test certain psychological variables on individuals, real deliberative forums will always be plagued by these social factors. They will also inevitably play a part in disrupting online deliberative procedures.

Despite this, we know that social media is still nevertheless held up by commentators as holding great opportunities for users to become active in disseminating information in the public sphere. Others, however, remain sceptical, not least because they feel that the likes of Facebook and Twitter promote an individualist culture that is opposed to the sort of communalist principles they wish to cultivate among members and potential recruits. Fenton and Barassi (2011), for instance, discovered in their ethnographic study of the UK's Cuba Solidarity Campaign that many of its full time staff and activists felt that campaign work undertaken through social media (writing a blog for instance) was often too individualistic and missed what was thought to be a more collective sense of belonging. They therefore favoured already existing alternative media such as newsletters, websites and printed magazines as tools for campaign work because they believed these fostered a more collectivist activist spirit among members.

But this example raises a number of other interesting issues about social media, not least trying to ascertain exactly what potential it does in fact hold for the public sphere and how, if at all, it contributes towards an individualised neoliberal form of dialogue in the public sphere. We now turn to these issues. Without pre-empting all of the arguments to be presented, we will see that one important function of social media (among many other functions) is that it produces a type of networked activism that inadvertently supports and bolsters an individualist neoliberal culture that can then frustrate building grassroots activism within civil society.

FIVE

Social media and the
neoliberal subject

Introduction

In *Communication Power* Castells (2009) differentiates between what
he terms as 'mass communication' and 'mass self-communication'.
The former emerged with the rise of new technologies in industrial
societies. Newspapers, radio, TV and so on all enabled messages to be
communicated to mass audiences. With the rise of the internet, however,
a different and more interactive form of mass self-communication has
become the norm. More commonly associated these days with social
media sites, mass self-communication is a global medium that enables
media convergence to proceed apace through the likes of digital
networks and the production of self-generated and self-communicated
messages. As a result, Castells is fairly positive about the democratic
potentials and possibilities of mass communication (Castells, 2009,
pp 54–5). Arguably, he therefore works, albeit critically, within a
'liberation technology' perspective in so far that he sees social media as
a means to 'expand political, social, and economic freedom' (Diamond,
2010, p 70).

But, while Castells describes social media along these lines he says
less about its relationship to the deeper processes of neoliberalism
(Fenton and Barassi, 2011, p 191). This is an important point because
there is another critical sense in which social media also depoliticises
public activism by promoting enjoyable neoliberal ideals to users. After
all, social media sites urge people to upload amusing, emotional and
personal information about their Selves to others, including information
about consumer and leisure pursuits. At the same time, it encourages
users to 'manage' and 'market' their everyday Selves through popular
culture and everyday personal experiences. Through sites like Facebook,
individuals can in effect modify their identities and assemble their
Selves into competent online 'brands'. To gain a critical perspective on
social media it is vital to understand that this occurs through emotional
elements of popular culture. By having fun, heated discussions, swapping
the latest gossip about celebrities and so on, individuals are often less
likely to care if information from their personal 'brand' is then collected

and harvested by major companies for profit-related purposes. Social media thereby delineates a new type of fetishism and ideology in society that on one level at least is compatible with the constitution of a neoliberal subjectivity. And, as an ideology, social media mystifies contradictions associated with neoliberalism.

The next section begins to explore these arguments in more detail. First, it considers what the 'social' in 'social media' denotes and how it has helped to reconfigure ordinary relationships in society. Following this, the idea that social media represents a radical transformation of society is critically investigated. For example, we will see that social media regularly reproduces existing social divisions and social hierarchies and frequently does so through conventional state and political mechanisms. If this is the case, then a space opens up to explore how social media might contribute towards strengthening neoliberalism and competence in society in ways that complement the competent workfare public sphere. None of this is to deny the many purposes served by social media in society. Its ability to articulate a neoliberal ideology and prevent new modes of public activism from emerging is only one, albeit compelling, moment to social media. More positively, social media also clearly offers new democratic opportunities for activists and social movements to get their voices heard in the public sphere. Indeed, later chapters will explore the emancipatory possibilities inherent in social media. For now, however, the present chapter is more concerned with how social media is an expressive medium for neoliberal ideology.

Web 2.0 and the 'social' in social media

Arguably, social media has helped to transform the boundaries between public and private spheres in new ways. In her study of 54 YouTube users aged between 9 and 43, Lange (2007) identifies two principle ways that this occurs. First, Lange suggests that YouTube can create a 'publicly-private identity' for some. This happens when a YouTube participant will share their private experiences by revealing personal identity information to others. 'Tags' and 'friends only' options can limit videos to a close circle of friends. An uploaded video can nevertheless be read publicly by somebody else in a completely different manner than was originally intended. Second, Lange identifies a 'privately-public identity'. This refers to the attempt to make as many connections as possible with others while remaining relatively private as regards identity information. For example, individuals can assume 'characters' on YouTube that hide their real identity but widen their network circle of friends, contacts or fans. Even so, the person uploading the video does not necessarily have to engage in dialogue with their associated social network. What Lange therefore conveys well is the reworking of not only public–private boundaries but also presence–absence boundaries. Social media sites like YouTube enable users to be both present by uploading media content or posting a comment, and absent by hiding their real identity. Lange similarly highlights a distinction between patterned and random interactions. After all, there is no inherent reason why a particular clip on YouTube will suddenly be viewed by thousands, sometimes millions, of viewers across the world. Yet the sudden randomness of connecting multitudes of people together through watching a YouTube video also generates patterns of interaction among these users (Farman, 2012, p 70; see also Keenan and Shiri 2009).

Social media sites likewise open up opportunities for users to 'perform' social ties with others. Facebook, for example, presents its users with a multitude of ways of performing emotional and expressive acts of friendship to different degrees. Even the act of just adding another Facebook page as a contact to one's own page contains a number of expressive meanings, from being a friend, to being a fan, to showing empathy with a social or political cause, to appreciating a joke and so on (Grimmelmann, 2009, pp 1154–5; see Tufekci, 2008). But such is the 'newness' of the networked relations unleashed by social media sites that some argue that these new modes of technology signal a profound change in communicative public spheres and a qualitative transition in the very meaning of what constitutes the social.

In 1997 a new website, SixDegrees.com, came onto the market. While it closed in 2000, due to declining profits, SixDegrees.com is generally acknowledged as one of the first social network sites on the internet to encourage people to create profiles, initiate friendship lists and navigate across other Friends lists (boyd and Ellison, 2007). Nevertheless, SixDegrees.com was just one of a number of interactive online sites that started to grow in popularity through the likes of bulletin boards, multi-user domains and e-mail lists, along with popular blogging sites and businesses experimenting with interactive services (Allen, 2013, pp 262–3). By the mid-2000s the term 'Web 2.0', promoted by key new media personalities and innovators like Tim O'Reilly, became a popular one to describe the interactive properties of digital technologies like digital platforms, collective intelligence, widely used and distributed software and active types of data processing. 'User-generated content' is another expression commonly associated with Web 2.0 and social media. It refers to the amount of power users have to customise, determine and produce content on a site in the form of audio interviews, blogs, citizen journalism, music and videos, which can then be uploaded to various sites. Today, we know that many platforms encourage users to access and contribute data in a variety of formats, whether these be photos, reviews or videos (Postigo, 2011, p 184; Blank and Reisdorf, 2012, pp 538–9).

Social media sites are especially known for their social networking functions. boyd and Ellison (2007, p 211) define social networking sites (SNSs) as web-based services that allow individuals to construct a public or semi-public profile inside a bounded system, compile a record of users who share a similar interest and view and navigate a list of connections between oneself and others in a network system. boyd and Ellison also distinguish between social network sites and social networking sites. The latter, 'social networking', term refers to those sites that initiate relationship connections between strangers. boyd and Ellison prefer the former, 'social network', term because they believe that when people use SNSs they are not necessarily trying to meet up with new people. Instead, participants frequently communicate with others who are already a member in their extended social network. Social networks thus assist a person to make contact and facilitate social interaction with others around similar interests, be these in art, education, literature, music, politics, religion, sports and so on.

Some, though, are critical of boyd and Ellison's definition. Beer (2008) suggests that to define SNSs in such broad terms so as to include all social networks, as boyd and Ellison do, misses what is specific about SNSs, which is exactly their ability to initiate and maintain friendship networks.

> The difficulty that boyd and Ellison's use of the term social network sites creates is that it becomes too broad, it stands in for too many things, it is intended to do too much of the analytical work, and therefore makes a differentiated typology of these various user-generated web applications more problematic. (Beer, 2008, p 519)

boyd and Ellison's explanation is not helped either by their insistence on distinguishing between physical friendships that obviously exist in real time and space and virtual friendships that exist only in computer-mediated interactions. Beer believes that this constructs untenable divisions between the physical and virtual. After all, online relationships are often converted into physical relationships, and vice versa. Beer therefore prefers the umbrella term Web 2.0 because it enables one to differentiate products and websites from one another in terms of online sharing and collaboration among users. SNSs, wikis, folksonomies and mashups can indeed all be defined through their capacity to facilitate online sharing and collaboration (see also Beer and Burrows, 2007). For Beer, then, SNSs are a particular form of Web 2.0 whose unique properties reside in building friendship networks in both the physical and virtual worlds.

In making these claims Beer also draws on theorists like Scott Lash to claim that we now live an era of a networked knowledge capitalism. As we saw in Chapter Two, this vision of capitalism argues that life is centred on a cultural form of economic accumulation based in a 'creative' informational economy. Importantly, for Beer, one crucial element of this new capitalist formation is the belief that social life is now founded on a portal system in which data tracks our every move and in fact actively searches and finds us. Data systems anticipate our desires 'through strategic data mining and classification, and search us out rather than the reverse' (Beer and Burrows, 2007, p 2; see also Beer, 2009). Debates about the effects of databases and surveillance in everyday life are explored in more depth in the next two chapters and so there is no need to cover these issues here. Instead, the next section explores whether the data systems attached to social media indicate, as Beer and others suggest, that we now live in what has been termed a 'post-hegemonic' age. This will then provide a basis to present an alternative view of social media's impact on society.

Social media and the question of hegemony

Beer builds his arguments in part on Lash's broader claims that we now live in a 'post-hegemonic' order (Lash 2002; 2007). According to Lash (2002, pp 111–12; 2007, pp 67–8), capitalism has moved towards a 'mode of communication' through the circulation of non-linear and self-organised technological assemblages. These assemblages are reflexive systems that develop through feedback loops whereby outside 'noise' is selected to be converted into information that can be used by an informational system. This is different from an older industrial past where texts, TV, think-tanks, political groups and states articulated a hegemonic discourse to homogeneous national populations. Under these circumstances hegemony was structured externally to people, whether this was through a politician, bureaucrat, journalist, author and so on. In a post-hegemonic order, however, the world gets more complex. Informational societies are dominated by digital codes articulated through Web 2.0 technology. 'Most important is the ubiquity of code, of mediatic code pervading more and more regions of beings' (Lash, 2007, p 70). Self-organised networks are thus immanent to the very existence of everyday life. Without being coerced to do so, individuals produce media content through 'confessional' outlets such as blogs and SNSs. Whereas people might have once 'resisted' hegemonic power relations at the level of the everyday – for example, through pop music (think of punk music as a mode of 'resistance' to dominant hegemonic mores of the day) – people are now increasingly complicit in the subversion of everyday resistance as they gain enjoyment and pleasure by letting new media objects occupy mundane and routine popular spaces.

In the confessional arenas of social media, then, dominant power relations become part of our very being. Hegemonic power now operates through the self-organisation of Web 2.0 applications and software. People are seemingly complicit in this development (Beer, 2009, pp 994–5). EdgeRank, an algorithm designed by Facebook, is a case in point. EdgeRank basically assigns a grade to the information that appears on a Facebook page such as status comments, likes, updates and so on. How these are ranked by EdgeRank will determine if they appear in the Top News feed on a Facebook page. For Bucher (2012), however, this algorithm works with a built-in bias. It ranks activity highly if there is a large amount of participation around it. So, for instance, if a post gets many comments from other friends, then that post will be ranked higher than a comment that attracts less activity from others. Bucher thus argues that EdgeRank helps to form a Facebook 'norm' made up of a networked participatory subject (Bucher, 2012, pp 1175–6).

This point is important because it implies more broadly that systems can 'spontaneously' generate data about us by mining information on our desires, and then feed this information back to us in the form of consumer lists for particular consumer products. Naturally, these profile lists are based on algorithms, but they are also grounded in our own behaviour in using these sites and constructing profile lists. As Andrejevic (2002, 2009a) notes, online consumption patterns increasingly rely on modes of surveillance such as personal demographic files/data. Sites like Amazon bring together production and consumption through algorithms so that we, the consumers, generate our own demographic information for companies in the very act of consuming goods. Somewhat ironically, then, interactivity on Web 2.0 sites can actually negatively affect our capacity for critical reflection about what we consume, because when we shop online we automatically create new personalised advertisements for ourselves.

These arguments are well taken and do indeed serve to flag up some of the novel practices that SNSs and other social media sites bring to society. Yet, much of the post-hegemonic thesis exaggerates and overstates the impact of recent technological developments in society. For example, many users of social media are in fact conscious of the amount of information posted and uploaded to these sites and they try to manage this in a 'considerate' way. One study found that numerous people on Facebook were well aware that too many status updates are unnecessary and annoying to those friends connected to their profile (McLaughlin and Vitak, 2011). Anyhow, others rarely engage with much that is posted on social media sites to any significant degree. Wikipedia, for example, has made a huge contribution to knowledge acquisition by ordinary people. It is equally true to say that numerous pieces of information posted on Wikipedia are of an esoteric nature and of little interest to the vast majority of people (Lam and Riedl, 2011).

More problematically, the post-hegemonic thesis is part of a rather implausible argument that says that so-called 'industrial' modern societies and nation-states have been surpassed by a late/post-modern informational network formation. To understand why this is an implausible argument let us for a moment focus on the assertion that the nation-state is losing many of its organisational and regulatory powers over society. In a post-hegemonic order, argues Lash, people are no longer politically constituted or controlled from the 'outside' by a state but are instead ever more formed through 'self-organisation' by communication networks around a series of interrelated and often complex events (Lash, 2007, pp 60–2). As a result, when a terrorist attack of the magnitude of 9/11 happened, the target was not the US state but a communicative symbol of global power, namely the World Trade Center (Lash, 2007, p 66).

Nevertheless, even if we accept that Lash makes some perceptive observations on the nature of contemporary global societies, this in no way, shape or form implies that the post-hegemony thesis about the nation-state must also be accepted. Let us take the case of 9/11 and terrorism. As we see, Lash wants to insist that 9/11 is an indicator of a new global order based on flows and networks of communication. Indeed, other theorists make similar claims about the changing nature of terrorism. Some suggest that terrorists conduct their activists through decentralised global networks that mostly avoid central command structures in favour of semi-autonomous inter-networked terrorist cells. According to some experts, this has led to an increasing proliferation of so-called 'netwars'. For Arquilla and Ronfeldt (2001), netwars can be defined as an emerging mode of conflict (and crime) at societal levels, short of traditional military warfare, in which the protagonists use network forms of organisation and related doctrines, strategies and technologies attuned to the information age. (Cited in Anderson, 2003, p 26)

As Anderson goes on to note, netwars are not necessarily predicated on terrorists using only the latest technological gadgets. In fact, most terrorist groups will draw on old and new technologies to commit terrorist acts. Even so, terrorist groups generally find that networked forms of communication are extremely useful in furthering their aims. Posting information and images on the internet is relatively cheap and they can be uploaded quickly. Sharing information through e-mails and video conferencing is likewise a useful tactic for terrorists. They also allow a degree of flexibility in designing and then adjusting tactics to suit changing circumstances.

A related term to netwars is that of 'cyberterrorism', first employed during the 1980s. Title 22 of the United States Code, Section 2656f(d) defines cyberterrorism as:

premeditated, politically motivated attacks by sub-national groups or clandestine agents against information, computer systems, computer programmes, and data that result in violence against non-combatant targets. (Cited in Conway, 2002)

To be clear, terrorists who use computers in daily interactions are not necessarily involved in cyberterrorist activities. If somebody who is a member of or is aligned to a terrorist movement is simply reading a website about political issues, then it does not follow that that person is also involved in terrorist acts. However, if that person went on to commit a terrorist act by using a computer, or by targeting a computer system and its accompanying digital networks and digital infrastructure, then it would be possible to say that he or she was involved in cyberterrorism.

Some analysts and scholars would therefore no doubt agree with Lash, arguing that contemporary terrorist groups like al-Qaeda are indeed representative of new globally networked and technologically sophisticated terrorist groups. Such groups are also seen to be motivated by religious ideology, to use weapons of mass destruction and to employ new media for indiscriminate killings (Kurtulus, 2011). In addition, and this is a view maintained by theorists like Lash who claim that we live in an informational society, netwars are inescapably linked to the fact that the digital public sphere is now an integral part for the reporting of terrorist acts. It goes without saying that this still occurs through mainstream media outlets, but it also ensues through the internet. Citizen journalists, as well as conventional journalists, thus gain a voice in public debate about global terrorism (Anderson, 2003). Such is the belief that netwars and cyberterrorism are real threats that governments and security services across the world have been involved in monitoring hundreds of suspected terrorist websites.

Yet, and contrary to this informational view of violence, many other experts dispute this interpretation of terrorism, claiming instead that 9/11 indicates a continuation of terrorist activities over the last few decades. Past terrorist organisations like the IRA also worked within loose global networks and operated in semi-autonomous cells, while today it is probably correct to say that terrorists currently function within both loosely organised and semi-structured networks that also feed into more centralised command points. This is further related to the point that few terrorists are actually involved in cyberterrorism. After all, high-risk targets like military infrastructures are generally not connected to the internet, while only a few people actually have the capability and knowledge to launch cyberterrorist attacks. Anyhow, terrorists generally use digital technology to coordinate their activity rather than to initiate terrorist attacks. Some groups occasionally employ hackers to deface and disrupt a website of the enemy, but overall few have been actively involved in perpetrating cyberterrorism (Conway, 2002). Moreover, many of today's terrorist groups might claim to be motivated by religious goals, but once one digs a little deeper it soon becomes apparent that they actually have secular and political aims too, such as demanding the withdrawal of external military forces from a particular country. As such, 'new' terrorists often have political as well as religious goals directed at specific nation-states. Think about terrorist activities in Afghanistan or Iraq. These actions are directed at changing the policies of particular governments and state structures. Furthermore, so-called 'new' terrorists today, again like past terrorists, use conventional weapons to gain publicity for their cause. Terrorists do not commit random acts, but instead more often than not carefully select targets for maximum publicity (Field, 2009; Spencer, 2011).

This last point is significant because it hints at how the state is still a crucial moment in network formations. Indeed, as Chapters Three and Four demonstrated in some detail, and as Chapters Six and Seven will also show, the neoliberal workfare state remains a powerful hegemonic force in capitalist societies. As a result, to imply that the state is somehow losing its organisational and regulatory powers to global 'flows' of global networks simplifies what is a far more complex picture of the world. As J.S. Davies (2011, p 102) observes, much of the post-hegemony thesis seems to conflate certain discourses about globalisation – the idea that nation-states are losing many of their powers to other global governance bodies, or the idea that digital codes act in a semi-autonomous manner in how they govern social life – with the actual realities of how the global world has indeed changed in the last 30 years or so. Just think about how governments regularly seek to order, govern and regulate global 'flows' of migrants entering their territorial borders, and frequently do so by summoning up nationalist and racist discourses so as to gain hegemony for specific government policies around these and other issues (Turner, 2007; Finney and Simpson 2009). Far from Web 2.0 sites indicating that we live in something called a post-hegemonic society, it still therefore seems plausible and entirely reasonable to argue that state hegemony is a hugely important factor for governments in order to win support from sections of a population for a political programme and to regulate and govern territories.

New technology thus creates and reproduces hegemonic power relations associated with 'normal' political and social practices, as well as instigating new ones. It shows a continuum in how social and political technological practices replicate and refract relations of dominance (cf. Feenberg, 1999, p 86). To think otherwise is to present a de-contextual account that fails to give due weight to hegemonic, especially state-led, processes and their integral relationship to forces in civil society, let alone broader capitalist power dynamics. In many respects, then, the idea that Web 2.0 represents a qualitative transition in how society operates misses subtle ways in which ordinary people subvert neat linear divisions between 'old' and 'new' technologies and in so doing underestimates how these technologies are still framed and mediated by wider capitalist relationships of exploitation (Christensen, 2011).

But, if this is the case, then we still need to understand how exactly we might analyse the 'social' in social in a more adequate manner. More precisely, we need to develop less 'thin' and transcendental theories about social media – the non-historical and rather transcendental idea, for instance, that communication networks have become all-encompassing attributes of life – and acquire instead more historically relevant ideas that situate social media in the contradictions of capitalist social relations (Johnson, 2007, p 102). Building on arguments and observations already made in previous chapters, the rest of the current chapter therefore shows in more detail how social media contribute in their own way to the articulation of neoliberal and competence themes in civil society.

The neoliberal social media self

We saw in Chapter Two that one prominent argument suggests that many organisations have moved towards a 'post-bureaucratic' formation based on horizontal cells, networks and organisational fluidity. In the business world this is often associated with a belief that these flows of knowledge need to be managed in a competent manner in order to gain competitive advantage. 'Knowledge management' therefore underlines the conviction that the world has become more complex, chaotic and unpredictable, and during these times of turbulence there is a requirement to allow employees some flexibility, space and initiative to draw on their acquired competence, know-how and intelligence to creatively respond to the opportunities thrown up by these conditions (Alvesson, 2004, p 6). ICTs are an important source in capturing the changing nature of knowledge, calculating its potential and storing information about its possible use and application (Earl, 2001, p 220). Discursive and semiotic assets are also often thought to be valuable properties of organisations in this respect. Tacit knowledge embodied in the likes of 'process manuals, articles of association, contracts, the inventory, records of property transfers, daybooks' coordinate knowledge acquisition between different individuals and groups (Davenport, 2002, p 1041).

Knowledge management thus embraces the idea that tangible and intangible resources are of equal importance in promoting success in business. A passion for solving a problem and the willingness to share different experiences and knowledge are as crucial as a formal set of skills in order to accomplish goals (Williamson, 1999; Pan and Leidner, 2003). Narratives embodied in the likes of policy documents thus help to articulate these passions across a firm and often emphasise soft character traits such as commitment, learning and self-discovery (Day, 2001, p 733). This is noticeable in some new work practices where there is an increasing propensity for employers to encourage their employees to competently express their emotions in the workplace and produce positive synergies between an organisation and its workforce.

Social media has many ideals similar to that of knowledge management. Collaboration and the sharing of knowledge is after all a key moment to social media sites, and this encapsulates key knowledge management characteristics. Wikis, for example, are online spaces where users can edit, update, generate, share and view knowledge. As such, wikis offer an opportunity to draw on tacit knowledge and convert it into explicit and available knowledge, collect information in one locality, distribute information across networks and connect people together. For O'Leary (2008), these benefits show how wikis provide an outlet for people to directly share knowledge that they are passionate about, as well as setting out transparent rules for accessing and uploading information. Moreover, wikis thrive on the 'wisdom of crowds' philosophy, in so far that 'content draws on a wide range of contributors with varying perspectives and expertise' (O'Leary, 2008, p 37).

Social media therefore shares a number of principles with management ideological themes. Perhaps this is unsurprising, especially considering that many of the specific words and terms used in social media products are employed by the business and management community. Van Dijck and Nieborg (2009) argue that Web 2.0 ideology reproduces new management ideals, particularly through the writings by management gurus. Their books and manifestos promote the belief that we live in profoundly revolutionary times, that we need to surf on the wave of liberation thrown up by them and grasp the opportunity for change (van Dijck and Nieborg, 2009, p 858; see also Collins, 2000; Huczynski, 2006).

To get to grips with this ideology, think for a moment of the word 'collaboration'. From new media academics to business gurus, 'collaboration' is utilised to describe a new world of cooperation between individuals so that synergies might be produced between a whole array of 'partners', be they ordinary individuals in their homes, businesses, charities or local politicians. These are frequently said to go beyond old-fashioned hierarchies and move instead towards a flat world of technologically sophisticated networks in which we are all equal. 'mass collaboration', 'smart mobs', 'creative clusters' and so on, denote a homogeneous mass of anonymous users who can all equally and actively contribute to content and learn from one another. But, as van Dijck and Nieborg point out, studies in fact suggest that the vast majority of 'users' are mostly inactive and passive spectators or consumers and so provide a good marketplace for business to tap into. 'The term "user" turns out to be a catch-all phrase covering a wide range of behaviour, from merely clicking to blogging and uploading videos. Mass creativity, by and large, is consumptive behaviour by a different name' (van Dijck and Nieborg, 2009, p 861; see also van Dijck 2009).

Another illustration is 'platform', a term frequently applied in new media rhetoric. A seemingly innocuous term, 'platform', as Gillespie (2010, pp 350–2) observes, in fact contains a number of ideological themes. At its simplest, 'platform' conjures up the image of a raised level from which a certain amount of activity will transpire. Moreover, there is an agenda of equality in the application and use of 'platform' in so far that a platform welcomes anyone to stand on it. In terms of social media it suggests that the architecture and software of particular Web 2.0 sites are available for all, to be used as a platform for self-expression and for communication between all. Creativity is aligned to interactivity. These are deeply progressive sites, so the narrative continues, because they empower users to connect to others across the world and, in the process, enable them to engage in a journey of self-discovery, of knowledge building, by creatively displaying elements of their individual identity. The 'You' in YouTube suggests as much (Gillespie, 2010, p 352), as does the 'My' in 'MySpace' (Coté and Pybus, 2007).

Those who uncritically embrace these ideological terms will often miss how these words mystify other social processes. To see this let us return to the idea of collaboration through social media. One recent form of collaboration is that of crowdsourcing. Emerging as a new utterance in 2006 from a piece written by Jeff Howe in *Wired* magazine, crowdsourcing is employed by individuals, groups and organisations to co-opt the 'collective intelligence' of others through digital networks in order to solve a problem and gain specific outcomes. Frequently, it is said that crowdsourcing encourages ordinary people to contribute knowledge gained from their 'amateur' interests to a whole array of formal organisational concerns, from fashion to politics. Crowdsourcing is thus thought to 'democratise' the input of ordinary people to provide innovative knowledge and help solve problems in society. Much that goes under the umbrella term of crowdsourcing is, however, a myth. Brabham (2012) convincingly shows that many contributions from so-called 'amateurs' in the realm of crowdsourcing are actually anything but. For example, Threadless.com, a clothing company encouraging crowdsourcing from online members in the guise of submitted graphic designs for T-shirts, in fact provides a space for professional freelance designers to submit their pieces, get them viewed online and then, with any luck, win new contracts (Brabham, 2012, p 399; see also Tkacz, 2010). Creativity unleashed by Web 2.0 sites does not therefore imply that people using the site in question gain real empowerment.

Countless people are of course aware that their personal data is being collected for the purposes of advertising and selling, but these very same people also use social media for popular types of education (Crick, 2012). What these terms like 'crowdsourcing' gloss over is of course the immense power that corporate business media services wield. They further normalise a set of assumptions about the world that serve a neoliberal perspective; or at least a competence-based perspective in the guise of management ideals like knowledge management. Owned by Google since 2006, YouTube, for example, uses the 'platform' utterance as a means, in part, to open up commercial opportunities for advertisers and big media producers to circulate their money-making goods and wares (Gillespie, 2010, p 358). From 2008 Google began to sell YouTube homepage space as well as key words so that ads will appear on the side of its web page. Soon, other major media companies such as MGM started to upload their own programmes and movie clips onto YouTube. YouTube has therefore steadily moved from user-generated content (UGC) to professional generated content (PGC), with the implication being there is now a real possibility that 'PGC will overshadow UGC, marginalizing individuals' own creations' (Kim, 2012, p 62).

Similarly, MySpace empowers people to learn to produce a networked subjectivity made up of consumer tastes, images, needs and so on. Public profiles of users rest on a networked subjectivity based on the friends that each person can generate through their profile and the degree to which these friends write comments on their page. Popularity can then be built up through this feedback loop and this helps to extend one's network. MySpace consequently has an inbuilt device for collecting information about, and encouraging users to be engaged with, personal tastes in music, film, TV, books and so on. As a result, users provide rich data of information to companies (see also Cohen, 2008).

Social media sites therefore demonstrate that consumers are no longer static, unchanging, quantifiable groups but are, rather, sites where production, circulation and consumption blur into one another. This makes social media sites wonderful places for businesses to venture into in order to capture and profit from this sector. No wonder, then, that many social media sites are keen to let third parties have access to this data so that they can then target specific users (Coté and Pybus, 2007). As Andrejevic (2009b) observes, this is one of the important traits of social media in so far that they denote a struggle among major corporations for access to and control over user-generated data. Personal consumer habits and lifestyles can thereby be mined for profits through social media sites.

Take Google as an illustration. In 2012 it earned $50 billion in total revenue, and the majority of this came from advertising. One notable program developed by Google in this respect is AdWords. As Google explains:

> With AdWords, advertisers create simple text-based ads that
> then appear beside related search results or web content on

our websites and on thousands of partner websites in our Google Network, which is the network of third parties that use our advertising programs to deliver relevant ads with their search results and content. Most of our AdWords customers pay us on a cost-per-click basis, which means that an advertiser pays us only when a user clicks on one of its ads. (Google, 2012, p 5)

AdWords combines with other devices such as DoubleClick to target the online behaviour of users both on Google and on other websites accessed via Google. Along with these and other advertising devices, Google gives advertisers the opportunity to target the personal tastes and consumption patterns of users. The so-called 'prosumers' of social media therefore do not create or generate surplus value (see also Chapter Two). It is truer to say that prosumers distribute surplus value from industrial capitalists to capitalists in the media and entertainment industries. Media capitalists, for instance, rent out space in their daily operations for industrial capitalists to advertise their products. Through rent, media capitalists thus capture an already generated portion of surplus value (Caraway, 2011, p 701).

A critical assessment can therefore see 'prosumption' as primarily an ideological means to co-opt consumers into the hegemonic project of neoliberal consumption. On one level at least, prosumption signals the individualisation of human interests and human growth through network connections with others and the need to be included in endless interactive consumption (Comor, 2010, p 320). What, after all, is the mantra of Web 2.0? First, that ordinary people are required to gain competence in how social media sites operate, but also, and just as importantly, to develop this competence in respect to their own desires, interests and innate skills, whether this means uploading photos, posting a message on a site, watching videos, playing games and so on. Second, one must be up to date in acquiring competence by keeping abreast of the latest technological developments. Competence in this respect is related to obtaining the latest 'versions' of new technology. 'Version' thus becomes another key ideological theme in the quest to create competent technological personalities and competent consumers of technology. Indeed, 'a discourse of versions reassures consumers that they were right to buy the product first time around, but also informs them that they must buy again' (Allen, 2013, p 264). Public discussions about a social media object, about a technological 'thing', thereby become the very space for co-option of individuals into the upgrade culture.

Looking at the question of 'prosumption' in this manner transforms it into an ideological issue, not necessarily a socioeconomic one. As Andrejevic (2009b, p 418) again notes, we need first to understand how users are persuaded to hand over their personal data and accept that it might be very well be mined by social media companies for commercial purposes. It is to this subject we now turn.

The fetishised individual of social media

When Apple embarked on a marketing campaign, launched in 2006, called 'Get a Mac' it drew heavily on the creative individualism that is strongly associated with the information society. Comparing two ideal-typical characters – PC and Mac – the ad campaign clearly associated the latter Mac character with creative and fun personality traits at ease in moving between the spheres of work and leisure, where flexibility in life, personified by a Mac computer, produces a healthier lifestyle. Obviously, the ad campaign made sure that Mac personality traits never mentioned the realities of real social inequalities and instead it tried to become a universal point of call for all those who want to enter Apple's creative technological utopia (Livingstone, 2011).

This ad campaign was of course drawing on the sort of individualistic ideology already rooted in interactive media. Think, for example, about how digital television has helped to individualise media consumption. It allows ordinary viewers to establish their own temporal frames for watching programmes and its highly interactive form lets audiences transgress normal modes of watching programmes. Viewers have the option to pause a programme at any moment or, by recording programmes, are able to compress time by watching programmes within their own temporal frameworks. And once programmes are recorded individual viewers can rewind or fast-forward segments of programmes so that time is not wasted but, rather, saved (Moshe, 2012, pp 73–6). Given that social media also operates through interactive participation by users who, by the very fact that they are interactive also create personal ads for themselves, then these sites represent a new development in the objectification of technology. As Kang and McAllister (2011) insist:

> The interactive web services are also seemingly free but more customizable, the targeted ads are personalized and match our interests and web content as if by magic, and how our data is collected, used and monetized is automatic,

instant, and largely masked. (Kang and McAllister, 2011, p 151)

One can recall what Marx notes about the ideological features of the fetish in this respect. A society based on universal private labour itself presupposes the existence of a specific contradiction founded on the dispossession of labour from the means of production. Workers thus become commodities – free wage labour – and are therefore necessarily exploited by capital because capitalists accrue unpaid surplus value from workers. Yet, in a concrete marketplace workers also appear to freely enter into an equal bargain with capitalists based on the principle of 'a fair day's wage for a fair day's work'. But it is at this point that the *ideological* part of the fetish reveals itself. For it is those ideas that seek to justify the inverted appearances of capitalist social relations at the level of everyday marketplace interactions, appearances that mystify underlying inverted contradictions in the realm of production, that count as ideology (Larrain, 1983, pp 126–7). Marx is clear about this. He notes that in the sphere of circulation – 'within whose boundaries the sale and purchase of labour-power goes on' – there emerges the ideological assumption that capitalism is fostered through 'a very Eden of the innate rights of man' (Marx, 1988, p 280). This assumption is maintained through an array of ideological categories, not least 'freedom' (for example, people are determined only by their own 'free will' in capitalism), 'equality' (for example, exchange between two people in the marketplace is based on an exchange of equivalence), 'property' (for example, each person exchanges only what is theirs) and 'self-advancement' (for example, one looks to further only their own self-interests and advantage) (Marx, 1988, p 280).

Comor (2010) picks up Marx's points on the abstraction of particular words and their ideological status. 'Prosumer' is a case in point, explains Comor, because what is contained in this word is the belief that a person actually can express himself or herself directly by consuming objects. Similar to words like 'equality' this is not entirely deceptive but does signal a meaningful experience in which individuals gain some empowerment over their everyday lives. 'As such, the commodities she co-creates *really* do provide her with more meaning. Moreover, the goods and services she consciously prosumes *really* do tend to be more (materially and psychologically) useful than those that are mass produced' (Comor, 2010, p 314; original emphasis). As Comor goes on to observe, the sort of prosumption encouraged has many alienating effects, not least the fact that on one level it contributes further towards the fetishisation of 'voluntary' labour by the separation of manual from mental labour.

One key ideological image in this respect is that labour is given freely to capital and without coercion. 'Prosumption' suggests that people voluntarily work on products the moment they consume them and by so doing engage in feelings of self-empowerment. Yet this obscures the fact that such self-empowerment operates in the overall confines of exchange relations in which labour becomes an abstract measurement of concrete human worth. Objects of prosumption are thus 'things' that *individual* concrete labour works on but does so while remaining within the confines of capitalist social relations. This contradiction is reproduced in new age digital ideology about collaboration. This ideology claims that the more people share information and collaborate in building new ideas with one another, the more everyone benefits. At the same time, however, new media companies also 'share' the collaborative information generated by their users with advertisers for profit-related purposes. Yet these very same companies explain this practice in a friendly, neutral manner that serves to stymie the commercial, business-related ideology underlying this message (John, 2012, pp 177–8).

But more than this, social media sites, through their banal ubiquitous functions, have become an integral part of many people's everyday lives. Using Facebook, for example, is a ritualised and habitual act for many. Even the gossipy element of the news feed, towards which many users sometimes express a degree of ambiguity, often draws people in and becomes a source of everyday information about the lives of others. Those that regularly use social media, suggest Debatin et al (2009), thus gain a sense of gratification from their ritualistic experience, and any concerns about privacy violations are considered to be threats to others. So, while there might be a 'knowingness' by people about privacy issues on Facebook, users still nevertheless upload personal information onto their respective Facebook page without protecting this information in the first place. And this occurs even though Facebook has been beset by problems around privacy since its inception.

Abe (2009) similarly notes that many social media users just do not care if they are being subjected to surveillance. There are a number of reasons to explain this phenomenon. First, social media users are usually granted some power over who views their individual social media page, or at least how much information can be viewed. Other social media sites allow users to be anonymous. Both give users the feeling of empowerment. Second, there is an obvious enjoyment factor at play in spending time on a social media site, along with other emotional states such as desire, expectation and so on. Third, social media sites sell themselves to the public as being transparent. Even those surveillance mechanisms found on social media sites are created to make interactivity safer and more fun. Fourth, people simply lack information about how their activity online will be subject to surveillance. Fifth, it is thought that if individuals make a personal choice not to be concerned with the likes of surveillance on social media sites, then this is fine. Finally, most users just feel that they have nothing to hide when they go online, so they equally have nothing to worry about by subjecting themselves to surveillance (Abe, 2009, p 78). Technology, then, can and indeed does communicate hegemonic ideas and practices to audiences to such a degree that these ideas and practices often feel natural to ordinary people and thereby remain concealed (Feenberg, 1999, p 86).

Conclusion

Far from Web 2.0 sites indicating that we live in something called a post-hegemonic society, it is still the case that state hegemony and governance is a hugely important factor for governments in winning support from sections of a population and in regulating and governing territories. To think otherwise is to give a de-contextualised account that fails to give due weight to those political, especially state-led, hegemonic processes and their integral relationship to forces in civil society. Social and political change is inevitably bound up with different forces competing for hegemonic power, and this includes state power.

Those critical theorists who do not stress this element tend to view social media as a qualitatively new form of power and, in the process, provide a complementary analysis of new media to that given by those who advocate a 'liberation technology' perspective. Both tend to argue that social media represent qualitatively new technological potentials in relationship to democracy and power, but in so doing underestimate the capitalist form of social media (Christensen, 2011). At the same time they also often fail to fully understand how social processes that operate through ICTs are both different from and the same as past technological processes and hegemonic power relations.

But if this is the case, then we need to develop less 'thin' and general theories about new media – for example, the non-historical and somewhat transcendental idea that digital technology is an indicator to show how communication networks have become all-encompassing – and develop instead more historically relevant ideas that situate new media in the real contradictions of capitalist social relations in space and time, which in turn disrupt and enhance public activism (Johnson, 2007, p 102).

The next chapter therefore continues the critical exploration of the relationship between new media and public activism by exploring the question of surveillance. In particular, it examines different surveillance mechanisms at that disposal of government officials, policy officials and planners in how they go about regulating modes of dissent. The chapter shows how officials are able to employ what might be termed as 'hybrid surveillance' mechanisms to govern public space and quell dissent. Hybrid surveillance is of course typified by database digital technology. At the same time, however, it is also characterised by 'old-fashioned' physical and practical modes of surveillance in the guise of legal statutes that zone cities into container units to make the monitoring of dissent and protestors easier. We will see that while the physical zoning of public space shows how civil liberties have been practically constrained in recent years, the use of surveillance through databases masks the extent to which this has occurred. This is because database surveillance normalises control in society in ways similar to how social media normalises a neoliberal subjectivity in civil society. Both physical and virtual zoning therefore work together.

SIX

Zoning public space 1: hybrid surveillance and state power

Introduction

On 28 September 1862 the Workingmen's Garibaldian Committee organised a sympathy meeting at Hyde Park, London for Giuseppe Garibaldi, leader of the Italian Risorgimento, who was injured and had been captured at Aspromonte during the Second Italian War of Independence. Garibaldi was an immensely popular figure among all sections of British society. Members of the working class applauded Garibaldi's perceived radicalism, while middle-class supporters considered Garibaldi to be a successful businessperson and a fine example of the virtues of political economy (Finn, 1993, p 205). At the meeting, attended by some 20,000 people, Secularists spoke on behalf of Garibaldi's republican offensive against Catholic Rome. Soon, scuffles broke out among the police and mainly Irish Catholic sympathisers (Gilley, 1973, pp 704–5; see also Richter, 1981, pp 51–2). The following week around 100,000 people came to Hyde Park to hear once again a number of orators speaking about Garibaldi. More disturbances ensued. The state was itself divided over how to govern this particular public space of activism. A Marlborough Street magistrate who presided over the trial of Garibaldian rioters recommended the outright banning of meetings; a view that was echoed by the Hyde Park superintendent.

Sir Richard Mayne, a commissioner of the Metropolitan Police, agreed that too many gatherings had occurred in the Park since the 1860s but he also realised that to ban them would be counter-productive. Based on their accumulated knowledge gained through surveillance, Mayne decided instead to let the police judge which topics were deemed 'popular and exciting' and to issue bans on such topics at their discretion. This was a considerable improvement over previous mechanisms of governing public demonstrations at Hyde Park. Through the Recreation Grounds Act 1859 parks managers could enforce byelaws, although they had no power to impose a fine. The Public Improvement Act 1860 improved the condition by conferring the power of making byelaws to the Bath and Wash Houses Act 1846, which enabled a penalty not exceeding £5 to be imposed on any person breaching a byelaw. Local authorities would often swear in park keepers and labourers as special constables to make sure members of the public followed these rules and regulations. In all these matters, the degree and extent of governance became the prerogative of local authorities themselves (Conway, 1991, pp 203–7).

Crucially, by arguing for the need of proper *police* surveillance at Hyde Park, Mayne contributed towards new thinking about the accumulation of knowledge of local public spaces by the authorities. Mayne not only recognised that the legal and governance mechanisms of the day were failing to curtail popular demonstrations in London's public parks, he also tacitly recognised that the distinct *place* of Hyde Park required more sophisticated mechanisms of governance. Simply banning demonstrations at Hyde Park was no longer a viable option in an age of organised radical groups. Regular police surveillance, along with gaining knowledge about how political agitators used specific public spaces, was now the preferred strategy.

By today's digital standards, Mayne's approach to governing demonstrations seems rather quaint and outdated. A network society is said to be powered through ICTs, which in turn means that knowledge and information can be accumulated in ways unimaginable to the Victorians. Digital modes of surveillance, so some argue, demonstrate that the state no longer has to rely on government police tactics. Databases are centres of computation through which various pieces of information about distinct populations can be fed. This includes not just 'normal' information about individuals such as their age, occupation and place of residence, but also DNA profile information that travels between databases through digital networks, across natural borders that connect subject profiles together in order to gather information in national jurisdictions (Prainsack and Toom, 2010, p 1125). Surveillance thus operates both transnationally, across borders, and locally, in situated contexts.

However, while much can be learnt about new modes of surveillance from this perspective there is also something amiss. In particular, there lurks an ever-present danger that this viewpoint perpetuates a dualist framework in which the networked nature of contemporary surveillance practices is given precedence over state-led governance and regulation. Yet, this considerably underestimates how new modes of surveillance are integrally related to the 'normal' actions of state power and political projects. Certainly, it *appears* to be the case that surveillance today is markedly different to that of the past. In past years the state seemed to be actively engaged in physically regulating the behaviour of defined groups in public space as well as subjecting them to modes of undercover police investigation. By way of contrast, the authorities in the present day appear to be preoccupied mainly with digital surveillance of specific populations in society. As we will also see in this chapter, however, while it is indeed true to say that police and security organisations currently draw on technologically sophisticated mechanisms to track and monitor political groups, it is equally true to say that they also draw on 'old-fashioned' physical means to control and pre-empt the activity of demonstrators in much the same way that Mayne did in the 1860s. Physically zoning public space helps the authorities to gain comprehensive knowledge of the actions of distinct political groups during moments of protest and demonstration. And these procedures are underpinned by state power and the strong arm of law and order.

Contemporary surveillance is therefore comprised of a hybrid mix of physical state regulation and digitally networked forms of accumulating knowledge and information about citizens. In this respect, hybridity is simply a process in which more conventional and older systems of surveillance — the physical zoning of public space, for example — are recombined with newer types of surveillance — the digital coding of discrete populations, for example. By bringing together past and present, old and new types of surveillance, novel forms of control, with their own strategic agendas, are brought to life (Chadwick, 2013, pp 14–15). These very specific forms operate within a wider surveillance system, but they also represent a distinctive response to a particular set of circumstances during a certain period. As such, they contain their own strategies for dealing with real and discursively narrated crises, dilemmas and problems in society that are also fought out in a battle over hegemonic projects. As Chadwick goes on to observe:

> Particulate hybridity is the outcome of power struggles and competition for pre-eminence during periods of unusual transition, contingency, and negotiability. Over time, these hybrid practices start to fix and freeze; they become sedimentary, and what was once considered unusual and transitional comes to be seen as part of a new settlement, but that new settlement is never entirely fixed. (Chadwick, 2013, p 15)

To begin to explore this hybrid surveillance at work in public space we first need to discuss new digital control mechanisms in more depth.

Codes, control and public space

City space is now inextricably tied up with new forms of technology. Of particular significance has been the creation of 'codes' – strings of numbers and letters that are generated through mathematical algorithms by means of software programs. Information systems track and monitor the movement of codes, differentiate them and assign them a unique identification. Different forms of identification codes can then be generated in a database depending upon whether the focus of attention is people, objects, information, transactions or territories (Dodge and Kitchen, 2005, pp 853–4). Through a database, codes are sorted into different types of knowledge and identification that track people and objects. These place people and objects into a number of profiles and populations, like that of criminality, homelessness or ethnicity. By performing these tasks codes have the power to pre-empt the movement of people and objects (Dodge and Kitchen, 2005, pp 858–9). The coming together of these devices results in new forms of surveillance; the rationalised accumulation of personal data to manage and control social environments. Surveillance techniques thus extract 'fragments' of data about 'virtual' selves that can be used 'as the basis of discrimination between one category and another, and to facilitate differential treatment' (Lyon, 2004, p 138; see also Thrift and French, 2002; Mackenzie and Vurdubakis, 2011).

Importantly, according to Deleuze (1990), these technologies mean that we have moved towards a control society based on how we are coded. This is different to living in a society based on discipline. Whereas discipline 'enclosed' and 'moulded' people, control is based on 'modulation', that is, on continuous change, mobility and variety. For example, education is no longer confined to the physical disciplinary location of the classroom but has become a continuous mode of learning throughout a person's life cycle (the continuous training and development of 'skills', for example). Whereas discipline sought to regulate the behaviour of 'individuals' located in 'mass' culture, control societies are grounded in regulating populations through codes and 'dividuals'. Our sense of being an 'individual' is now broken down into a multitude of codes which are then recoded in a variety of ways, thereby creating a number of profiles or 'dividuals' for each person located in a distinctive population. Elsewhere Deleuze says that this new condition represents a diagram, a cartography that is 'coextensive with the whole social field' (Deleuze, 1988, p 34). What Deleuze wants to alert us to is the manner in which codes spread across society as a whole through decentralised networks to manage specific populations of people and groups in society. No longer confined to physical locations, codes override the normal boundaries between different forms of existence. Indeed, they operate by unmaking realities and stable representations and by establishing continual and numerous points of emergence. Codes thus generate 'supple and transversal' networks of alliances that map strategic relations between forces beyond that of the state (Deleuze, 1988, pp 35–6).

The idea that control through digital technology now subsists primarily in non-state forms is one that is commonplace among some scholars and thinkers. Sure enough, Deleuze's arguments are persuasive. Furthermore, this new form of control no longer relies on governing individuals in localities through one central point of command in the guise of a state. More precisely, control operates through codes and databases that anticipate and, indeed, socially construct the behaviour of discrete populations. This is to argue that control operates by pre-empting the activity of formless and shapeless processes that it will eventually try to mould. Control is not so much concerned with the actual subjects as it is with 'the effects, the patterns of code that are continuously generated by "subjects" as they use their mobile phone, twitter, check their Facebook and MySpace pages, drive their car, do their shopping, or surf the web' (Savat, 2013, p 48). The internet provides a practical illustration of some of these points.

During the Cold War there had been much speculation in US government and military circles about whether a communication network might be able to survive a nuclear attack. At the RAND Corporation in 1959 an American scientist, Paul Baran, started to think through the implications of this question. His answer was to design a computer network that essentially escaped centralised control. At the forefront of this breakthrough was 'packet switching'. In this system messages break themselves apart into small fragments and each fragment goes on to find its own way to a destination through different interconnected networks. Arriving at their destination, fragments then reassemble into the message. Even if part of the network is subsequently destroyed there will always be other routes that a message can take to reach its end-point. Revolutionary at the time, this relatively simple idea provided the foundation for what later became the decentralised network formation that comprised the internet (Barney, 2000, pp 67–72). But the internet is also built around Internet Protocols (IP), which are the rules and standards that govern relationships in networks. IPs send packets of information to points across computer networks. If one packet goes missing, then a Transmission Control Protocol (TCP) can request that it is sent again. Hence, TCP is a layer within IP and addresses problems in communication between computers. Protocols are therefore uninterested as to the content of information, preferring instead to manage the formal structure of information (Galloway and Thacker, 2004). Protocols ensure that a number of decentralised, distributed and flat networks comprise the internet.[1]

According to Galloway (2004), however, a more centralised system is also noticeable on the internet in the shape of Domain Name Systems (DNSs). When a computer wants to send data to another computer it does so through the IP address, which is made up of numbers. In order to render these numbers intelligible to humans, DNSs transform them into an easily identifiable name. The Uniform Resource Locator (URL) or web address is the most common example in this respect. How IP addresses are matched with domain names is dependent on a hierarchy of computers and this implies a degree of centralisation and distributed control in the internet. So, while there are decentralised networks these can only successfully operate through centralisation (Galloway, 2004, p 13). But (de)centralisation is also a type of control in a Deleuzian sense that is qualitatively distinct from disciplinary power associated with the state. Protocols that govern the internet are contained in Request for Comments (RFC) documents. RFCs originated in 1969 and are today published by the internet Engineering Task Force in the US, but there are also other organisations that develop protocols such as the World Wide Web Consortium. In practice, this means that protocols are governed by a technocratic elite of scientists, professional bodies, committees and so on. New modes of control are thus maintained through decentred computer networks and through professional technocratic groups whose expertise lies beyond state power (Galloway and Thacker, 2004).

Another illustration of this Deleuzian pre-emptive control agenda can be found at airports. Amoore (2006) notes that airport personnel have been increasingly engaged in compiling and classifying data on individual passengers. Information is gathered from a variety of sources, including financial transactions and social security information. Advanced computer technology can use mathematical modelling techniques to then map 'normal' patterns of human behaviour. One technique at the disposal of American airport authorities and security is that of Automated Targeting Systems (ATS). Amoore (2006) notes that the purpose of ATS is to accumulate passenger data such as address, financial records, past one-way travel and seating preference in order to assign a risk score to individual travellers. Worryingly, scores can then be used to physically detain individual passengers or deny them entry to the US or elsewhere if the passenger in question is deemed a risk. In practice, the authorities are searching for the 'unknown terrorist' who has yet to commit a terrorist act. However, because a person identified might never have committed an act of terrorism it is unclear how they might challenge decisions made about them by security forces working at airports. This is especially difficult when a person is not even told why they have been denied entry to a country (Amoore, 2006; see also Marx, 2007, p 380).

Today, then, power and surveillance moves beyond the state and encompasses the whole of society. It is a less visible type of surveillance than in the past. But another question immediately presents itself in this respect. If this new form of control is now pervasive and ubiquitous throughout cities, why do people accept its governing mandate? One answer lies in a discourse of legitimation that often accompanies control societies. While not the only utterance employed to justify a new surveillance agenda, 'resilience' has nonetheless become important in demarcating security concerns in cities. Prompted by the belief that we live in a world of uncertainty and non-preventable threats in which risks can now flow through informational networks across the globe, 'resilience' highlights the need to take pre-emptive action to offset the worst-case scenarios of these risks. This is to insist that individuals, groups, organisations, cities, regions and so forth take control of their own risk-averse strategies in order to develop the potential to withstand and bounce back from shocks (O'Malley, 2010). Resilience is subsequently an utterance that helps to rationalise this pre-emptive (de)centralised new security agenda.

Stephen Graham's work is instructive here. He also employs, in part, Deleuze's ideas on modulation, and this leads him to argue that contemporary cities are today controlled through a number of computerised calculations linked together via global computer networks and databases. Management of distinct populations through these mechanisms of control has become increasingly merged with the surrounding urban fabric of cities (Graham, S., 2010, p 64). Congestion charges and smart highways are two illustrations. Notably, Graham subscribes to the idea that political power has moved beyond its embodiment in a central sovereign force. Power is now spread across a number of networks, primarily those associated with 'visual-technological popular culture, political economy and state practice' (Graham, 2012, p 137). More ominously, resilience and security have given rise to 'battlespaces' in everyday urban locales. Here, numerous objects become a site of permanent war. Military and civilian boundaries collapse into one another. 'Unpredictable' terrorist forces in cities, for example, justify the need for authorities to engage in a constant process of creating pre-emptive risk profiles of populations (Graham, S., 2010, p 31). For Graham, 'resilience' is a vital resource employed by authorities to defend and legitimate these practices. Announcing to their citizens that they have built a resilient infrastructure to tackle unpredictable threats becomes a means for authorities and governments to demonstrate that pre-emptive action of the sort described above is wholly justified (Graham, S., 2010, p 297).

The various approaches discussed above are indispensable for a critical approach to surveillance in contemporary cities. In particular, they highlight how surveillance operates through pre-emptive strategies that are opaque, subtle and enmeshed in various human and technological networks and which are difficult to hold accountable. Codes of surveillance embed themselves in everyday popular culture, they become part of our very being and therefore, like social media, their negative effects become harder to detect. As Gary Marx observes: 'When not hidden altogether, the new information gathering also seeks to be soft and relatively noninvasive and to avoid direct coercion' (Marx, 2007, p 380). Even so, many of these approaches also tend to assume in some way or another that the nation-state has relinquished many of its security powers to horizontal surveillance networks. But to what extent is this in fact true? Has the nation-state lost many of its powers, or does it work in parallel with, or even underpin surveillance networks? It is to these questions that we now turn.

Resilient surveillance of neoliberal competence

Haggerty and Ericson (2000) apply the term 'surveillant assemblages' to make sense of new surveillance devices. Taking their cue from Deleuze and Guattari (1988), Haggerty and Ericson claim that an assemblage is a multiplicity of heterogeneous objects that come together for specific purposes. Assemblages are unified through 'continuous variation' (Deleuze and Guattari, 1988, p 375) of different architectural forms, bodies, codes, discourses, groups, technological machines and so on that, when contingently brought together, create a qualitative entity in its own right. According to Haggerty and Ericson, the state captures the free-flowing nature of these objects and endeavours to construct them into specific assemblages in order to capture, control and striate these flows for political purposes. At the same time, argue Haggerty and Ericson, it is essential to see assemblages as operating across states and extra-state institutions. Commercial marketing companies, for example, construct exact profiles of different populations in society around the desires that people hold. These might be associated with dating, consumer goods, voluntary activity and so forth. Police departments can tap into these commercial databases for undisclosed investigative purposes. Here, surveillance can be said to move beyond hierarchical institutional control. It functions instead to create distinct assemblages (Haggerty and Ericson, 2000, p 615).

Haggerty and Ericson usefully demonstrate how surveillance survives and prospers through a number of interlinked objects that help to normalise a surveillance consensus between security agents and across society at large. In these surveillant assemblages it is no longer clear who is being included in security strategies. Is it the potential terrorist or is it somebody who is merely using his or her daily travel card to commute to work? At the same time, we are told that risks and threats have increased and are increasing across society. As such, 'the visibility of exclusion vanishes, while the power of exception and the production of normative imperatives amalgamate into a "governmentality" of uncertainty, unease, fear and (in)security' (Hempel and Töpfer, 2009, p 161). In terms of resilience, the focus is on those security and military discourses that underline the need to implement 'critical infrastructures' that adapt, survive and bounce back after an attack of some sort or another. Computer systems able to repair themselves after an attack are one obvious example (Lundborg and Vaughan–Williams, 2011, pp 271–2).

Yet, when we start to examine the way in which the regulation of urban space is enacted today we soon recognise that these accounts go too far in painting a picture between 'old' surveillance mechanisms associated with the policing and zoning of visible city spaces and newer, digital surveillance mechanisms. Without doubt, pre- and post-9/11 governments have intensified surveillance techniques that calculate, measure and pre-empt different forms of activism, including resistance-led dissent from political and social activists. But what is also interesting about these surveillance techniques is that they combine both new and old styles of regulatory governance. The new styles can be seen most readily with the installation of increasingly sophisticated machines that map human behaviour and subject it to surveillance. The old styles can be seen most readily in the passing of state legislation to monitor and contain dissent. In effect, then, what we see in our cities today is hybrid surveillance in which horizontal modes of surveillance are connected with vertical systems of command associated with some of the 'normal' and everyday strategies of state power. In other words, networks of surveillance are still heavily dependent on a central mechanism of authority and coercion, as well as a whole host of related governance bodies like public-private partnerships, in order to function properly.

We can begin to comprehend the significance of hybrid surveillance in relation to resilience in cities. In Chapter Seven, the issue of neoliberalism in cities will be explored in greater depth. For now, however, it is important to note that many cities have been constrained by the financial neoliberal imperative to market and sell their city to particular investors and groups. Obviously, this practice will exclude other interest groups from taking part in these local ventures, not least groups of residents (see Gibson, 2005; Marcuse, 2005; Kavaratzis, 2007; see also Chapter Seven). Significantly, however, resilience is often built into many narratives about marketing and selling cities for investment opportunities that at the same time highlight the need to adapt to short-term, pre-conceived plans that foster tight-knit relationships and networks between different public–private partnerships. Both adaptability and adaption therefore stress different moments of a city's ability to be resilient. Adaptability highlights a qualitative aspect, stressing that a city's fortunes require long-term planning for the future among loose networks of partners. Adaption highlights a quantitative moment, stressing how strong and strongly allied groups can plan for the future in the short term (Pike et al, 2010, p 67).

While there are obvious tensions between strategies of adaptability and adaption they can also work together to provide strategic responses to unpredictable ruptures and shocks in relatively stable governance systems and partnership networks. Such adaptive capacity is particularly useful for local policy makers in their quest to brand cities for neoliberal investment strategies. Recognising potential risks and engaging in risk management are often thought to be crucial in this respect. Emergent threats and disasters, whether these are financial risks, robbery, murder, environmental disasters or terrorism, need to be identified and programmes of action clearly set out by local policy makers for how theses will be isolated and contained. The London Resilience Forum, for instance, was established in 2001–02 with these needs in mind. Through the Forum, local politicians and policy makers in London could demonstrate to potential stakeholders and investors that the city would be able to 'bounce back' from potential risks and threats, should they occur (Coaffee and Rogers, 2008a).

Mega-events like global sports spectacles provide exceptionally fertile ground for resilience to become embroiled in visible and invisible neoliberal and security agendas. To give just one example, the Rand Corporation designed a model for the 2012 London Olympics that aimed to 'foresee' worst-case scenarios that could possibly erupt in London during this global event. By isolating three potential factors – adversary hostile intent, adversary operational capability and potential domestic and/or international influences – the Rand Corporation created what it considered to be 27 feasible 'future security environments' with different degrees of hostility, even though they were all seen as sharing equal possibilities. As Boyle and Haggerty note of this specific plan of action: 'Including such previously unimaginable scenarios reflects an ascendant precautionary logic in security assessment and planning that exceeds historical frameworks of proportionality' (Boyle and Haggerty, 2009, p 262).

If it is true that resilience is bound up with the neoliberal restructuring of cities, it is equally correct to say that it is tied in with ideas of competence and NPM. For example, one approach to resilience focuses in part on the pre-existing resources, competencies, skills and experiences at the disposal of a community to adapt to new circumstances and shocks. Competences in particular help to reorient a region or locality towards new knowledge networks and new strengths, all of which are said to eventually lead to path-dependent evolution and renewal of local businesses and communities (Dawley et al, 2010, pp 656–7). Some argue that a crisis can even be an opportunity for local officials to begin to develop new, innovative, resilient opportunities and policies for their regions. Being competent is therefore also about building up creative opportunities in meeting local needs and the needs of local business. Officials need to engage in imaginative approaches to tackle uncertainties and allow innovative projects to get under way. The Coalition government in the UK, for example, said that the 2008 financial crisis presents new openings for innovative economic thinking that escape from older socioeconomic ideas. Reskilling those who have not prospered as well as other groups over the last two decades is just one illustration (Raco and Street, 2012, p 1069; Shaw, 2012, p 291).

Making competent judgements in measuring resilience is, moreover, to co-opt members in a local community into a security agenda. Indeed, active engagement with community members is seen as an integral moment of thinking through the adaptive capacity of a city towards risks and uncertainties. Establishing working groups and partnerships with community forums and organisations is one way for local officials, the police and security agencies to encourage their residents to take responsibility for their own well-being in respect of potential risks they face. This everyday construction of resilience planning therefore aims to embed new security concerns into popular experiences and, in particular, to encourage residents to 'empower' themselves to take greater care of their local surroundings. Moreover, it normalises the use of private security agencies to help administer a resilience agenda in communities (Coaffee and Rogers, 2008b, p 111; Shaw, 2012, p 15).

As has also already been noted, the competent neoliberal resilience agenda is also underpinned by state coercion. To see more precisely how this is the case we now turn our attention to the relationship at work between state power and surveillance strategies in the US and in the UK.

Zones of hybrid surveillance in the US

In 1983, the American legal system formally adopted a three-part framework to evaluate which types of dissent might legally occur on different government-owned property. First, it was decided that the public has a right to use 'traditional' public forums like parks, public streets and sidewalks and so on for public debate. It was deemed that in these places the government has no intrinsic right to prohibit public assemblies, debate and legal dissent. Second, it was noted that in the past 'limited' public environments related to government property had been opened for public debate, a typical example being that of schools. It was decided, however, that the government has no obligation to ensure that these public spaces remain open indefinitely for public debate. Finally, it was found that 'non-public' spaces exist, such as prisons, military bases and airport terminals, in which no public debate is permissible. Sometimes, of course, restrictions also need to be placed on legitimate public forums that exist on government-owned property. But in these cases it was decided that three 'compatible use' tests had to be observed. First, government restriction on dissent and public debate in these public contexts must be neutral with regard to the content of protest speech in question. Second, restriction should be based on a substantial government interest. Third, restriction must ensure that other avenues for communication are offered to protestors (Nielsen, 2004, p 21; see also Zick, 2006a for specific examples).

Since the 1980s, the US has also witnessed the development of 'negotiated management' of public spaces of dissent. Negotiated management is 'based upon judicial interpretation of the doctrine to regulate the time, place, and manner of protest gatherings' (McCarthy and McPhail, 2006, p 234). In practice, this means that the 'right' to meet in a public space must be officially sanctioned to a protest group by acquiring a permit from the police. Importantly, the issuing of permits implies that the legitimacy of entering public property and public space to engage in public dissent lies in the hands of 'police officers standing on the street with handcuffs, guns, and only the most oblique understanding of or interest in legal niceties' (Dunn, 2005, p 329). As a result, the US police have considerable advantage in regulating and controlling public spaces of dissent. The establishment of free speech containment areas for protesters since 1988 has strengthened the police's hand in these matters. Through these areas, the police establish physical spaces for protestors to demonstrate within, and thereby restrict the areas in a city where demonstrators can legitimately proceed (Zick, 2006b, pp 589–98).

It is worth making four additional and interrelated observations about these legal changes in America. First, they are associated with the broader emergence of neoliberalism in cities. Designing and landscaping a city to make it an appealing investment opportunity for financiers as well as demonstrating its resilient traits are also increasingly related to the negotiated management of dissent. Indeed, some strategic sites for dissent like Washington, DC go as far as to employ professional consultants 'to negotiate the permit process, meet with police forces, arrange for stages, sound systems, preparation and clean up' (Mitchell and Staeheli, 2005, p 805).

Second, as indicated above, a change in the physical governance of public spaces for dissent was gaining momentum through new tactics of containment *before* the terrorist attacks in New York on 11 September 2001. The difference today is that the containment of dissent in US cities has grown since 9/11. Indeed, since 2004 'free speech areas' have been transformed into 'free speech zones' and 'protest zones' and have now even appeared in other places, like universities (Kohn, 2004, pp 39–41).

Third, the surveillance of public space in the US operates both horizontally and vertically. As Yesil (2006, p 403) points out, leading cities like Washington, DC, Chicago, Boston and Baltimore have all witnessed the installation of high-tech, often biometrically augmented, digital cameras to monitor public spaces. These cameras operate along a centralised police system in each city and some, such as those positioned in Washington, DC, can be connected to other cameras operating in everyday public spaces like schools, shopping precincts and privately owned businesses that deal with the public, as well as being connected to wider law enforcement agencies like the FBI (Yesil, 2006, pp 403–7). This increase in the video monitoring of public space is usually justified along the lines that it helps to deal effectively with anti-terrorist activity and ensures public safety. More importantly, it illustrates again that decentralised surveillance is connected to central state power.

Finally, penal and security services had been undergoing a noticeable change in policy direction in the US and elsewhere before 9/11. For example, for a number of years prior to 9/11 authorities increasingly deemed criminality as a social force that could not be defeated as such but that could be managed. As a result, many governments increasingly *estimate* the costs of *future* criminal activity (Zedner, 2003, p 159). In the post-9/11 US the Bush administration passed a number of laws with the aim, among other things, to calculate potential terrorist threats in order to take pre-emptive action against individuals suspected of having terrorist links, associations or sympathies. The US Patriot Act (Uniting and Strengthening America by Providing Appropriate Tools to Intercept and Obstruct Terrorism) of 2001 is one notable illustration of this tactic. This 2001 Act increased the powers of the government in its handling of immigration issues and has expanded the range of judicial powers in managing criminal activity, especially suspected terrorist activity. On 16 May 2011, President Obama extended three components of the Patriot Act for a further four years because they were set to expire. These are roving wire traps that follow a surveillance target, searches of business records and conducting surveillance of lone suspected terrorists. But the Patriot Act and similar pieces of legislation remain highly controversial, not least because their extensive powers are said by critics to diminish civil liberties, particularly of those from certain cultural and ethnic backgrounds. For instance, the introduction of a Special Registration Programme in November 2002 aims to register male foreign visitors aged 16 years and over who have entered the United States from one of 25 countries in which the government claims terrorist activity takes place (for example Iran, Somalia, Pakistan, North Korea and Eritrea). In 2003 it was reported that of 1,000 people detained because of the Special Registration Programme only 15 were charged with criminal activity, and none was charged with terrorist activity (Welch, 2003, p 6).

This new culture of security also affects the use of public spaces for protest. Dunn (2005) reports that since 9/11 anti-war demonstrations in New York have seen not only the increased use of new types of surveillance but also a more coercive police presence. Eight days of demonstration at a Republican National Convention in New York City, which began on 30 August 2004, saw the police arrest over 1,800 people for mainly minor offences. Many were arrested for just standing in public spaces such as sidewalks. Moreover, while New York stipulates that any person arrested for minor offences cannot be fingerprinted, it was discovered that the police had done exactly this to many of the protestors arrested (Dunn, 2005, pp 353–4; see also ACLU, 2003).

What is also noticeable about these coercive tactics is that they often assume different degrees of power, depending upon whether the authorities perceive protestors as engaging in non-resistance dissent or resistance dissent. An illustration of this point comes from a study of anti-war protests on 29–30 September 2001 in Washington, DC. Noakes et al (2005) found that during the protest the police dealt spatially with anti-war groups of demonstrators in different ways. The Washington Peace Centre (WPC) held its own rally and the police remained at a respectful distance from the members during their procession, primarily because WPC members respected the contained route of their march. But Noakes et al also note that the police treated another protest group, the Anti-Capitalist Convergence (ACC), rather differently. The ACC encompasses anarchist, communist and socialist groups in the greater Washington, DC area. The police had formed a more high-risk picture of the ACC for these reasons. While the ACC had not initially obtained a permit for its protest it did eventually agree a proposed route with police on the day of the march. Yet, when a scuffle broke out between some ACC marchers and the police, ACC demonstrators soon found their exit and entrances along their route blocked by the police. The ACC demonstrators were then forcefully contained in a two-block area demarcated by barricades, for nearly two hours. As Noakes et al note, clashes between the police and ACC demonstrators occurred not because ACC members disturbed spaces of power, such as that of the Pentagon, but because the ACC challenged and actively resisted police containment of its demonstration (Noakes et al, 2005, p 251; see also Vitale, 2005).

State surveillance has continued under President Obama's administration. In the spring of 2013, Edward Snowden, a former intelligence analyst who worked first for the CIA and then the National Security Agency (NSA), leaked information to the press that showed that the American government and intelligence agencies employ digital programs to engage in mass spying. These programs allow organisations like the NSA to capture internet and telephone conversations from over a billion users from an array of countries across the world. The revelations came in the wake of increased expenditure on surveillance under Obama's regime and the growing use of private companies to conduct surveillance operations in American society. As the American lawyer and activist Kate Epstein notes, annual spending on corporate security and intelligence in the US has doubled in ten years and currently stands at around $100 billion (Epstein, 2013). Epstein goes on to observe:

> A series of legislative developments since 9/11 have expanded the executive branch's surveillance and intelligence-gathering functions drastically, under the umbrella of the U.S. Intelligence Community ... These policy changes have loosened restrictions on intelligence gathering, expanded the definition of terrorism, inflated

the role of corporations in catching so-called terrorists and protecting 'critical infrastructure and key resources,' and created fusion centers (regional information sharing centers) under the direction of the Department of Homeland Security ... The seventeen agencies that make up the Intelligence Community reported a combined budget of $80 billion in 2010, a figure three times higher than when it was previously disclosed twelve years earlier. (Epstein 2013)

Zones of hybrid surveillance in the UK

Before the Human Rights Act 1998 was introduced in the UK, the British population had a 'negative' right of freedom of assembly. In practice, this meant that the legal right to hold *public assemblies* on UK highways was not *guaranteed*. Instead, individuals only had the right to use the highways in a 'reasonable' manner, while public assembles were not positively recognised by the judicial system; hence the negative right to hold public assemblies on the highways. The Human Rights Act changed this by allowing and guaranteeing the right of free, peaceful assemblies on highways (Beetham et al, 2002, p 49).

Still, there has also been a move in the UK to employ similar zoning tactics to regulate dissent, albeit in a less systematic manner than in the US. One of the most documented attempts has been the ratification of the Serious Organised Crime and Police Act 2005. Passed primarily to establish the Serious Organised Crime Agency (on which see Segell, 2007 for an overview), a Statutory Instrument of the 2005 Act under sections 132 to 138 also prohibited unlicensed protests within a radius of one kilometre around Parliament (Welsh, 2007, p 367). But these prohibitions extended far beyond Parliament, across the Thames to areas not occupied by government buildings. In 2011 the Police Reform and Social Responsibility Act was passed, which repealed sections 132 and 138 of the 2005 Act. Instead, the new 2011 Act restricts other prohibited activities around Parliament. Even so, according to the UK civil liberties group Liberty, the 2005 Act contains a number of other measures that negatively affect the rights of protestors and demonstrators in public spaces. Trespassing on areas designated as 'national security', for example, is now a criminal offence even though the Serious Organised Crime and Police Act 2005 does not define 'national security' (Liberty, 2005).

The 2005 Act has been part of an on-going number of legal measures introduced that have served in their own way to place constraints on dissent in public space. The Terrorism Act 2000, for example, grants police the power to zone areas of public space under section 45 in order to carry out section 44, namely the stop and search policy. As Moran (2005) notes: 'From 2001–2003 there was no part of London which had not been zoned for s 44/45 searches' (Moran, 2005, p 343). The Terrorism Act also allows the police to restrain protests that resemble conventional demonstrations. Obviously, all of this is not to suggest that the British government simply appropriated US-style methods of policing public space (see Jones and Newburn, 2002). Some nevertheless argue that it is possible to detect similarities between both the US and the UK to the extent that the key civil liberty idea of respecting each person's equal right to political speech in open spaces is being undermined by a new national security agenda. Weakening basic rights in this manner is often justified by authorities along the lines that such legislation in fact complements rather than diminishes civil liberties in our post-9/11 world (see Gearty, 2003, 2005; Ewing, 2010).

Others remain more cautious in their assessment of the current state of civil liberties in the UK since 9/11. Moran (2007) argues that civil liberties are still robustly defended in the UK through different legal measures. In addition, of 1.8 million Muslims who live in Britain, fewer than 4,000 are subject to stop-and-search policies on an annual basis under the Terrorism Act 2000 (Moran, 2007, pp 86–7). However, some argue that the Terrorism Act has 'racialised' stop-and-search policies in the direction of Asian communities. Blick et al (2006) note, for example, that while black people represent the group who are subject the most to stop-and-search policies under all UK legislation, when the figures are examined as related only to the Terrorism Act 2000, then this ominous accolade shifts to the Asian population *as a whole* and to 'Others'. 'The obvious conclusion', suggest Blick et al (2006, p 49), 'is that people who appear as though they might be Muslims are more likely to be stopped and searched.' Yet the success rate of arresting actual or potential terrorists through stop and search has been minimal (Blick et al, 2006, pp 49–50).

Of course, before the Terrorism Act, the Public Order Act 1986 had extended police powers in the remit of public disorder and violence. The 1986 Act also enhanced police powers over public processions. Section 14 of the Act states that 'to prevent serious public disorder, serious criminal damage or serious disruption to the life of the community' the police are empowered to impose conditions on public processions, for example, by specifying the number of people who can take part, the duration of the procession and its location. In many respects, however, the enforcement of the Public Order Act at actual events of dissent and resistance has remained ambiguous. As Waddington (1994) observes, the Act stipulates that the police must have 'reasonable belief' of the likelihood that serious disorder will break out if a procession goes ahead. But, Waddington asks, how should the police interpret the word 'reasonable' in this context? The same can be said of the word 'serious' in the phrase 'serious disorder' (Waddington, 1994, p 380).

To combat some of these ambiguities the Anti-Social Behaviour Act was passed in 2003 and this extended the 1986 Act by, among other things, enforcing police powers over public space. The police can, for example, legally remove a 'public assembly' of two people from a place if it appears that the two people in question are likely to cause 'serious public disorder, serious damage to property or serious disruption to the life of the community'. Under the Public Order Act 1986 the number of people deemed to constitute a 'public assembly' had to be 20 or more. New Labour similarly established 1,000 new criminal offences from 1997 to 2007 (Moran, 2007, p 89). According to James (2006), the UK's police force has been strengthened along more bureaucratic lines as well. In 1983, the Conservative government began implementing the culture of NPM into the police force, which effectively began the process of centralising police bureaucracy. The National Criminal Intelligence Service was established in 1991, to be followed in 1997 by the Police Act from which the National Crime Squad was born. These developments ran in parallel with a greater emphasis on 'community policing' and the division of individual police forces into 'micro-beats'. James (2006, pp 473–4) argues that both developments can be seen as increasingly sophisticated spatial tactics being adopted by the UK police services in order to manage, measure and pre-empt crime in places of risk.

What is also clear is that the UK police now enjoy more powers in the sphere of surveillance of electronic communication and public order, thanks to the British state. The Regulation of Investigatory Powers Act 2000, commonly known as RIPA, makes a distinction between intercepting private communications (phone calls and e-mails, for instance), which is generally seen to be the most intrusive type of surveillance, and intercepting communications data (a person's phone provider, for instance). RIPA makes another distinction between two types of surveillance. On the one hand, there is directed surveillance, which takes such forms as the following of a suspect that is likely to result in gaining private information about a person. On the other hand, intrusive surveillance involves the use of a surveillance device in a private residence or vehicle. RIPA thereby authorises internet service providers, phone companies and postal service operators to hand over detailed information to the authorities about customers who use their services. The Act also extends beyond the police to public authorities and other public bodies. Still, as Patrick observes:

> In virtually every other common law country, interceptions and bugs by law enforcement require a judicial warrant. This means that the police have to apply to a judge for permission before they can carry out surveillance. By contrast, an interception warrant under Part 1 of RIPA is granted by the Home Secretary. The only requirement for judicial scrutiny under RIPA was introduced in 2012, when Parliament determined that local authorities exercising surveillance powers should first be authorised by a magistrate. (Patrick, 2013, p 22)

Part XI of the Anti-terrorism, Crime and Security Act 2001 seeks as well to ensure that Communication Service Providers will retain communications data on users for a specified period. The 2001 Act also empowered the executive to detain somebody indefinitely if the Home Secretary thought they were 'international terrorists'. But this provision in the 2001 Act came unstuck when a House of Lords ruling found that it infringed the Human Rights Act. An Act passed in 2005 replaced the detainment provision with new control measures (Gearty, 2013, pp 89–91). Interestingly, another function of the Serious Organised Crime and Police Act 2005 has been to extend the power of non-policing organisations like private security guards, store detectives and Community Police Officers to detain suspects. Untrained and unqualified security personnel have therefore seen an expansion of their limited police and surveillance powers (Button, 2003, p 236). Private and public security and police forces have thus seen an increase in their powers.

Conclusion

The areas touched on this chapter are by no means definitive but they do suggest that over a number of years pre- and post-9/11 governments have introduced new ways of managing and ordering dissent. If one overall point can be made from the discussion in this chapter it is that pre-emptive action against different forms of dissent has been strengthened in recent years. Moreover, through these pre-emptive measures, from the everyday to the more visible spectacles of dissent are targeted by governments, who frequently employ the language of citizenship, human rights and civil liberties *against* the democratic practices of ordinary citizens. Governments have strengthened their coercive power as well in their endeavour to win the hearts and minds of certain groups in civil society towards a new security agenda. Digital media is implicated in these processes, but so too are older and more conventional police tactics such as the zoning of public space.

But while hybrid surveillance has developed new modes of control in cities it is not without its own problems. Coaffee and Rogers usefully note that while local policy makers push forward a resilience agenda in order to help stimulate regeneration in deprived and derelict city spaces, it is equally true to say that greater surveillance sometimes unleashes the coercive tactic of zoning off public spaces for purposes of safety (Coaffee and Rogers, 2008b, p112). More optimistically, despite the centre-right consensus that the new security agenda is necessary in an increasingly unpredictable global world, there is still a sizeable minority of ordinary people who continue to defend and support civil liberties for all UK citizens. These very same people also register some disquiet about what they perceive to be the erosion of these liberties in society (Pantazis and Pemberton, 2012, pp 661–2).

Coming from a slightly different angle, Coutard and Guy (2007) insist that many writers tend to develop a number of negative arguments about the impact of surveillance on city cultures. Nevertheless, what these writers fail to note, observe Coutard and Guy, is that technology is applied and used through the competing and contrasting actions of different groups. For example, those who own and control closed-circuit television (CCTV) cameras often argue that they lead to a decrease in crime, but in reality this is frequently not the case (see Chapter Seven). Coutard and Guy's point, then, is that, in overemphasising the coercive power of surveillance agendas, many forget that CCTV is beset by dilemmas that often lead to failure, or at least a malfunction, in elements of a security agenda in cities. The next chapter therefore continues this line of investigation to try to see more precisely how CCTV contributes towards the competent public sphere in urban space, and at the same time to tease out in greater depth some of the dilemmas that this creates in cities.

Note

[1] The same is true of the World Wide Web. Created by Tim Berners-Lee in 1990 while working at the Cern European Particle Physics laboratory in Geneva, this is a network of interlinked files accessed via the internet. The Hyper-text Transfer Protocol (HTTP) lays out the rules that enable their transmission between computers and thus operates through a horizontal formation.

SEVEN

Zoning public space 2: gentrification, community publics and CCTV

Introduction

Cities are not mere repositories of wider global processes. Huge swathes of economic activity still take place domestically, and indeed cities are structured through different local and regional strategic interests in which certain policies will favour some to the detriment of others. It is in this sense that architects and city planners become key organic intellectuals in local communities for the articulation of hegemonic ideas associated with specific state projects. City designers have a substantial input into the way in which rival demands for and over city space are deciphered and transformed into 'design products' for promotional purposes and for potential investors. Planners also often become caught up in the party politics of the day, in the sense that they become the medium through which hegemonic agendas gain practical application in spaces (van Deusen, 2002; Fainstein, 2005; Eisenschitz, 2008). Some, for example, have been co-opted and pressured by successive governments to incorporate a PPP agenda in how they envisage changes in cities (Jessop, 2002; Flinders, 2005; Gough et al, 2006). As we know, PPPs are also part of a wider neoliberal agenda aiming to deregulate international trade barriers, privatise business practices, stem the power of trade unions, reorganise welfare entitlements along workfare lines to ensure a steady supply of (cheap) labour for business and police spaces between localities in terms of 'value for money, the bottom line, flexibility, shareholder value, performance rating, social capital and so on' (Peck and Tickell, 2002, p 387; see also Gough, 2002).[1]

The aim of this chapter is to argue that the redevelopment of cities is indeed embroiled in the hegemony of neoliberal workfare. Digital technology is an integral element of this neoliberal formation by helping to classify distinct public spaces in new ways that then reproduce specific power relations. These points are developed in this chapter by exploring how digital technology in the form of CCTV exposes public space in cities to certain neoliberal moral and regulatory agendas, which exclude as well as include groups. Such technological mechanisms are important because they affect the right to the city and ordinary people's democratic input into how urban spaces are constructed, designed and managed. They subsequently pose serious challenges to the ability of community publics to challenge the hegemony of neoliberalism in their respective localities. The chapter begins by exploring how neoliberalism has shaped agendas around community regeneration in UK cities. From here, the chapter examines how digital technology classifies community publics. CCTV is then presented as one particularly prominent mode of classification and zoning of public space and community publics. However, the final section demonstrates that these practices also have contradictory effects in communities.

Neoliberalism, new public management and the regeneration of community publics

Mobilising an urban 'strategy' is a moment for policy makers to bring together the public and the private in ways that create new community publics.

> The strategy process is a mechanism to make people talk about their fears and desires, and brainstorm and collect their ideas. The political and the non-political, the private and the public are deliberately blurred as strategy invites conversations about facts and values. Strategy spins a grand narrative where the personal idiosyncrasies of an individual captured on a sticky note are placed next to global issues. In the vision of the future, the social division of the 'I' and the 'we' appear to be overcome. (Kornberger, 2012, p 99)

Strategy therefore assembles community members into distinctive publics so that they have a forum through which to deliberate with other 'partners' about local issues. Strategy is therefore a moment for 'partners' to be brought together and mobilised as one public sphere so that dilemmas and problems between them all are 'solved'.

One important urban political strategy is of course the need to market a city around an entrepreneurial image in order to attract private investment. This, though, is not a recent phenomenon. At least since 1945 major cities in the UK have sought to redevelop their urban landscapes in order to entice businesses to invest in their localities. By the 1960s this modernisation agenda had grown so that private business was called upon to 'provide capital and expertise' for local authorities and 'work with them directly and indirectly' on different local infrastructure projects (Shapely, 2011, p 519). Yet it is also true to say that this agenda was shaped to a considerable extent by Keynesianism, a welfare state and, in the case of some policy makers in Labour Party governments, the recognition that public ownership should play a crucial role in these development ideals (Ellis, 2012).

By the 1980s this had all noticeably changed. Under Thatcherism public managers now saw their finances cut and were forced to become 'enablers' of services rather than providers. One of the more conspicuous transitions towards a neoliberal localism in the 1980s occurred when the Conservative government started to push local authority officials to see business leaders as competent experts who could design and implement local social policies. The Thatcher government was also keen to establish specialist agencies and quangos to deal with the likes of employment training (for example Training and Enterprise Councils), community regeneration and private investment in specific regions. Peck (1995) suggests that one primary aim of Thatcher's Conservative administration in this respect sought to reduce the power and independence of local government. The rationale in doing so was to regenerate depressed urban cities through private finance and new modes of local governance, with the aim of side-stepping the perceived bureaucracy of local government. Increasingly the emphasis became one of wealth creation in cities and communities rather than of the redistribution of wealth, and this came to be achieved in part through market-based policies.

A number of schemes illustrate this new agenda. Established through the Local Government Planning and Land Act 1980, Urban Development Corporations were empowered to make an area attractive for private investment, and could do so by compulsory purchasing. Eleven Enterprise Zones were established in 1981, increasing to 24 by 1983. Aiming to regenerate run-down industrial districts, designated Enterprise Zones offered an attractive package to potential private investors that included exemption from local property taxes more relaxed planning controls. In the 1990s the Conservatives unveiled more regeneration schemes. City Challenge, originating in 1991, was designed to make local government less bureaucratic and more responsive to the needs of local community, with funds being allocated through competition between localities. Meanwhile the Single Regeneration Budget of 1993 pulled together 20 budgets that were previously administered by several departments. However, 'deprivation' as a reason for funding was increasingly shelved in this particular programme (Peck, 1995).

What were the consequences of these schemes? One notable effect identified by Peck and others (for example Lavin and Whysall, 2004) was that by the 1990s unelected business specialists from quangos increasingly started to enjoy more policy-making powers. These were individuals whose professional competence in dealing with private business ventures in the public sector gave them opportunities to be invited onto local government committees involved with policy areas like housing, education, health and policing. Another important effect was to implant the ethos of competition and PPPs at the heart of the public management of cities. This transition occurred even though some independent studies demonstrated the failure of many private initiatives to achieve their goals. For example, Enterprise Zone initiatives were mostly unsuccessful in generating new industrial activity in designated areas. One survey published in 1984, which explored the initial 11 zones, 'found no differences between employment generation, investment activities, or production of companies in zones versus outside the zones' (Papke, 1993, p 47). These results dovetail with similar findings from other studies.

In an age of a hollowed-out welfare state this neoliberal ethos in city regeneration is now firmly established. Public management creates new 'enabling' mechanisms and partnerships in order to facilitate investment opportunities in the localities it governs (Noordegraaf and Newman, 2011). Public space has thus become a vital resource in promoting a city to outsiders as well as in garnishing support for redevelopment schemes from some of those located inside its boundaries. To all intents and purposes, designers and planners are well aware of the need to project visually stimulating 'utopias' in their proposals to redevelop city spaces, especially in an age when city space is an economic and a cultural resource that melts into one. The 'right' to the city, and how a city sells and markets itself, is now as much about being passionate for late-time clubs, bars, restaurants, comedy and music as it about trading goods. But these passions are also encapsulated in the attempt by different 'partners' to redesign and rebrand cities and public spaces so that they are seen as being 'hospitable' both to a diverse range of local community identities and to commercial and business travellers and investors (Amin and Thrift, 2007; Bell, 2007). At this level the redesign of public space is believed to possess wholly positive effects for all in a community and, if successfully implemented, planning strategies can contribute towards greater economic prosperity (for example, better housing and shopping facilities), more integrated communities (for example, people from all walks of life come together in pleasant public spaces), healthier lifestyles (for example, people are more willing to take walks in nicely designed public spaces), reductions in crime (for example, carefully planned open spaces can offset petty crime) and healthier environments for children to grow up in (CABE Space, 2004).

Importantly, the pursuit of these soft virtues has propelled national and local governments to engage publicly with people, groups and organisations in civil society through community publics and public consultation forums. The emphasis here is on state personnel to appreciate the life context and experience that the impact of regeneration has upon residents. People are no longer to be viewed as mere aggregates. Rather, there is a need to publicly engage individuals' own culture so that state personnel are forced to establish public spheres that continually reflect on 'the real world situation' of local residents (Crawford et al, 2003, p 444). For some, this new policy agenda has the potential to reinvigorate democratic possibilities at a local community level. New modes of governance and the willingness of the nation-state and public sector to devolve core competencies to community publics highlight the attributes of *negotiation* between affected groups in developing a specific policy. Conflict *and* consensus are thus believed to be crucial mediating variables in establishing outcomes agreeable to all.

Pierre and Stoker (2002, p 42) therefore claim that one of the benefits of the new governance agenda and public sphere is that it allows government to ascertain possible stakeholders of a policy venture and to then devise connections between them. Once these connections are established, government can then help to steer these relationships to produce 'desired outcomes' and 'effective coordination' between all parties involved. This approach values the deliberative input of citizens to developing policy ideas. It also envisages the role of policy improvements as simultaneously empowering the democratic capabilities of local citizens (Gustafsson and Driver, 2005, p 533). Nowhere is this clearer than in the case of voluntary activity.

In 1998, and in line with its workfare-oriented Third Way philosophy, Tony Blair's government encouraged the voluntary sector to work more closely with local government and PPPs by introducing separate 'compact' documents for England, Scotland, Wales and Northern Ireland (see Fyfe and Milligan, 2003, pp 402–3; see also Roberts and Devine, 2004). Then, in 2001 a National Strategy for Neighbourhood Renewal was unveiled that was linked in with the New Deal for Communities (the remit of which was to invest in 39 neighbourhoods over 10 years). Among other things, this initiative established 35 Neighbourhood Pathfinders the remit of which was to ensure that conventional service delivery was successfully maintained in deprived communities. To ensure that public, private, voluntary and community sectors worked together, 'local strategic partnerships' were established in 88 neighbourhood priority areas so that community empowerment networks supported voluntary and community participation (Taylor, 2007, p 299).

In 2001, the government also created the Active Community Unit (ACU). Financed to the tune of £300 million, the ACU supported the third sector and voluntary activity through a number of programmes. The Treasury established a Charity and Third Sector Finance Unit in 2006 to work on fiscal policy for the third sector, while the Department of Trade and Industry set up a Social Enterprise Unit in 2001 to explore and support the potential of social enterprise in helping economic regeneration (Alcock and Kendall, 2011, pp 457–8). By 2006, the Office of the Third Sector was unveiled. Based at the Cabinet Office, the Office of the Third Sector merged the Active Communities Directorate from the Home Office with the Social Enterprise Unit from the Department of Trade and Industry. The rationale for the merger was to push the voluntary and third sector agendas into other government departments and to broaden their programme of activities to encompass 'voluntary and community organisations, charities, social enterprises, cooperatives and mutuals both large and small' (Alcock and Kendall, 2011, p 458). The Coalition government launched the Office for Civil Society in 2010, which at the time of writing preserves this broad agenda for the English third sector, with Northern Ireland, Scotland and Wales having their own devolved third sector governance structures.

These, then, are just a few examples of changes that have occurred to the third sector over the last few decades. Arguably, what they illustrate is how the connection between neoliberalism, public management and community publics has grown over the years. As neoliberalism and a hollowed-out workfare state have become more firmly embedded in society, so have the state's expectations of the role that voluntary organisations will play in society noticeably altered. Since the 1990s successive governments have expected the voluntary sector to take charge of more service provision with other partners. As S. Davies observes, New Labour increased the resources available to voluntary organisations, doubling the amount it spent on the voluntary sector to £11 billion during its time in power (Davies, S., 2011, p 643). However, this money was not evenly spread, with less than one quarter of charities receiving government funds.

New Labour also altered the relationship between the voluntary sector and government by introducing a more competitive ethos into the relationship, in line with NPM thinking. Charities and voluntary organisations could no longer simply expect funds but instead had to enter into a contract with the public sector in order to provide services. This transformed the culture of voluntary organisations in so far that they restructured their internal arrangements to become more efficient and compete successfully against other voluntary bodies and private businesses for public sector contracts. For Davies, this could mean that extra mergers occur between charities and voluntary bodies to cater for economies of scale, the elimination of some smaller and specialised charities and the continual transfer of staff between public, private and voluntary sectors, depending on what organisations win which contracts (Davies, S., 2011, pp 645–6).

These all represent concrete illustrations of the hollowing-out of the welfare state and the slow encroachment of the workfare state into civil society. First, voluntary work is seen by some politicians and policy makers to be a productive activity that 'encourages' ordinary people to invest in their human capital when 'helping out' in a community. In other words, voluntary work should be viewed less as an amateurish way of working and more about gaining formal skills and knowledge when taking part in community projects. Second, politicians and policy makers are keen to emphasise the links between volunteering and the creation of social capital. Voluntary work brings people together as a collective unit, so the arguments goes, and thus encourages them to rely on one another for mutual support, rather than on the welfare state. Finally, voluntary work is also a useful way to embed a neoliberal ethos in society. Indeed, by 'helping out' one another, people start to become 'passionate' about forging networks of reciprocity with their fellow community members and, by default, become less 'passionate' about building structural networks of welfare in society. This is a type of (neoliberal) politics based around 'soft' virtues like community feeling, trust and voluntary contribution, which are said to have positive effects within communities. Through these soft virtues, *individuals* are thought to *learn* the requisite skills to *become* competent community members (cf. Wilson and Musick, 1997; Rose, 1999; Walters, 2002). Later on in the chapter we will see how this project is contradictory, but for now we turn our attention to the new media agenda that is also embedded within it.

Zones of coded classification in local communities

Public space is comprised of multiple ways to map social behaviour, from the more visible methods like a police presence, architectural design, laws and so on, to more intangible methods associated with codes and programmes (see Crang, 2000; see also Chapter Six). Digital codes contribute to spatial ordering as they mobilise numerous networks and 'partnerships' around specific matters of concern within distinct zones (Amin and Graham, 1997). A city 'zone' is thereby a space in which variation and diversity between technologies, people and procedures has been diminished through common types of measurement, connections and standards (Barry, 2006; see also Lash, 2002, pp 28–30).

Graham and Marvin's ideas on 'splintering urbanism' provide a useful analytical framework to think through some of more concrete practices involved in zoning community space through new technologies. 'Splintering urbanism' refers to the way in which access to local public services and amenities has been 'unbundled' by measures associated with privatisation and new technologies. One example that Graham and Marvin present relates to the geodemographic software industry, which creates detailed images of neighbourhoods along with information about consumption habits, house prices, local amenities and so on. Such information about consumers is handed to private businesses like estate agents to target the 'right' people in a locality. Accordingly, geodemographic systems assist in establishing urban zones. These then open up opportunities for rich groups to demarcate 'secessionary networked spaces' in cities and close themselves off from other groups and urban ways of life (Graham and Marvin, 2001, p 268). Spatial inequalities thus work alongside architectural, political and financial practices to separate off the lives of these elites from those of the 'poor'. New opportunities, likewise, arise for 'powerful users' in cities to build upon their already advantageous positions by taking advantage of premium-networked spaces that have 'splintered' away from their urban localities and that are connected up to networks of economic, social and cultural information. Those who benefit from these new sources of information can gain and act upon knowledge about a whole host of data on the gains and losses to be made by living in particular neighbourhoods. While it might be the case that Graham and Marvin are too ready to pose a rather too neat distinction between an older, industrial standardised urban service infrastructure and a newer, post-industrial networked urban infrastructure (see Coutard, 2008), it is also true to say that they nevertheless provide some extremely useful indicators about how new technology is being applied to 'splinter' and gentrify urban space.

Ellison and Burrows follow Graham and Marvin to the extent that they believe that UK city space has been split into a number of zones along the lines of social, cultural and economic divisions. For example, some middle-class families utilise geodemographic and other ICT systems to gain information about particular areas and then 'colonise' specific local services (for example education, employment and housing) when they move into those areas. This can be contrasted with relatively deprived urban areas where residents are more likely to engage in a defensive activism of communities. To make sense of these processes Ellison and Burrows divide city spaces into different zones. First, they identify proactive zones of disengagement, which refer primarily to contiguous middle-class communities living next to 'other' communities (for example working-class communities). These middle-class groups withdraw into their own enclaves and disengage from the wider community. Second, there are zones of proactive engagement, which refer primarily to middle-class members living in contiguous communities who selectively 'colonise' strategic points in a city for their advantages (for example schools). Third, there are zones of defensive engagement and these relate to both regenerated areas and deindustrialised spaces. Zones of defensive engagement include those places where inhabitants seek to preserve their way of life and communities from what they perceive to be encroachments from various regeneration schemes. Fourth, zones of disengagement refer to those places of deprivation whose 'random, disorganized violence' is 'best understood as a defensive reaction to socio-economic ills ranging from crime, poverty and high unemployment, through poor housing and environmental conditions, to intrusive and intensive policing' (Ellison and Burrows, 2007, p 309).

However, while these zones have created new divisions in society the urban pictures becomes even more complex when the relationship between dissent, public space and neoliberalism is posed. This is because there is no simple mapping of activism, its regulation in public space and the sort of zones analysed by Ellison and Burrows. This leads some to argue that while cities have been subject to some neoliberal commands over the last few decades, not all processes of redevelopment can be brought under the neoliberal label. Business Improvement Districts (BIDs) provide an illustration of this point. BIDs map out areas in a city where businesses can opt to pay additional fees in order to help improve the area in question. In his analysis of four Canadian cities, Lippert (2012) discovered that private and public processes are certainly involved in a BID scheme. However, many of the districts studied also wanted to enact a 'clean and safe' security campaign that ensured that spaces were free of refuse and risk so that consumers might walk down and around the surrounding streets feeling comfortable and secure. For Lippert such illustrations demonstrate that other non-neoliberal factors – clean and safe campaigns, for instance – are involved in BID assemblages. In a different but also related argument

Waiton (2010) questions the claim that city space has been subject to increasing modes of neoliberal governance, preferring instead to see new technological regulation in cities as part of an imposing regulatory state seeking to govern a risk-averse society. In this account, CCTV cameras represent not the enforcement of surveillance congruent with a neoliberal entrepreneurial urban agenda but, rather, the management of communities by ever-increasing regulatory bodies.

While Lippert and Waiton present some extremely interesting and thought-provoking arguments it is nevertheless difficult to see why the processes they each describe cannot be said to be part of neoliberal processes. Naturally, much of the debate around these topics depends on how neoliberalism is first defined. There is a common way of defining neoliberalism, which is simply to equate it with free markets. However, as we have seen in other chapters, this is a rather limited definition. Explanations that are more convincing demonstrate how neoliberalism is enacted and developed through social, political and economic hegemonic projects directed by the state. This last point is particularly apposite because scholars like Lippert and Waiton often say very little about the centralisation of neoliberal power in the state, preferring instead to investigate power in its contingent and empirical guise as being comprised by an unstable networked configuration of objects. Yet, as we know, governments have constructed regulatory zones of public space and then continue to order them (see Chapter Six). This in turn highlights once again the power of states to govern dissent in our global times, which sometimes seem to get lost in overly eager celebrations of the complexity and chaos that are undoubtedly important features of globalisation. The next section discusses how zones of public space in cities have been constructed by states to this effect.

Neoliberalism, CCTV and the rezoning of community public space

As we have already noted, in an age of neoliberal economic and political governance many cities are constrained by the necessity to market and sell their city to particular investors and social groups. In parallel with the rise of redevelopment schemes, like Enterprise Zones from the 1980s, there has also been the redesign of cities and public space which has come to be known as gentrification. Broadly speaking, gentrification brings together a number of different processes, not least attracting investment from private business to redevelop abandoned industrial districts, to improve the surrounding social environment, to build both affordable and private housing and to provide an attractive location for future businesses to come, invest and relocate some of their operations.

There is, though, some debate about the effects of gentrification and the extent to which it allows middle-class residents to 'perform' their social identities in public space, which then helps to create exclusionary middle-class zones (see Butler, 2007). Certainly, it would seem to be the case that gentrification assists in its own way in fashioning a neoliberal narrative in a particular locality. Davidson (2007) studied architects and developers in London along the River Thames and found that an imaginary neoliberal global narrative influenced their designs. For instance, one element of their architectural remit was to design 'metropolitan buildings'. Yet they broadly imagined metropolitan buildings to be associated with a globally connected, high-density architectural aesthetic, which the developers and architects thought would also attract investment. This imaginary aesthetic was also connected with an image of international and cosmopolitan residents who would buy apartments in these buildings. Gentrification was thus not only part of 'middle-class identity' but also part of perceived global neoliberal capital realignments. What Davidson additionally notes is that local neighbourhood and community needs were not high on the list of priorities for developers and architects.

Davidson's analysis of gentrified spaces is borne out in some respects by other studies. London Docklands, located in the east and south-east of London, is held up as one of the shining examples of regeneration. Regeneration in the area, once a declining industrial port, started in 1981 and has been pursued ever since. Today, London Docklands is internationally recognised as the heart of the City of London and thus as a global financial centre. While acknowledging some of benefits that have accrued to the surrounding communities through these developments, Brownill (2010) in equal measure recognises the uneven nature of regeneration programmes. In 2005 one London borough that sits within London Docklands, the borough of Tower Hamlets, 'was ranked fourth nationally in terms of combined levels of poverty, poor housing, education levels, and access to services, and over one-quarter of residents had incomes below £15,000 per year' (Brownill, 2010, p 138). What this reveals is that while a redevelopment scheme might adopt a rhetoric of inclusive regeneration for all, in reality it promotes itself to more affluent sections of the community or to affluent 'outsiders' in the belief that these individuals will also bring their wealth to a community through (for example) local taxes paid. But in order to promote itself in this way a city or locality frequently sends out the same standardised message to the effect of its being the hub of creative potential (see Gibson, 2005; Kavaratzis, 2007).

The result of these processes is often the appearance of new, gentrified middle-class zones in the form of the so-called 'gated communities', 'fortress cities' or 'revanchist urbanism'. Here we see the middle classes retreating to places designed to shut out those deemed 'undesirable', like the homeless, theunderclass or those from a particular racial or ethnic background. Or we see policies designed to forcefully remove 'undesirables' from public spaces such as public parks in order to generate new, entrepreneurial, visibly 'clean' spaces (Mitchell, 1995; MacLeod and Ward, 2002; see also below). Under these circumstances, gentrification retains a class perspective in the sense that much that goes under redevelopment projects in cities serves to displace members of the working class or groups suffering deprivation from a locality so that middle-class residents can then occupy those spaces. New Orleans is a case in point. After Hurricane Katrina in 2005 the local authorities have sought to rebuild the devastated areas of New Orleans where the most deaths occurred during the storm. In reality, a gentrification approach has displaced many working-class black residents from central city neighbourhoods (Slater, 2008, pp 212–13).

Surveillance is also an integral moment of the neoliberal realignment and re-zoning of urban space. In particular, surveillance is implicated in neoliberal gentrified urban space through CCTV. Once associated with analogue technology, CCTVs are now integrated with digital technology in cities and the monitoring of public and private space by security forces (see Chapter Six). One of the first examples of video surveillance was in Time Square, New York, in 1973 to deter crime in this public space. Interestingly, this experiment was deemed a failure, and yet more CCTVs were rolled out in America over the years (Yesil, 2006). In the UK the first large-scale surveillance of public space was installed in Bournemouth in 1985 (see Norris et al, 2004). Since then, CCTV has proliferated in the UK. Estimates as to the exact number of CCTV cameras in the UK vary from 1.85 million to about 4.2 million. However, in his analysis of various research projects conducted on the effectiveness of CCTV cameras to deter crime in the UK, Webster found that while CCTV cameras did sometimes reduce crime levels in some areas, this certainly was not the case in other areas. Indeed, one report published in 2005 that examined 14 detailed case studies of CCTV use in different localities in the UK found that only one case study showed a statistically significant reduction in crime that might plausibly be related to the presence of CCTV (Webster, 2009, p 17).

So, if the crime reduction rates of CCTV are poor, to say the least, why is it still being used in public space? Two plausible interrelated reasons exist. First, the increased use of CCTV is part of the NPM, competence and workfare agendas and the need to reorient public space in line with these agendas. As previous chapters have shown, PPPs have been one prominent route to achieving these goals. After New Labour came to power the number of PPPs grew substantially, so that by 2010 the Treasury could report that there were nearly 700 PFI schemes in operation, accounting for nearly 10% of annual government spending (Hodkinson, 2011, p 914). CCTV similarly helps to foster this partnership agenda and the hollowing-out of welfare provision. In 1998, the Home Office introduced a new crime management strategy by devolving some state-related responsibilities for crime reduction to local authorities. Local authorities had to work more comprehensively with other crime-reduction agencies and 'partners' and to 'incorporate components of new public managerialism including the establishment of clear and quantifiable priorities and targets and, in achieving them, the development of performance indicators and tangible goals' (Fussey, 2008, p 126).

Second, CCTV has the capacity to construct virtual exclusions that connect up with the gentrified zoning of public space. This is because CCTV assists in creating and making visible specific grievances associated with particular spaces, which then translate into wider imaginary risks. Imagine, for example, that at a particular place a person suffers a serious assault. The assault is captured on CCTV and part of the footage is relayed to members of the public through other media forms. Circulating the footage may lead some to argue that this particular grievance is part of a wider risk associated with unsafe public areas in cities. Once constructed, the risk then feeds back into the original grievance and legitimates the deployment of yet more surveillance techniques in a wide array of public spaces (see Hier, 2004). The same can be said of CCTV images of sex workers, which are often used to justify the policing of what are constructed as dangerous sexual spaces (Cook and Whowell, 2011).

CCTV thereby contributes to the circulation of public information in the public sphere, which itself relates to iconoclasm, or the struggle to control images about what can be spoken about in society (Finnegan and Kang, 2004). In the case of CCTV, images are used that define a particular version of reality as part of taken-for-granted 'shared assumptions, values, perceptions, and beliefs for matters identified explicitly as topics of discussion' (Asen, 2002, p 351; see also Woodiwiss, 2001). Visual images in this respect engender a type of visuality, of images and imaginings in everyday life that are capable of acting as the social precondition for activating claims about, say, who has the right to inhabit specific public spaces. What is considered to be in the 'public interest' in terms of who is allowed to go where and how one senses a city is thus incorporated with spatial, technological, and (new) media practices. At the same time, however, CCTV is frequently employed to regulate community publics in line with particular regeneration projects and also to monitor and control dissent. But this contradicts the emphasis that governments place on encouraging residents to become involved in new community publics and forums in their immediate localities. We now explore these contradictions in more depth.

CCTV, neoliberal regeneration and contradictions in new community publics

Lowndes and Squires (2012) observe that governance partnership networks sometimes provide opportunities for new collaborations between different groups in communities. Creativity often flourishes in such circumstances because it pushes people together from different backgrounds so that they learn from one another and generate innovative solutions to common problems. Indeed, 'in a climate of cuts, partnerships cannot afford *not* to harness the benefits of creativity' (Lowndes and Squires, 2012, p 406; original emphasis). Some evidence does indeed seem to support this sentiment. Choi and Choi (2012, p 235), for instance, discovered in their survey of 414 US cities that where collaborative partnership occurs between community groups and police departments, the police are more likely to do their job more effectively and efficiently, as measured by crime rates. Community groups can press police departments to address particular types of crime, and police in turn build relationships of trust with community groups.

Wills (2012) similarly demonstrates how new modes of governance and a new politics of localism ushered in by successive governments since the 1990s have enabled community activists from different backgrounds to come together and campaign on common issues. She illustrates her point through The East London Communities Organisation (TELCO), which is affiliated to London Citizens. TELCO was the founding 'chapter' of London Citizens and was established in 1996. Other 'chapters' in London have been launched over the years so that London Citizens is now includes '200 different member institutions including religious groups, trade union branches, schools and community groups (Wills, 2012, p 115). What is unique about these groups is that they recognise and respect each other's beliefs and differences but campaign on common social issues such as the battle to gain a living wage for all.

There is no doubt that the neoliberal workfare agenda provides many benefits for communities, not least its propensity to build new modes of socialisation and politicisation (on this point see also Elwood, 2002). Yet we know that neoliberalism contains deep contradictions that in turn reproduce qualitatively new strategic contradictions and dilemmas in more everyday contexts. Those active in community groups are therefore never simply disciplined by those in power but do of course manage to take advantage of different contradictions in order to assert their own interests (Pollock and Sharp, 2012). In cities this is manifest in the tensions that surface between community organisations campaigning for better public spaces and private developers who will potentially gain much from the contracting out of public space (Biddulph, 2011, p 97). Yet, it is equally true to say that these contradictions and tensions often serve to depoliticise community activism. Wills (2012, p 124) recognises some of the problems evident here when she notes that many individuals and groups in the poor communities served by London Citizens often remain outside the affiliated member institutions, and these usually belong to the most vulnerable groups in communities.

This in turn is related to another strategic dilemma, that of community elites. Sure enough, if community organisations come together in one forum, then there is potential for many positive outcomes, not least local officials or developers consulting the forum in question. However, none of this further implies that community leaders in a community forum have legitimacy in their own respective communities, nor does it imply that community leaders represent a united community voice. Beebeejaun's (2006) research on race, ethnicity and community planning is instructive in this respect. In one of her case studies in Smethwick, West Midlands in the UK, Beebeejaum found that race and ethnicity were both key determinants in facilitating, or not, public deliberation with local residents over land–use planning. Smethwick has a large Asian community. Planners consulted with the Asian community about a new housing scheme under a formal umbrella group, Sandwell Ethnic Minority Umbrella Forum, which represented a number of racial and ethnic groups in the area. A male Asian business group, who made their views known to the planners, represented the Indian group. The planners agreed to their concerns. However, as Beebeejaum notes, a survey that was carried out reported that some Asian residents had different concerns. Yet, by believing that the Asian business group was a legitimate voice of the Indian and Asian community, planners neglected other community voices associated with women, the young and the old.

But in a neoliberal workfare environment we also know that the idea of what a 'community' is and how it is defined is a deeply divided one at different levels and between different 'partners'. Ordinary residents who 'help out' in their neighbourhoods will hold ideas and views about 'community' that compete with those of more business-led partners. Volunteers, for example, frequently say they 'help out' for reasons other than neoliberal, market-based ones. Mutual aid and being involved in the community are given as preferred reasons for volunteering, rather than investing in human capital (Baines and Hardill, 2008). Social planners, on the other hand, are involved in a competitive process to win planning contracts. If they do indeed win a contract they are then often forced to complete a development in a short amount of time. Under these pressures community becomes a somewhat fluid concept and invariably succumbs to internal tensions

> between capacity building and achieving 'hard' development outcomes, between focusing on long-term versus short-term change, between broad community-change ambitions and aligning expectations with the scale and nature of interventions supported. (Sites et al, 2007, p 530)

In a neoliberal environment the danger always exists that the needs of the community and assurances that democratic frameworks are adhered to will be demoted in favour of the needs of business. Private sector maintenance of local public service delivery might then entail, as Sager (2011, p 164) observes, higher user fees, decreasing equity between groups, less transparency and accountability around development issues as private companies restrict inspection rights, and might show a bias towards property rights over the social rights of community members.

What seems to be occurring, then, is that major cities have increasingly transformed themselves into regimes of good governance based on the principles of public deliberation with residents, but also on the surveillance and policing of public space for the purposes of neoliberal accumulation. Liberal democracy is thus publicly celebrated by government officials and policy makers because they say it is working properly at a community level while in reality the content of what in fact is publicly debated by local residents has altered. 'Stakeholders' and 'partners' become the preferred ideological utterances in this instance, with new modes of management taking the place of 'normal' local politics (MacLeod, 2011). Again, however, this agenda develops its own contradictions.

A powerful image to emerge from CCTV relates to recent changes in public space. Over the last few decades public space has shifted from public parks, streets and the like and has moved to 'quasi-public' spaces such as shopping centres, housing developments, leisure centres, and airports. This heralds a move towards the (semi) privatisation of public space. To give one illustration, public officials and business are becoming aware of the income that can be generated from housing projects located in or near public parks. It is said, for example, that in the US there is a positive impact of 20% on property values next to a park area that is 'passively' used by the public (Crompton, 2005, p 216). Issues of security are also closely bound up with the privatisation and marketing of space, to the extent that many cities sell themselves through 'a spectacle of security in the shape of ... highly visible manned entry points and the prominent network of cameras throughout the area' (Gold and Revill, 2003, p 41).

These issues come together through the way in which some who manage public and quasi-public spaces are utilising CCTV as a means to 're-visualise' the morality of the space in question. Shopping malls are a case in point. Acting as an aesthetic as well as commercial sign of recovery in a once deprived area, shopping malls also subject those visiting them to moral surveillance. For example, managers of shopping malls primarily see these spaces as sites of consumption, and not as places for deliberation about social or political issues. A 'community' of interests among different 'partners' might therefore exist in a shopping mall, but only to the extent that it abides by the requirement to consume. CCTV assists in monitoring shopping malls and in removing any people who do not 'belong' to this narrative; all of which is done of course in the name of public safety (Staeheli and Mitchell, 2006; Voyce, 2006).

But the regulatory parameters of CCTV are much wider than shopping malls, and in fact encompass wider procedures associated with gentrification. After all, CCTV can displace visible signs that attract a politics of dissent around tangible issues like urban inequalities. This occurs when palpable symbols of social deprivation like homelessness are translated into criminal and/or deviant issues through CCTV images. As Coleman observes, 'CCTV can be understood as an attempt to disguise-through-exclusion the flip side of neoliberal city building' (Coleman, 2003, pp 34–5). Legislation underpins this agenda. In the UK the Crime and Disorder Act 1998, for example, explicitly associates low-level crime with anti-social behaviour in public space. Low-level crime thus becomes equated with 'deviant' lifestyles and serious offences as well. In these circumstances CCTV became a means to identify those in communities who had fallen into these moral categories (Fussey, 2008, p 130). Subsequently there is more than a ring of truth to Lovering's observation that neoliberal planning has been focused on the need first to improve the image of a city than it has been on promoting real socioeconomic and democratic advantages for most ordinary residents (Lovering, 2010, p 237).

In this regard, Akkar (2005) usefully distinguishes between public space and 'publicness'. Planners and designers alter the 'publicness' of public space by either opening up or shutting down access to the public space in question. As De Magalhães (2010) notes, planning policy has the potential to regulate the rights of access and use, as well as the ownership and control of public space, through contractual relationships between governance bodies that deal with the coordination, regulation, maintenance and investment of public space and 'stakeholders' (for example business, visitors, and residents) who use public space.

Undoubtedly, these schemes do bring citizens together in order to gain contracts to then manage selective public spaces for their own benefits and enjoyment. However, there are also democratic costs incurred in public–private redevelopment schemes. A shopping area in Washington, Tyne and Wear in the UK, known as the Galleries, was privatised in 1987. This particular public space in the north–east of England was thereby transformed into a 'quasi-public space'. After privatisation the Galleries was redesigned and policed to ensure that the area was devoted solely to the experience of shopping. When, a few years later, a stall was set up in the Galleries to collect signatures against a proposed plan to build on the remaining green area in central Washington, the owners of the Galleries thought the actions of the petitioners were 'unacceptable' in this quasi-public space and promptly had them removed. An appeal by the petitioners to the European Court against their unfair removal and loss of the right to peaceful assembly was not granted (Bottomley and Moore, 2007, pp 183–5). This case illustrates how struggles over the rights of public space are associated with the publicness of public and community spaces. Moreover, this struggle is associated with 'ordinary' forms of publicness, such as the architectural design and surveillance of public space along with images and narratives about the changing use of such space.

The extension of CCTV surveillance across cities also has considerable impact upon legitimate dissent and protest. In Manchester, UK, an industrial dispute arose in May 2003 at a building site in the city centre. At the picket line, striking workers were subject to intense surveillance by five CCTV cameras. Part of the reason for the strike was because of unsafe working practices at the site. Strangely, however, none of the cameras directed its gaze upon these unsafe working practices, even though the building site was within their range (Coleman et al, 2005, p 2517). CCTV is thus a powerful mechanism for bringing people, discourses and objects together around constructed issues and demonstrates that the struggle to control images and their meaning is also a struggle over space, technology and the 'public interest' of who is allowed to go where.

Conclusion

David Harvey (1989) suggests that urbanisation is plagued by both creative potential (for example, the aestheticisation of cities) and destructive potential (for example, perpetual inequalities) and it is this contradictory mix that constantly opens up new opportunities for places of dissent to arise in cities. Activism arises from and often draws on local community voices and resources to mobilise opposition and create new community publics against a 'thing' causing frustration. In this respect the redesign and redevelopment of urban space can be conceptualised as a means to regulate these ordinary 'interstitial spaces' and in so doing attempt to pre-empt points of dissent through a strategy of 'including' ordinary community voices in development schemes. It is in this respect that designers and planners also belong to a group that includes 'scientists, urbanists, technocratic subdividers and social engineers' who impose order upon social spaces through (for example) architectural designs, symbols, codes and language to promote vested and dominant interests (Lefebvre, 1991, pp 38–9).

One way of assessing this point is to explore the quality of consultation with relevant interest groups before the redesign of public space occurs. This chapter has shown that what is of particular significance here is the value and worth of collaboration with planners, local officials and voices of dissent from local residents towards the development scheme in question. On the one hand, designers and local officials might want a public space to appeal to a wide cross-section of public and private interests. Local residents, on the other hand, might want a local public space to retain a functional use for an existing community, such as a recreational playing field (McInroy, 2000; on public consultation see Barnes et al, 2006). This in turn has knock-on effects for how planners and local officials consult with community leaders over the redevelopment of public space, especially since deliberation between different 'partners' can produce tensions among them. It is during such moments that further disputes can arise between all key players and 'partners' that go on to open up a broader public debate about other contradictions and dilemmas in a community and beyond.

We have also considered how these events generate their own contradictions that disrupt the formation of community publics, but also unintentionally provide resources for them. Yet, others believe that one way to empower community publics is for them to try to make social and political connections with other community and social movements that work in and beyond formal political mechanisms at local, regional, and global scales. In other words, some have argued that we need to move beyond standard institutional and state-led governance of the public sphere and towards an emphasis on social movements and their construction of autonomous public spheres of activism, communication and dissent. For many this makes good sense if for no other reason than the fact that at least since the 1950s commentators and academics have been arguing that class-based politics has been eclipsed by the emergence of 'new social movements', 'the politics of difference', 'identity politics', 'urban movements', 'the urban left' and so on. No longer is there a class subject as such, but rather a subject defined across social boundaries campaigning on a whole range of social issues such as environmentalism, gender, sexuality, race, 'or, more generally, humanity as a whole' (Scott, 1990, p 29). To what extent, though, can these new global social movements pose a serious challenge to the competent workfare public sphere and ignite a new wave of anti-neoliberal public activism in society as a whole? We now turn to this question.

Note

[1] Global institutions act as organic intellectuals in this sense too. To give just one illustration, in 1998 the OECD noted, for instance, that the private sector 'would have to participate more directly in the policy planning phase of regeneration efforts' through 'tripartite' partnerships with the public sector and civil society (cited in Theodore and Peck, 2011, p 30).

EIGHT

Global social movements: beyond the competent public sphere?

Introduction

In *The Power of Identity* Castells (2010) notes that the move towards global network societies has given people a 'reflexive' awareness of the world around them. We can now be constantly connected to one another through the likes of digital media and this brings about a continual awareness of the world. Castells also argues that globalisation has created what he terms as 'project identity'. Based on a number of cultural and social attributes, project identities give rise to new forms of belonging and meaning that redefine the position of particular social groups in society. Groups campaigning for women's issues and gender equality are typical illustrations in this respect (Castells, 2010, p xxvi).

Project identities are closely associated with the distinctive beliefs and ideals of global social movements (GSMs). According to Cohen and Rai (2000, pp 8–10), there are six factors that make a social movement 'global'. First, different transnational institutions have slowly eroded the powers enjoyed by the nation-state. Many of these institutions make decisions that affect local communities as well as larger populations. GSMs often mobilise to confront and challenge these powers. Second, global communication networks have made it easier for social movements to organise themselves across borders and converge on sites of demonstration and/or be involved in different campaigns across the world. Third, corporate and transnational business interests have become powerful socioeconomic organisations. 'Political activity has thus to adapt to a larger terrain, particularly in the case of the international labour movement and movements allied with it' (Cohen and Rai, 2000, p 8). Fourth, political and social movements can no longer simply think about putting forward solutions to combat social ills at a national level. Globalisation implies that we require global solutions and transnational coordination among movement activists. Fifth, many activists across the world are united by global values like anti-war values, environmentalism, and human rights. A truly global social movement must then work with these global values in order to tackle global oppressions. Finally, global social movements work to provide alternative global spaces for different democratic ideals, and are willing to accommodate a plethora of democratic expressive identities. In all of these instances, then, a range of global processes has made a significant impact on identity formation among people and, as a result, these have forged new types of politics around distinctive projects.

To what extent, though, do GSMs provide genuinely new outlets for campaigners and ordinary people to engage in public activism? Is their unique employment of new media a help or a hindrance to them in gaining supporters for their different causes? Does the predominance of their global identity serve to preclude regular politics allied with the nation-state? Do GSMs represent a challenge to the competent workfare public sphere? This chapter will explore these and other questions in order to examine some of the main characteristics of global social movements and their use of new media. The next two sections outline how GSMs have helped to instigate a new global public sphere that draws heavily on images and spectacles to rouse supporters into action and campaigns in and around specific global issues. Several concrete examples are presented to illustrate the points made, including those taken from the Arab Spring, culture jamming and hacktivists. The third main section presents a number of critical observations on GSMs. In particular, this section demonstrates that the very global and networked nature of many GSMs leads to dilemmas and problems in leadership structures in these movements. Moreover, the fact that they are 'global' in nature often implies that activists involved in various GSM campaigns fail to engage in and with the politics of nation-states. This, though, is a rather weak strategy to adopt because it means that one is less able and prepared to struggle against neoliberal competence articulated by nation-states. The conclusion, however, flags an alternative type of politics that is developed in the next, final chapter.

Global social movements and the global public sphere

GSMs have proliferated in the last few decades and their increase in numbers has been strengthened by their use of available technologies. Created through transnational social networks that coordinate the activity and actions of different civil society groups around a specific issue or set of issues, GSMs engage in modes of protest and single-issue campaigns that are in turn developed against common targets at both national and global levels. Some of the more well-known movement campaigns include Our World Is Not For Sale (trade issues), Third World Network (fair, equal and ecologically sound distribution of world resources) and European Network Against Arms Trade (peace).

Many involved in social movements around the world are also associated with anti-globalisation politics, and this type of politics is often allied with small-scale activist groups who are connected to various global networks. These decentralised groups can shift in and out of global networks in order to forge alliances as need be during long drawn-out local campaigns. Some anti-globalisation movements like Earth First! have global activists who also create groups specific to particular countries. So, Earth First! groups exist in, among other countries, the UK, Canada, Australia, the Netherlands and the US.

Just as a language is comprised of many different meanings that name specific events, so is it the case according to some that GSMs produce communicative meanings, forms of life and social relationships that name and draw attention to social, economic, political and cultural events across the world. Think of intellectual property. Intellectual property is obviously tied to economic production and so, where it can, capital will convert scientific ideas into patents and private property. However, this is not just an economic question but also a political question because the monopoly upon knowledge obviously is concentrated in the wealthy northern hemisphere. At the same time, it is a cultural question because access to knowledge is inexorably related to artistic and cultural expression in the form of access to digital rights (cf. Hardt and Negri, 2004, p 284). With its criss-crossing communicative networks, the very nature of global capitalism is therefore one in which many activists can monitor its operations and coordinate their own activism across the world with one another (Hardt and Negri, 2004, p 340).

Taking their cue from Hardt and Negri's analysis, Chesters and Welsh (2006) observe that global civil society harbours an antagonistic movement in the way it is organised. Accordingly, one of the most recognised GSM groups, the anti-globalisation movement, represents an elementary challenge to the way in which the production and distribution of social, economic and ecological goods is carried out. Importantly for Chesters and Welsh, the anti-globalisation movement provides a good illustration of a combative social force combined through many diverse global networks. These are structured through different nodes and weak links that permit the anti-globalisation movement some flexibility in developing emergent properties in order to adapt to new contexts. Such networks are therefore durable and global precisely because they are decentralised and yet occupy global informational linkages. As Hardt and Negri explain:

> The global cycle of struggle develops in the form of a distributed network. Each local struggle functions as a node that communicates with all the other nodes without any hub or centre of intelligence. Each struggle remains singular and tied to its local conditions but at the same time is immersed in the common web. (Hardt and Negri, 2004, p 217)

Activist public spaces therefore serve to intensify GSM networks by acting as 'plateaux' – a moment for networks to converge, to exchange experiences, stories, reflection and practical activities and to think about future actions and campaigns.

One notable activist public space, or plateau, has been the World Social Forum. Holding its first meeting in Porto Alegre, Brazil in 2001, the World Social Forum has met every year since. Such is the success in mobilising activists that smaller regional forums have been established, like the European Social Forum. Comprised principally of social activists, social movements, NGOs and intellectuals, it is a public sphere in which a multitude of people exchange information on the problems of globalisation and propose solutions to them. Activists and organisers at the World Social Forum have built on pre-existing associational networks, seen most evidently at Porto Alegre, which brought together both Brazilian activists (for example the trade union federation and the movement of landless peasants) and European activists (Yiä-Anttila, 2005, p 431). The World Social Forum has been particularly apt at assembling media representation about global campaigns and, as a result, instigating a global public sphere around issues and campaigns discussed.

This non-linear complex interaction between networked activists and networked spaces implies that 'one individual or a small group of individuals can dramatically transform the process of building the public sphere' (Sinekopova, 2006, p 514). This is ever more the case in a world in which people neither are directed by one political party concerning what can be spoken about in the public sphere nor remain autonomous and separate from one another. For some, the varied nature of GSMs and global civil society has meant we must take account of both the institutionalisation of public debate and its symbolic representation and performance. This is a mode of global citizenship in which the struggle for rights, justice and inclusion in the democratic public would simultaneously struggle against social divisions based on race, ethnicity, gender, nationality, popular/high culture and nature/culture (Stevenson, 2003). Through participatory forums like the World Social Forum, GSMs have helped to foster the belief in the possibilities of a cosmopolitan citizenship, and one in which differences are respected while a common humanity is promoted. At the same time, GSMs have also presented new and innovative techniques for employing digital technology for campaigns, demonstrations and protest. We now turn our attention to this issue.

Global social movements and new media

Pickerill (2006) notes that GSMs have employed new media technology from its earliest stages to further activist causes. Use of e-mail lists and newsgroups by social movements in the late 1980s and of the web in the early to mid-1990s was already noticeable. Often this was simply to advertise a group's existence but it also demonstrated a strong commitment by social movements to employing digital technology. Some movement activists also joined arts-based groups, who then engaged in projects that combined arts, critical theory, technology and activism. Arguably, though, three events have firmly established the link and possibilities between new media and GSMs.

The first event occurred on New Year's Day 1994, when a group living in the mountains of south-east Mexico and known as the Zapatistas embarked on a 12-day uprising. The aim of the rebellion was to liberate the indigenous people of the Chiapas. Since this time, the Zapatistas have been engaged in a constant war of manoeuvre and attrition with the Mexican government. What is distinctive about the Zapatistas, according to Tormey (2006), is that they refuse to talk *for* the people of Chiapas but instead talk *with* them. Through talking *with*, the Zapatistas engage in a 'post-representational politics' that refuses to speak on behalf of 'the People'. Instead the Zapatistas are accountable to the Clandestine Revolutionary Indigenous Committees (CCRI) comprised of local and regional bodies and elected representatives. In turn, the CCRIs are accountable to about 40 autonomous communes and answerable to any delegate from a specific community; all of which implies that local public spheres are established based upon the principle that it is the views of indigenous people themselves that are the most important in setting agendas. Such democratic practices appeal to the decentralised command structure of many GSMs.

The activism and politics of the Zapatistas is also important because the insurgents made use of new digital technology to further the cause of their uprising almost from the outset. Through digital technology they were able to publicise their insurgency and thus demonstrate the power of new media to communicate a local rebellion to a worldwide audience. During the first few months of their uprising, information about the actions of the Zapatistas was posted on numerous listservs in various websites and through e-mail lists. Obviously, these technological networks have developed and transmuted in size and scope over the years, so that publicity surrounding the Zapatistas flows into a range of local, national and global networks. For example, Global Exchange, a human rights organisation based in San Francisco, sends volunteers to Chiapas communities to act as peace observers. Global Exchange then distributes information gathered in these indigenous communities to a wider cyber audience (Olesen, 2004).

The second event arrived in December 1999, during a World Trade Organisation (WTO) summit meeting in Seattle where thousands of protestors converged to force the WTO to abandon its meeting. A riot soon ensued between demonstrators and the police. But the importance of the 'Battle of Seattle' is more than the fact that a riot took place. It demonstrates instead the opportunities afforded by GSM activism and digital media. For example, the Independent Media Centre, or Indymedia, was established in 1999 to provide independent media coverage of demonstrations against the WTO in Seattle (see Platen and Deuze, 2003). Soon Indymedia centres were set up in other parts of the world, along with a number of other independent and activist media networks such as Common Dreams and Take Back the Media. These were and are loosely organised networks of groups that post information about demonstrations, campaigns and reports about social and political issues on websites. Since then, alternative media outlets have become sites for easily accessible information that poses a challenge of sorts to the information circulating in the mainstream media. GSMs are thus attracted by the opportunities afforded by new technologies and they like its decentralised structure. In addition, ICTs can bring individuals together around single-issue campaigns, ensuring that a sense of obligation and commitment ensues between participants (Langman, 2005; Garrett, 2006; Pickerill and Chatterton, 2006).

The third event is the more recent case of the Arab Spring. Erupting in Tunisia in December 2010, the Arab Spring soon spread to other countries in the region, including Egypt, Libya, Oman, Syria and Yemen. While they were diverse, some common themes nevertheless united many protestors across Arab countries, including greater democratic rights, an end to political corruption in Arab states and greater social protection from socioeconomic inequalities. This event is important not only because it represents a more contemporary illustration of the relationship between social movements and digital technology,, but also as we will now see, because it is often held up as an excellent example of how social media can be mobilised for revolutionary purposes.

Some large mainstream public media institutions such as BBC Arabic TV (launched in March 2008) and BBC Persian TV (launched in January 2009) started to draw on UGC arising from different Arab countries during the Arab Spring. Indeed, from 2009 both channels established links with the BBC UGC hub in order to process UGC streaming out of Arab countries, so as to cover events of the Arab Spring as they were happening (Hänska-Ahy and Shapour, 2013). For sure, a new, mediatised Arab public sphere had already been formed some years previously, through new satellite channels like Al-Jazeera, while digital technology, especially in the guise of the internet, meant that an Arab digital public sphere had been steadily growing throughout the late 1990s and 2000s. The first Iranian blog, for instance, emerged in 2001, but just two years later one study placed the number of blogs in Iran at around 13,000 (Khiabany and Sreberny, 2007, p 564). However, the relative cheapness of new media products like iPhones and the relative ease and cheapness of setting up social media websites ensured that protestors discovered new outlets to publicise the Arab Spring. Facebook became available in Arabic only in 2009, and yet more than a quarter of the protestors in Egypt first heard of demonstrations taking place there on Facebook (Tufekci and Wilson, 2012, p 373). One study estimated that Egyptian activists spent on average one to three hours per day on social network sites to share and gain information about what was happening on the streets (Mansour, 2012, p 143).

Three further observations can be made in this respect. First, the Arab Spring demonstrates how new media in general and social media in particular lower the costs of communication while increasing visibility. For example, some Arab readers posted their own opinions on the online comment pages in western newspapers to set the demonstrations in their proper national context. These readers thereby offered up alternative opinions to those of mainstream western journalists (Christensen and Christensen, 2013). Social media undeniably played a role in publicising important information among activists and protestors about the demonstrations (Hussain and Howard, 2013).

Second, new media helps to empower those who privately hold oppositional views to a government regime and then translate these into public expressions of opposition. This 'information cascade' was particularly noticeable in Tunisia and Egypt, whereby 'the courageous early movers sent a signal to a generally sympathetic public of the valuing of joining in' (Lynch, 2011, p 304).

Finally, new media hold the potential to document abusive authoritarian practices of corrupt government officials in Arab states (Lynch, 2011, pp 304–5; Youmans and York, 2012, p 317). Social media in particular was believed by some to have made a substantial contribution to mobilising protestors during the Arab Spring. It created an independent Arab media space that at the same time was fused with popular culture and popular Arab experiences. Through this space, so it is said, corrupt officials and governments could at last be held accountable through increased transparency brought about by social media (Cottle, 2011, p 651).

What all of this underlines for some analysts is the potential of new media, especially social media, to initiate deliberative forums in and around social and political issues that are then expanded in the wider global public sphere. Indeed, some evidence suggests that reportage of initial events of the Arab Spring transpired mainly through citizen journalism. If we momentarily focus once again on Egypt we see that during the initial phase of the revolution in January 2011 citizen media outstripped the mainstream media in reporting protest events. On 25 January 2011, for example, 76% of all videos uploaded to the internet detailing demonstrations came from citizens, while journalists produced only 24% (Nanabhay and Farmanfarmaian, 2011, p 385). A few days later mainstream journalists started to upload their own videos of events. In one important respect, then, the work of citizen journalists was taken up by the mainstream press and 'amplified' in the wider public sphere.

These three events – the Zapatistas, the Battle of Seattle and the Arab Spring – therefore demonstrate more broadly that the visibility of citizenship has markedly changed in recent years. Political and social life is now more mediated than has ever been the case. Politicians strive for a positive mediated public existence and realise that their words and actions are accepted or rejected by voters to the extent that they maintain an intangible aura of credibility and trustworthiness. In a world where apparently class politics is no longer in play, politicians would be perceived as being somewhat peculiar if they paraded the same old assurances. Rather, they must maintain a reputable and trustworthy character on the public stage in an age of sophisticated journalistic investigative reporting and popular media forms.

> Hence it is not surprising that *struggles for visibility* have come to assume such significance in our societies today. Mediated visibility is not just a vehicle through which aspects of social and political life are brought to the attention of others: it has become a principal means by which social and political struggles are articulated and carried out. (Thompson, 2005, p 49; original emphasis)

We now explore this point in more depth.

Global social movements and image events

In *Media Matters* John Fiske (1994) argues that media events are increasingly important channels of information through which to convey news to people. At the same time, ordinary people challenge mainstream media images by staging their own media events, ensuring that these become points of struggle in the public sphere over social and political issues. In this respect, Fiske claims that there are three elements to a media event. First, there must be a topic or area of social experience that people can relate to and that initiates public discussion. For example, the Iraq War was initially an issue that provoked discussion in the public sphere. Second, he claims that social positions need to be constructed so as to make sense of and narrate the media event in question. In the case of the war in Iraq, two obvious social positions were the anti-war movement and those mainstream politicians who supported the war. Finally, a repertoire of words, images and practices that explain the media event in question (for example 'terrorism' or 'illegal war', in the case of the Iraq).

DeLuca and Peeples (2002) present a similar argument but develop it to make sense of GSMs and digital media. They say that global media networks have formed not only public spheres of political activism, but also 'public screens' of activism. Whereas the public sphere is premised on dialogue between *people*, the public screen is premised on dialogue among *images*. Media images speed up information, but also vastly expand geographical consciousness and knowledge for most people. For, among other things, new media images are generated through *hypermediacy*. To give one illustration, an online news website is not just a window on the world but also opens up windows to other media forms. From this simple example a broader point can be made that suggests that we now live in a pictorial age in which publicity is gained through images and representations. Political activists can therefore stage 'image events' and articulate their political standpoint to others through media spectacles.

While image events are often associated by the mainstream media with serious disturbances in the guise of demonstrations of the sort witnessed in Seattle in 1999, they are in fact also frequently imbued with humour. One notable element of GSMs is that they often have visual humorous displays. Culture jamming is a case in point. Associated with various media techniques by social movements, culture jamming is roughly defined as those protest tactics designed to disrupt corporate messages to consumers. Such disruption proceeds by imitating corporate advertisements or subjecting them to parody and satire (Carducci, 2006). Mixing humour with protest is thus a clear aim of culture jammers, and through this mix different emotions are released during the actual moment of culture jamming. For instance, Wettergren (2009) notes how at one incident a group of culture jammers entered a Wal-Mart shop in New York and proceeded to push empty shopping carts in a Zombie-like fashion, in an unbroken line, up and down the shopping aisles. They thus articulated various emotions in around the work practices of Wal-Mart. Other culture jammers aim to create an 'image event' in which protest action is a highly staged moment that also incorporates media mechanisms (Delicath and Deluca, 2003) to highlight negative corporate practices. Through the humour involved in such practices new emotional spaces are opened up for dissent to take place.

Some culture jammers are also involved in the hacktivist movement. Hackers can be traced back to the Massachusetts Institute of Technology in the late 1950s, where a group of computer programmers could produce and repair codes at an amazing rate. Many hackers today believe in free access to computers and information, they hold a mistrust of central authority and they feel that they should be assessed by their computing talents alone (Jordan, 1999). Hacktivists are political hackers who use their skills to further their political and social beliefs. A number of hacktivists, for instance, are critical of the centralisation of the internet by corporations. To combat this they produce open-source software programmes that can then be used freely by movement activists. But hacktivists also sometimes engage in culture jamming tactics and do so by targeting a specific corporate or military web page and rewrite the page in question along more political and humorous lines. This form of culture jamming is related to other online hacktivist tactics like virtual sit-ins or blockades, whereby coordinated requests to access a targeted website to cause that website to overload (Taylor, 2005).

Hacktivists are interesting for another reason as well. As Coleman and Golub (2008) show, hackers and hacktivists belong to a variety of groups that hold different political ideals. Some groups defend liberal theories of privacy. Established in 1992, Cypherpunks, for example, are advocates of privacy technology and cryptography and so seek to extend and embed liberal rights more fully into mainstream society. Open source software hackers similarly campaign for the free flow of information across communication networks. In many respects they wish to defend and extend a liberal notion of free self-expression. All of these hacktivists therefore seek to challenge narrow views of property rights, and believe that knowledge should be enjoyed, shared and distributed to others (Coleman and Golub, 2008).

These latter points are interesting in so far that they show in a roundabout way that some global social movements are not necessarily radical in a left-leaning sense of that term; or at least in a socialist sense. Some can in fact seek to embed and widen existing liberal freedoms across capitalist societies. Fundamental core principles of capitalist power are not subsequently challenged by them as such, but are simply reconstituted. After all, liberal freedoms always operate within the institutional boundaries of the capitalist state, and extending liberal freedoms does not confront the class-based authority of the state. Of course, extending liberal freedoms across society as a whole is not an inherently negative deed to undertake. Indeed, it has many benefits. However, it also shows up the limits of those global social movements that undertake these actions, especially those that seek to reform the 'system' within existing liberal frameworks. The next section develops these points by exploring some links between the global civil society and GSMs.

Global civil society and the limits of global social movements

From some GSM literature, it is easy to be left with the impression that global civil society exists as a network of associations through which people, groups and institutions can come together to empower themselves and offset the non-democratic traits of globalisation. But, as Amoore and Langley (2004, p 102) insist, global civil society is more ambiguous and contradictory than this narrative suggests. There is in fact no one, single vision about what 'empowerment' actually means in practice. Non-governmental organisations like Oxfam, Greenpeace and Amnesty International are seen as key players in the democratisation of global civil society, in the sense that they frequently campaign against global injustices and they marshal public opinion against these injustices. But in a neoliberal, albeit 'humanitarian', world NGOs can easily be compromised in their policy provision, especially since the current global climate lacks political transparency and is plagued by competing state interests. To be effective, NGOs might therefore have to make concessions in their respective projects and goals to gain the cooperation of specific states. And, lest we forget, global neoliberals encourage the growth of global civil society because they see it as a realm in which entrepreneurship can flourish. The term itself – global civil society – does little to help matters in this respect. Its all-inclusive nature makes it a rather indistinct concept and it tends to cloud issues of how nation-states still have an immense impact on ordinary people's lives (Wilkin, 2000; Munck, 2002; Olesen, 2005).

From a global social movements perspective, the picture is equally ambiguous. In the UK, for example, there is a whole array of competing social movements. There are those associated with the Marxist Left, like the Socialist Workers Party, to anarchist groups in the Anarchist Federation and anarchist-related artistic/cultural groups like Reclaim the Streets who advocate the use of images, space and architecture as modes of protest, to far right groups like the British National Party. With such diverse groupings and strategies there is an ever-present risk that a coherent anti-globalisation strategy, let alone an anti-capitalist movement, will be lost. It is then easier for government forces to grant concessions to some movements at the expense of others, thus furthering divisions within global oppositional forces and weakening their impact (Worth and Abbott, 2006). These divisions are evident in the dilemmas encountered in movement activism. While certain decentralised traits of movement activism may contain many advantages, there is also the perennial danger that such activism will suffer through weak coalitions, leaderless organisation, conflicting goals and inconsistent ideas about how activism should proceed (Bennett, 2003).

These divisions are mirrored in global media public spheres. A few years ago, for example, the Indymedia network received a $50,000 Ford Foundation Grant to instigate an Indymedia conference. Yet the Argentinian Indymedia network blocked the grant on the grounds that acceptance would compromise the status and work of Indymedia (Pickard, 2006). Here, a decentralised command structure caused confusion over tactics and strategies. Yet such strains and tensions are evident too in the World Social Forum. In principle, the World Social Forum is an 'open' space, whereas in practice it harbours competing interests and politics and maintains some hierarchical structures that often favour professionalised NGOs (Biccum, 2005). The consequences are all too clear. Elements of the anti-globalisation movement claim to 'speak on behalf' of those whom they quite rightly feel to be dispossessed, without necessarily understanding the real everyday political and social experiences of the dispossessed. This is not to criticise every social movement, but it is to suggest that some who claim to speak on behalf of other communities do so without understanding the distinctive political constituency of the communities in question (Kiely, 2005). The main point to make on this issue is that many social movements have not in fact been as successful as their supporters arguably suggest. Even a major alternative organisation like the World

Social Forum receives little publicity in the mainstream media and has minimum impact on ordinary people's lives (Ugarteche, 2007, p 66).

Chandler (2004) goes further by arguing that some social movements create a fictitious community of interests that in reality abstracts away from engaging a political electorate (Chandler, 2004, p 161). Indeed, electorates tend to see themselves as national citizens whose concerns and interests are inescapably tied to national and local governments and only partially tied to global institutions like the EU (Axtmann, 2002, p 106). This is true not only of advanced capitalist societies but also of developing countries. Grassroots struggles against dominant class interests in developing societies are often confronted with robust, explicitly defined and more exact (authoritarian) elites and parasitical state interests than those in advanced societies. The Zapatistas, for instance, are not merely a local movement who have pushed their demands to a global level, as one would be led to believe by reading some GSM scholars. Rather, as Otero (2004) observes, the Zapatistas are intent on helping to organise (some) movements in Mexico's civil society, particularly indigenous groups, to push forward their *political* demands to the Mexican *state*. The Zapatistas are therefore well aware of the need to work within and against the Mexican state, to engage various political electorates in Mexican society and to campaign on traditional political and social issues like housing, education, healthcare, land and work (Otero, 2004; see also the similar points made about global civil society by Colás, 2003 and Saccarelli, 2004).

However, some involved in global campaigns use consumer images to help to construct a universal community of interests among the population at large that, at the same time, unfortunately ignores important social divisions between people based on factors like social class. To develop this point consider, briefly, how globalisation is portrayed to us through the likes of everyday objects. One conspicuous everyday visual image is that of the 'blue globe' that figures prominently as a logo on various TV stations, especially news and current affairs programmes, and as a logo for some Hollywood studios. For Szerszynski and Urry (2006) this image represents Earth as a universal moment in time where nations are not divided along borders. 'Outside' no longer exists in this visual representation. Instead, the image projects the idea of an abstract, borderless and universal space through which we can all travel, be morally connected to one another and consume other places. Such ordinary global images therefore help to create 'banal cosmopolitanism'; the way in which, at a daily routine level, we are told that all human beings belong to one moral domain and in principle have obligations towards one another across that domain. As a result, the 'private' daily consumption of everyday goods is irrevocably connected with a global public rather than with real grassroots activism and real social divisions that people face in their everyday lives.

There has been a propensity of late for some charities to tap into this socially constructed ethical and universal global public sphere and incorporate a consumer-driven celebrity culture at the forefront of their campaigns, while simultaneously drawing on notions of 'ordinariness' on their websites. The ONE Campaign is emblematic of such practices in this respect. Launched in 2004, ONE aims to mobilise ordinary people to become lobbying activists on issues in and around government funding for international aid programmes. While ONE has thus managed to capture the public's attention through high-profile celebrity endorsements, its actual website promotes the image of *individual* ordinary people becoming active lobbyists on behalf of ONE's goals. In this respect Tatarchevskiy (2011) notes that ONE's website has a performative element to it in so far that ordinary people are encouraged to create 'events', such as writing to politicians about international aid, which will then serve to publicise ONE's ethical and humane message. ONE is thus representative of an online ethical politics based in and around images and standardised activist packages rather than real political activism in and around struggles against state hegemony. Like many large-scale charities, ONE also employs professional lobbyists to do its actual campaigning work. These professional lobbyists, however, serve to strengthen an existing unaccountable elite of political cliques. As Tatarchevskiy (2011, pp 308–9) goes on to observe, ordinary individuals involved in ONE unintentionally add value to this professional lobbying elite because they present an 'authentic' public face based on a rather fabricated 'people's power' and grassroots mobilisation that lends credence to what is in effect an unaccountable political layer of professional lobbyists (see also Chapter Four).

These critical points are related to another theoretical point in that many movement activists see the public sphere as a good in itself that will lead to increased *autonomy* for individuals and a greater sense of community between participants. Autonomy and community are thus believed to be positive attributes for the extension of democratic procedures because they produce citizens who are more engaged with others in their communities. More problematically, though, this viewpoint reproduces a binary opposition whereby a fluid and open space occupied by resistance movements is seen as a good in itself because it gains some freedom from visible and hierarchically structured forms of global governance. Occupied social centres provide an empirical illustration of this dilemma. These are unused or condemned public buildings that are transformed by specific social movements into spaces for political and social activism. Such spaces build on and contribute towards daily, face-to-face campaigns, cultural pastimes and wider movement networks such as new media groups like Indymedia. While noting the benefits of occupied social centres, Hodkinson and Chatterton (2006) also demonstrate how these frequently become hubs for self-enclosed groups of activists. One knock-on effect is to assume that those who attend particular occupied social centres are attuned to the activism being undertaken within their walls. Subsequently, organisers within occupied social centres fail to project their aims and goals to wider, ordinary community forums in local areas, and this is especially the case in the language and ideas frequently used by activists (Hodkinson and Chatterton, 2006, p 312).

What has been stated so far is associated with one further point, which is that many who celebrate GSMs have a habit of reproducing another binary opposition between 'older' social movements that campaigned around nation-states and relied on media such as newspapers and 'newer' global political activists, who employ the likes of newspapers but also interactive social media products. Again, however, such dualisms frequently obstruct an exploration of more complex relationships between activism, dissent and media technology. Some evidence in fact suggests that political activists sometimes exploit Web 2.0 sites for purposes of *inactivity* that are similar in principle to older, Web 1.0 sites. In this respect activists will simply post information on a social media like Facebook without engaging in any other type of interactive activity, much like when activists would post information on e-mail lists in the 1990s. By engaging in this tactic, they develop new web practices that both deconstruct banal celebrations of 'new' technological developments and seek to move beyond ideological themes associated with business-led buzzwords like 'collaboration' (Barassi and Treré, 2012, pp 1280–1).

We know, moreover, that capitalism is dependent on the nation-state to support it in regulating events of struggle in civil society in order to govern the public sphere. This is especially the case in our current times, which have witnessed a *strengthening* of the state in civil society. This in turn affects the ability of social movements and other political activists to utilise the democratic potential of (new) media apparatuses for their various causes. We now explore this point in more depth.

The neoliberal state and global social movements

In order to underscore the point that the state has a prominent bearing on the actions of social movements, Sparks (2005) discusses the example of MED-TV, a Kurdish-language satellite TV channel broadcasting to Kurdish communities in the Middle East, with its headquarters based in London. Kurds have long struggled for recognition of their right to form an independent Kurdish state and MED-TV was associated with this struggle. A high percentage of the Kurdish population live in Turkey, and in the 1990s the Kurdistan Workers' Party (PKK) was at war with the Turkish state. The Turkish government complained to the Independent Television Commission (ITC), the British organisation responsible for granting broadcasting licences, that MED-TV supported the PKK against the Turkish state. One of the conditions the ITC placed on granting the licence to MED-TV was that the broadcaster would observe rules of impartiality. For this reason, ITC withdrew its licence for MED-TV. From this example Sparks observes that the 'fate of satellite broadcasters lies with governments as much as does that of terrestrial broadcasters' (Sparks, 2005, p 39). In other words, the idea that global communication produces in its wake a deterritorialisation of communication networks that empowers global civil society underplays the ability of states to govern those very same communication networks.

State and other governance mechanisms have acted as a conduit for constraining the activism of social movements through global institutions as well. One illustration can be noted in the shape of the UN-sponsored World Summit on the Information Society (WSIS), undertaken in two phases (Geneva, December 2003 and Tunis, November 2005), which sought to bring together various stakeholders to discuss how to combat the global digital divide. Four 'open and inclusive' meetings between the WSIS events facilitated by the Working Group on Internet Governance (WGIG) tried to gather information from civil society, governments and private organisations about 'the equitable distribution of resources, access for all, stable and secure functioning of the internet, and multilingualism and content' (McLaughlin and Pickard, 2005, p 360).

Yet, the global public spheres generated by both WSIS and WGIG were framed through a neoliberal agenda at the outset, suggesting as it did that the power of information technologies could be used for entrepreneurial activities in less developed countries and so result in positive outcomes for economic and social needs. A Civil Society Declaration in December 2003, issued by civil society organisations increasingly frustrated by this neoliberal agenda, appealed for a more social programme to stem the global digital divide. When it seemed that those heading the WSIS would effectively ignore the Declaration, some civil society groups decided to leave the deliberations, while others remained. McLaughlin and Pickard note that in many respects this outcome was inevitable. After all, the neoliberal agenda had been established from the outset of the deliberative proceedings, and the UN and corporatist business interests were both attuned to the need to appeal to selective social movement identities. Indeed, one would expect nothing less under a post-Washington consensus that claims to advocate a more 'humane' neoliberal free market agenda. Nevertheless, 'it became apparent early on that, in allegedly offering a venue in which all stakeholders were welcomed, the WSIS process would unfold in such a way that, with few exceptions, everyone would remain in their place' and neoliberal ideas would retain their predominance (McLaughlin and Pickard, 2005, p 367).

In many respects, both the local and global neoliberal governance of global social movements can also be found at work in the Arab Spring. In fact, even calling the Arab Spring a 'media event' is problematic to a certain degree, in so far that it encourages one to explore a real revolutionary situation in terms of the media rather than in terms of broader socioeconomic and political dynamics. While it is therefore true to say that the Arab Spring represented a moment when social media was used for the first time to help galvanise revolutionary activism against political regimes, it is equally important to note that corporate hegemony had been operating in the media infrastructure of many of these countries for a number of years prior to 2011. For example, Sakr (2002) notes that the first two private satellite companies created to serve the Arab world were the Middle East Broadcasting Centre (MBC) in 1991 and, in 1993, the Arab Radio and Television (ART). From the outset, however, both stations had close links with the Saudi ruling family. This meant that they both gained lucrative contracts not only in the Saudi Kingdom but from elites residing in other Arabic states too. These political and private intermeshed relationships are also tied into other business networks. ART is a member of Dallah Al-Baraka, a transnational organisation made up of a group of companies that has a stake in manufacturing, trade, shipping and tourism (Sakr, 2002). Satellite channels in the Arab world are thus, like their counterparts in the west, owned by the super-rich with support from political elites (Murphy, 2009, p 1148).

Corporate media companies are allowed to get away with these actions because a neoliberal environment had already been established some years previously by the state and global governance bodies.

During the 1980s many Arab states moved towards a neoliberal mode of governance. In return for loans made by them, International Monetary Fund and World Bank demanded that countries like Algeria, Egypt, Morocco and Tunisia should follow market-based policies. As a result, the public sector was severely scaled back, which in turn led to increasing inequalities among their populations. In addition, states no longer sought to make large-scale investments in the public provision of education and health, which served only to exacerbate the problems being faced by families already affected by the imposition of neoliberalism. Lower wages, higher unemployment among the youth and marked increasing social divisions became the norm. By 2009, youth unemployment stood at 30% in Tunisia, 25% in Egypt, 35% in Yemen, 20% in Bahrain, and 77% in Syria (Hatem, 2012, p 406).

These are important points because they offer a balance to those perspectives that overly celebrate the use of social media in providing an important trigger to the Arab Spring. Extensive media use employed by activists to publicise political and social dissent in fact often *follows* from the painstaking work over many months and years of building and channelling the discontent of numerous groups against their governments into motivated groups willing to take to the streets to voice their complaints over their material conditions. One study 'showed a rapid growth in the number of users and uses of Facebook and Twitter during the first four months of 2011 – *after* the onset of the Arab Spring. In many of the countries that experienced uprisings, such as Tunisia, Egypt, Yemen, and Bahrain, the growth rate of Facebook users was *twice as high* as the growth rate a year earlier' (Wolfsfeld et al 2013, pp 128–9; original emphasis). In other words, the material conditions were already in place for the uptake of social media by copious numbers in the Middle East to voice their disquiet against their respective governments.

Conclusion

Many social and political theorists welcome the formation of global civil society as an international space for emancipation and empowerment of the multitude (see Hardt and Negri 2000, 2004; Goodhart, 2005). Moreover, they argue that the remedy for current ills in global democratic participation lies, at least partially, in creating new global political mechanisms because the effectiveness of the nation-state to implement democratic capabilities is dying out in the global world. Castells (2012, p 8) similarly notes that while it is wrong to ignore the centralised power of the nation-state, it is equally if not more important to underline the need for GSMs to mobilise the resources of the network society in order to create autonomous spaces at some remove from the nation-state (Castells, 2012, pp 11–15). Therefore, Castells believes that GSMs are at their most commanding when they occupy these autonomous spaces of deliberation at some distance from the state. This further implies that GSMs are not constituted through formal leadership structures with formal political agendas and programmes, but instead foster networks of cooperation, solidarity and multiple demands through networks that aim to change the values of society (Castells, 2012, pp 224–6).

While these aims of GSMs are laudable, they also demonstrate some fundamental weaknesses at the heart of many of their actions. For it is still the case that these demands need to be channelled into a *political programme* that challenges the *capitalist* basis of both state and economic power. In spite of everything, capitalism is not primarily defined in relation to the extension of liberal rights such as the freedom of expression. Capitalism is a system that seeks to expand and deepen the exploitation of life into the whole of society. Self-expanding value in the form of M (money)–C (commodities)–M1 (an increase in money) is the mainstay of capitalist accumulation. Price signals, not social goods like equality or fairness, activate capital's quest to innovate and transform production. The objective pressure to accumulate profit will therefore always take priority over social justice (Albritton, 2010). State power underpins this structural imperative by its very form, which rests on its separation from civil society and its monopoly of force to regulate both law and money in civil society (Clarke, 1988). What all of this further suggests is that a critical analysis of how to extend the democratic potential of the public sphere must be integrally related to the realities of how capitalism operates.

The next and concluding chapter starts to outline an alternative approach to activism and dissent in new media public spheres. This is achieved by exploring the Occupy Movement, people's forums and trade unions. By looking at these examples it will be argued that to be fully effective social movements need to articulate a socialist political programme among civil society. Only a socialist political programme is capable to providing a realistic challenge to the power of capital and its relationship to the state. While Castells, Hardt and Negri, and other contemporary social theorists of a similar persuasion provide some astute insights on this matter, they frequently do so by abstracting away from some of the determining characteristics of contemporary global social relations. To put the same point differently, what their respective analyses lack is a value-theoretic approach to new media activism. The chapter therefore argues that we need to move beyond a network approach in order to take seriously structures of domination in the competent capitalist world. We need to build socialist public spheres in civil society.

NINE

Conclusion: the Occupy movement, community activism and 'incompetent' public spheres

Introduction

The previous chapter identified a number of shortcomings to GSMs. What it did not do, however, was take note of new protest alliances that have emerged in recent years between global social movements, community groups and other progressive organisations like trade unions. The most notable of these alliances has of course been the Occupy movement. It sprang into life on 17 September 2011 in New York City, when campaigners and protestors buoyed by the Arab Spring and the campout movements in Spain, and swept along by anger at the 2008 financial crisis, responded to calls to occupy Wall Street by the online radical journal Adbusters. The initial rally in September attracted 2,000 people, and following this nearly 200 people set up camp in Zuccotti Park near Wall Street. Hacktivist collective Anonymous distributed information about the movement through the hashtag #Occupy Wall Street (Juris, 2012, p 261). Soon other Occupy groups were set up across the US and throughout the world in places as far apart as Armenia, Belgium, Brazil, Hong Kong, Malaysia, France and the UK. It seemed that within a relatively short period in time Occupy had been transformed into a global movement that attracted people who would not normally consider themselves as 'political' activists. While the majority of Occupy campsites were evicted by January 2012, many saw Occupy as a success. As Bessant observes:

> The movement was inclusive, relatively broad and successfully managed to engage in 'will formation' and to inform public opinion in ways that shaped policy agendas, discourses, government policy and law. In the US, for example, New York Governor Cuomo reconsidered his opposition to extending the millionaire's tax, which saw the implementation of legislation for a higher tax for the wealthy. (Bessant, 2014, p 38)

What is interesting about the Occupy movement is that it combined elements from both GSMs and conventional social and political organisations in local communities. Like GSMs, the Occupy movement was organised around horizontal networks, it arranged its campaigns through a variety of social and political issues with no domineering political perspective and it employed new media to create image events and to publicise activism at both local and global levels. At the same time, the Occupy movement was aware of the need to galvanise support from local residents and from existing and on-going campaign groups in local communities. Like other GSMs, however, Occupy has been criticised for its lack of a leadership structure and clear political goals. These are thought to have hampered its continuing progress in building a cohesive opposition and alternative public sphere to that of neoliberalism and the competent workfare public sphere.

This final chapter takes stock of the Occupy movement by exploring its successes and failures in order to understand the extent to which its ideals and principles offer a genuine and realistic alternative to neoliberal politics. In the next section some of the key characteristics of the movement are sketched out in a little more depth. We will see that while Occupy was largely successful in expressing a new mode of opposition to financial neoliberalism it also demonstrated major drawbacks and limitations in this task. In particular, its ultimate failure to build a coherent political project meant that it was dogged by disagreements about how to proceed politically and what alliances it should form with other social and political groups. Following this, the chapter then considers whether community activism based in neighbourhoods and ordinary civic public spheres represents a better way forward for organised opposition to the neoliberal imperative. Without doubt, community activism has great merits and in many respects holds many advantages over a social movement like Occupy. By themselves, however, it is doubtful that community groups will present a clear and coherent national opposition to neoliberalism, especially since they are rooted in the diverse everyday experiences of residents and cultural specificities of localities.

What both Occupy and community public spheres require, therefore, is a force that will unite these diverse strands into a united political and economic hegemonic project against neoliberal capitalism. One such a force, it will be argued, can be found in trade union public spheres. The reason for saying so is that trade unions have the potential to act as the collective interests and bargaining power of labour in their struggle against capital to own and control the surplus created by workers (Hyman, 2001, pp 3–4). Consequently, trade unions possess the capacity to unite both economic and political forms of democracy. By campaigning on better wages and better representation in the workplace, trade unions stress that real democratic progress encompasses the expansion of economic and political rights of workers. Unions thereby underline the need to overcome the capitalist wage relation in favour of developing enterprises where people work together as fellow socioeconomic citizens with full democratic rights (Smith, 2006, p 303). To be effective, this socialist political project must be extended to communities in order to provide a real challenge to neoliberal workfarism. We begin the discussion with the Occupy movement.

The Occupy movement and its limits

From the outset, digital and social media were at the forefront of the Occupy campaign. In its 2012 survey of 500 Occupy US activists, the Occupy Research and Data Centre discovered that a majority of respondents (64%) said that they had used Facebook for Occupy-related activity within 24 hours of taking part in the survey. However, just as important for these respondents was the need for face-to-face communication with fellow activists, with almost half of the respondents (43%) stating that they had been discussing Occupy with another person physically present with them within 24 of taking part in the survey (Costanza-Chock, 2012, p 379).

As noted, Facebook was a particularly useful digital medium for Occupy campaigners. It enabled activists to post personal narratives of their experiences about local events and to make connections with Occupy members in other localities and countries. The phrase 'I am the 99%' was often employed by them to signify their emotional attachment to what they saw as both a local and a global movement (Gaby and Caren, 2012, p 371). Twitter too inhabited an important space in the Occupy movement. Videos of different types of activism were tweeted with relative ease, which meant that Occupy publics had another network that connected them together. Still, one study found that not all Occupy videos uploaded onto YouTube were tweeted. In the main, though, the study suggests that tweeted videos tended to be more professionally edited than those non-tweeted videos, the latter of which contained raw uncut footage of Occupy events. In general, Occupy hashtags brought different videos together and that then went on to create their own narrative about the protests (Thorson et al, 2013, pp 434–41).

Another important characteristic of Twitter is that it circulates information, images, texts and videos in a way that 'allows protestors to very quickly build a geographically dispersed, networked counterpublic that can articulate a critique of power outside of the parameters of mainstream power' (Penney and Dadas, 2013, p 88). This is combined with Twitter's special feature of allowing individuals to use only 140 characters per tweet. As a result, people are motivated to condense what they say into eye-catching rhetorical flourishes. For many of those involved in Occupy this meant posting information on Twitter that was succinct, straight to the point and catchy (Penney and Dadas, 2013, p 88). Tweets regularly served to strengthen network ties and in general provided an important source of up-to-date information for activists as well as facilitating face-to-face meetings.

For DeLuca et al (2012) the Occupy movement represents a moment of 'panmediation'. Smart technology allows people to 'live in and access mobile spaces of multiple media immersed in the wi-fi cloud' (DeLuca et al, 2012, p 487). This radicalises DeLuca's original ideas about public screens discussed in the previous chapter. Nowadays, observe DeLuca et al, public screens are with us all the time. We no longer have to travel to them because, through gadgets like smartphones, we can instead simply keep them in our bags or in our pockets. Occupy activists thus employed social media to disseminate their own image events and watch other image events online. Social media empowered protestors and supporters to legitimise their grievances and overcome the framing of their events by right-wing bloggers and writers. As a result, argue DeLuca et al, Occupy simultaneously challenged the monopoly over images by corporate media power in so far that the use of social media by activists showed the world that it is possible to create alternative public screens of possible worlds (DeLuca et al, 2012, pp 500–1). For example, those at Occupy Wall Street were conscious of creating and then disseminating performative spectacles across various media. The 'people's mic' was one of the most noticeable tactics used in this respect. In order to transgress New York's restrictions on the use of megaphones an Occupy speaker would make a speech, pausing after every few sentences. This then permitted those listening close by to repeat the sentences in unison to the rest of the crowd. Not only did this strategy overcome local laws about the use of megaphones, but it also 'provided an opportunity for spectacle' across the world (Hambrick, 2012, p 9).

For some, Occupy subsequently represents both a continuation and a departure from previous GSM activism. It represents a continuation to the extent that Occupy operated through decentralised networks, or 'horizontalism'. Becoming more prevalent in social movement activism since 2001, horizontalism is a term used to capture more participatory ways of representation. Rejecting hierarchical modes of democratic participation predicated on formal political apparatuses, horizontalism builds people's assemblies that actually empower members and not leaders. As such, the voices of all those involved, and not just those belonging to single political parties with fixed political programmes, are given an opportunity to be heard. Horizontalist movements thus have multiple goals because these will encompass multiple groups and multiple voices (Maeckelbergh, 2012; Sitrin, 2012). At Occupy Wall Street activists set up a General Assembly based on horizontalist principles. In practice, this meant that during each evening Occupy members gathered to discuss issues and reach solutions without voting but through consensus. Agreement among the Occupy community was thereby founded through collaboration. The boundaries of what constituted Occupy Wall Street were therefore constantly being renegotiated. Rules, regulations and limits internal to the movement thereby changed and shifted so that how the Occupy community of activists was constituted remained in a continual process of becoming (Mulqueen and Tataryn, 2012). Social media alongside other digital technologies as well as old media were also put to use by Occupy members to publicise issues, galvanise support and contribute towards a horizontalist identity. At the same time, these resources helped activists to establish a shared community of becoming among those involved, based on narratives, personal experiences and common values. Correspondingly, an online presence provided familiar spaces for activists to gain access to resources of protest. Howtooccupy.org is one illustration of an online site that became a movement plateau for campaigners to exchange stories of activism with one another, obtain tactical information about legal rights, engage in online discussions and submit reports about on-going Occupy activity in a particular locality (Tewksbury, 2013, p 17).

Occupy was therefore noticeably different from other, earlier GSMs. Juris, for example, notes that previous social movements have been established through a logic of networking in which pre-constituted campaign groups connect with one another through decentralised, horizontal and open networks of communication and coordination. Occupy, however, represents not so much a logic of networking as it does a logic of aggregation built on people gaining their sense of identity in part through social media, then coming together as *individuals* in public space. Yet, as a group of individuals, their collective identity is always in danger of breaking apart. '[H]ence, the importance of interaction and community building within physical spaces' (Juris, 2012, p 266). Social media is especially well placed to build these campaign ties. After all, social media enables individuals to post quick bursts of information while simultaneously engaged in public spaces of dissent.

Certainly, some of these characteristics helped the Occupy movement to have successes. Occupy activists at Wall Street built alliances with other community groups, including trade unions, churches and anti-poverty groups. As Rehmann (2013, p 6) notes, this quality of the original Occupy space meant that the activists made meaningful connections with broader social initiatives, thus ensuring that Occupy was both a political and a social movement. In other words, it recognised the crucial point that any meaningful leftist movement must see activism as a way to connect politics with economics. Moreover, by forging links with other community-based movements, Occupy activists sought to include 'ordinary' people in their programme of action. An attempt was thus made to surmount a criticism made of GSMs in the past, which is that they have tended to ignore ordinary people in their communities, preferring instead to focus on global causes rather than community-led issues. Rehmann (2013, p 9) usefully notes that Occupy managed to tap into some people's common-sense beliefs that increased socioeconomic inequalities in America meant that something had gone drastically wrong, along with a discontent with government bailouts of failed financial speculation by major banks since the 2008 economic crisis.

Rehmann (2013) further observes that the Occupy slogan, 'we are the 99%', drew on this dissatisfaction among some groups and managed to create a unifying and collective symbol to draw people together from different social backgrounds. 'We are the 99%' signified the majority of the population whose very sense of being had been thrown into doubt through the rash, stupid and undemocratic socioeconomic actions of the richest in America. Dube and Kaplan (2012, pp 2–3) claim this slogan was therefore a powerful reminder of the excessive wealth accumulated by 1% of the US population. They note that in 1970 the top 1% of the population in the US made less than 10% of total pre-tax income. By 2007 this had increased to 23.5% and much of this increase has come from financial means and mechanisms. Meanwhile, from 1970 to 2007 the top marginal tax rate for this 1% group fell from 60% to 35%. Such figures lead Dube and Kaplan to observe: 'Overall, a focus on the 1 percent concentrates attention on the aspect of inequality most clearly tied to the distribution of income between labour and capital. This type of inequality is seen as being the least fair, as economic rents and returns to wealth are often seen as unearned income' (Dube and Kaplan, 2012, p 4).

At the same time, the Occupy movement has many notable problems that demonstrate some fundamental weakness in challenging capitalist power. The first point to make in this respect is that the Occupy movement exhibited what Campbell (2011, p 44) notes is a 'togetherness' but not necessarily 'solidarity'. 'Togetherness' signals an emotional and physical connection among members, whereas solidarity signals unity structured around a political programme. Occupy members themselves recognised this drawback. Some activists in Los Angeles said in October 2011 that lack of consensus around strategies and tactics was one reason why divisions eventually opened up among activists. Indeed, 'the unclear goals and strategy of the Occupation' meant that some protestors split off from the Los Angeles Occupy movement to create new alternative spaces across the city (cited in Lang and Lang/ Levitsky, 2012, pp 104–7).

But this was one illustration of a wider problem. Without a coherent political programme it proved difficult to reach agreement among Occupy members as to what demands it should push forward. And without a clear set of demands it was difficult to be equally clear about which existing political mechanisms Occupy activists should engage with and which political alliances should be built. Indecision about whether or not Occupy activists should engage with existing political mechanisms meant that many of the demands that eventually were made seemed more like eye-catching slogans rather than clear, concise and concrete requests (Roberts, 2012, p 758).

Many Occupy members were also suspicious of becoming closely associated with existing and formal political and economic groups such as trade unions. Certainly, as already noted, members did forge some alliances with already established community groups. Some trade unions likewise forged links with occupied spaces. For example, the Professional Staff Congress (PSC) in New York joined Occupy Wall Street and helped to organise a rally and labour march in October 2011 that included other unions, community groups and Occupy activists (Shepard, 2012, p 124). Yet, it is also true to say some members of different Occupy spaces wanted minimal contact with unions. In the US some activists at a few Occupy camps. were not strong advocates for pro-union policies. For instance, 'Occupy Oakland organized a shutdown of the city's port in December 2012 despite the active opposition of the major unions' (Roberts, 2012, p 759). A few Occupy groups declared that formal political organisations like unions were mere lobbying bodies that had no role in the movement.

Moreover, lack of solidarity towards a unified political programme and political demands among Occupy members led to some disastrous results. Protestors at Occupy Oakland, for instance, had refused to engage with the local police on the need to apply for permits for their activism and to set the terms for the negotiated management of their protests with the authorities (see Chapter Six on negotiated management). The police, though, could not act against them because most of Occupy Oakland's activity did not contravene the law. Unbeknown to many of the activists, however, a small group of protestors had incorrectly applied for a permit to erect a tepee in Oscar Grant Plaza. Once this had occurred, the police now had a reason in place to criminalise other Occupy Oakland activities on the pretext that they were outside of the legally sanctioned permit (King, 2013). As we see, then, the police could move to criminalise these protestors because lines of communication did not flow in a coherent and uniform manner among the Occupy group as a whole.

If it is indeed the case that notable problems were evident in the Occupy movement, maybe it is advisable to look to other local grassroots social movements to see if they represent challenges to neoliberal capitalism. This is particularly important because a number of people argue that new opportunities have opened up for local grassroots movements in cities to push forward their respective demands and programmes for change. Pearce (2013), for example, suggests that novel spaces have appeared in urban centres in which ordinary people are able to forge new cooperative associations and subjective identities that forego dominating relationships of power. In her studies of different community and voluntary groups in the north of England, Pearce discovered that many members of these groups were aware of dominating power associated with the likes of formal political structure, while also being aware of the power gained by working in cooperative relationships with other local residents to bring about positive changes in their communities. Their aim is to transform local social relations through decentralised, diffuse and horizontal engagement. Accumulation of power is not the prime motivation for these individuals. The goal is, rather, to make small changes and build cooperative networks of trust among people 'through which diversity can live and breathe' (Pearce, 2013, p 660). We now look to see if this represents a more preferable type of activism.

Community activism, trade unions and being incompetent

Community programmes formed under the auspices of neoliberalism are of course especially vulnerable if socioeconomic crises occur. In the UK, the Coalition government used the 2008 financial crisis as a reason to restructure the voluntary sector in an even more draconian neoliberal direction. This much was obvious from a consultation paper – 'Supporting a Stronger Civil Society' – issued by the Office for Civil Society in 2010 (cited in Macmillan, 2011). The paper made clear where the Coalition government's priorities lay with respect to voluntary organisations. Underlining the need for the voluntary sector to 'improve their business skills' and become 'more entrepreneurial', the paper noted that 'civil society organisations (charities, social enterprises and voluntary groups) must embrace new skills, partnerships and organisational models if they were to seize the opportunities that lie ahead' (cited in Macmillan, 2011, p 119). For Macmillan, the consultation paper signalled the forging of a new government agenda based on a business-led approach to the voluntary sector that encouraged low-cost capacity-supporting procedures through bursaries and horizontal partnership networks (Macmillan, 2011). This agenda was also noticeable in relation to philanthropy. The Coalition government clearly wanted to promote a greater role for major donors and corporate organisations in giving their time and money to charitable and voluntary causes. Yet the government expressed these policies in part through the language of 'philanthrocapitalism', in which charitable giving is associated with a '"strategic", "market conscious", "impact-oriented", "knowledge-based"' discourse that yields returns to the donor (Daly, 2011, p 1086).

Still, for all of his talk about the Big Society, David Cameron cut even further into the social fabric of voluntarism. While the Coalition government released several further papers and reports signalling its commitment to the third sector – for example, its 'Unshackling Good Neighbours' report of 2011 (cited in Alcock, 2012), which emphasised the need to establish employee-owned cooperatives to deliver some public services – this was in parallel with drastic government cuts to public services. As Alcock observes, the Office for Civil Society and the Cabinet Office had to endure nearly 60% in cuts in the first two years of the Coalition government's stay in power. As a result, many infrastructure third sector schemes under Strategic Partnership plans were reduced or simply stopped. Local authorities also saw their budgets cut, which again had a negative impact on third sector funding (Alcock, 2012, pp 6–8). But if there are on-going problems in forms of community activism, then how might we proceed in trying to transgress the social constraints imposed by the neoliberal competent public sphere on society?

Silver et al (2010) note that debates on participatory and deliberative democracy in cities are often premised on a simplistic binary opposition between establishing a consensus among community actors from different sectors versus the conflict that arises between them due to their diverse interests. This is related to another binary opposition between respecting established procedures of deliberation and participation versus underlining the need to continually challenge democratic procedures. Silver et al argue that the boundaries between these two oppositions are in fact more blurred than antagonists in each camp suggest. Consultative forums in communities can, for example, open up real opportunities for ordinary people to have their voices heard. Participative governance should not therefore be seen merely as a tool of neoliberal governance. As they say: 'The common tendency to argue that participation is either neoliberal governance or an empowering, inclusionary, progressive implement can and should be confronted with a battery of questions: Where? When? By whom? For what purposes? To what effect?' (Silver et al, 2010, p 472).

A similar argument has been put forward throughout this book. It has contended that the contradictory nature of neoliberalism implies that gaps open up for some groups to put forward alternatives to neoliberal governance. At the same time, it is the very nature of capitalism as a system based on necessary relations of exploitation and, by default, a number of necessary contradictions, that ensures that those who advocate deliberative democracy will never succeed in fully implementing the deliberative ideal. On a more optimistic note, however, we have seen that some movement activists in the guise of Occupy do make genuine attempts to reach out to already existing community groups and vice versa. Indeed, such was the learning experience between the two that Occupy continues to exist in other community-based forms. Occupy Our Homes in the US, for instance, grew out of the original Occupy groups and seeks to campaign for and defend those facing eviction from their homes if they default on mortgage repayments (Manilov, 2013, p 208).

Why is it important to breach divides between social movements of the type involved in Occupy and already existing community-based movements? Mayer (2013) is correct to observe that alliances between the two lend visibility to each other's struggles. Occupy's progress on housing issues brings some added publicity to those being evicted from their homes. In addition, it leads to greater unity in campaigns around the deepening inequalities in housing brought about by the financial crash and the irrationalities of neoliberalism. Community-based groups and Occupy activists harmonise their campaigns and efforts in order to build relationships of solidarity with one another against the damage wrought by financial neoliberalism.

As these campaigns have been getting more coordinated, they scale up local struggles, turning them into regional movements that occasionally protest the same banks at the same time and often attend each other's rallies; participants increasingly see themselves as part of national and international movements (Mayer, 2013, p 15).

Nevertheless, what we have also seen in earlier chapters is that capitalism operates through a specific set of historical processes and logics. This is related to the historical and social form that labour assumes. Under capitalism, labour is not merely an additional factor of production but is instead socially constituted by contradictory and objectified social relations whose abstract alienated form is reproduced in the concrete substance of class struggles (Bonefeld, 1993, pp 24–5). These processes develop through to advanced capitalism where labour reproduces itself through labour power and the acquisition of surplus value by capital (see Chapter Two). Historically, therefore, the peculiarity of labour in capitalism is that it both objectifies itself in everyday commodities and reproduces objectified and alienated social relations (Postone, 1996).

However, why is it important to highlight these points? One reason concerns those solutions advanced to solve some of the social ills associated with information technology. In May 1997, for example, the United Nations Commission on Science and Technology for Development (UNCSTD) adopted a resolution that, among other things, called for national governments and other stakeholders to ensure that 'ICTs are used to satisfy the basic needs of all the population and that their production and use contributes to economic and social objectives' (UNCSTD, 1997). To achieve this and other similar goals, UNCSTD also recommended that governments and relevant stakeholders should implement concrete policies to achieve greater socioeconomic integration among ICT programmes between the developed and the developing world. Introducing new education curricula, training programmes and learning skills suitable for the production and use of ICTs in supporting development within distinct regions in specific countries, along with measures to encourage and facilitate research and development networks and collaboration among science and technology research groups, were just a few such proposals put forward.

Without doubt, these are all laudable propositions, which, if successfully implemented, have the capacity to improve the lives of people in developing countries. At the same time, there are noticeable problems with some of them. For example, UNCSTD implied that a number of contingent factors create social inequalities that can be tackled on an empirical level. As we have seen throughout the book, however, capitalism is not simply founded on a relationship of empirical inequality derived from the exclusion of some social groups and countries from certain resources. Capitalism is instead driven in the first instance by the voracious appetite to accumulate money and profits for the sake of accumulation, irrespective of the social consequences in doing so. Thus, social life is first mediated through contradictory, alienated and irrational social forms that shape individuals and their lives from the moment they enter the topsy-turvy world of capitalism. Any concrete policies designed to alleviate social inequalities brought about by these abstract processes must acknowledge this basic fact if they are to enjoy a degree of success. In our present times, this of course means confronting the irrationalities of neoliberal financialisation.

Three further critical points are worth making at this point. First, if it is indeed the case that capitalism is constituted as a contradictory and exploitative system, then any emancipatory project must seek to rid society of what it is that causes capitalism to assume this identity. From the perspective adopted throughout the book, this means trying to rid society of the dominance of abstract labour and its substance in the form of socially necessary labour time. An irrational way to structure society, socially necessary labour time rewards atomistic behaviour in markets rather than truly planned public markets for the benefit of everyone. This latter precondition can be achieved only through democratic ownership and control of the means of production (Levine, 1988; McNally, 1993). To even think about mounting a serious challenge to the abstract dominance of capital we therefore need to recognise, as indeed many in the Occupy movement did, the necessity to build a politics based on collective interests. Unlike the Occupy movement, however, this collective politics must pose a fundamental challenge to the class basis of capitalism, because only then will we really be able to address its exploitative dynamics. After all, capitalism gains its identity and its energy not by exploiting some workers at the expense of other workers but by exploiting the labour of everyone (Gough et al, 2006, p 226).

Second, and following on from this point, if it is the case that labour constitutes and establishes the capitalist world, a world that then turns around and imprisons labour in relations of ceaseless exploitation, it makes no sense to construct boundaries between the communicative potential of people in civil society and that of labour in the economy. Labour is not merely an instrumental activity bent on creating objects to satisfy needs, while meaningful, free and creative communication resides elsewhere outside of the grim world of work. Prevalent in much public sphere literature, this perspective essentially separates the relationship between civil society, politics and the economy, and fails to note that capitalist societies are not fragmented but are essentially a contradictory whole. In reality, labour represents the most important communicative sphere in capitalist society, even if the collective class interests of this communicative potential to confront capital are constrained and stifled. Even at an abstract level, a workplace is mediated by distinctive relationships of communication that include cooperative relationships and technical expertise among and between workers, management and owners. At the same time, workers must follow rules laid down by management and owners about how the workplace in question is organised and governed, which is itself underpinned by questions over allocation and distribution of the surplus created in the workplace. Conflict and inequality therefore invariably appear as each group struggles over access to the social product created, labour conditions and relationships of exploitation and power (Gough, 2003, p 33). If labour does act in an 'instrumental' manner it is because it has become alienated from its communicative and collective nature by the abstract dominance of capitalist social relations (Clarke, 1991).

Third, what the preceding points suggest is the need to embed struggles against neoliberalism with struggles to establish and extend democratic rights in the workplace. One of the most potentially effective movements to achieve democratic rights in the workplace is trade unions. Why is this so? As has already been noted, labour is the point at which capital obtains surplus value. Labour thus represents the social constitution of capitalist society. It is therefore at least conceivable that trade unions have the potential to represent the collective interests of groups of workers in and against the interests of capital. Naturally, some trade unions are often bureaucratic, lack democratic participation by members and work in unison with management. In other instances the reverse is the case. Nevertheless, the causal power of trade unions partly rests on their ability and capacity to disrupt the core exploitative practices of capital. Unlike other social movements, trade unions thus signify one of the most potent forces with which to confront the irrational tendencies of capital.

None of this is to deny the importance of so-called social movement or community unionism, which is premised on unions and community groups working together on campaigns to protect one another's interests. For example, some women's groups, gay rights organisations, human rights groups and so on have started campaigns to protect different workers' rights, while some trade unions actively seek out community organisations in order to forge activist links with them and carve out new campaigns (see Wills and Simms, 2003; Fine, 2005). Nevertheless, it must also be borne in mind that social movement unionism is often defined in relation to a host of diverse community interests and social identities that lack some exactness as to their meaning and goals. This is related to the point that some campaigns that help to spark these community union initiatives can soon wither away once certain activist demands are seen to have been met by the authorities (Stewart et al, 2009, p 12). Moreover, social movement unionism frequently classifies itself against 'old' industrial labour movements and in the process shows support for new, post-industrial informational movements that move beyond social class. Despite changes to socioeconomic relations over the last three decades or so, we know, however, that class politics remain an integral feature of contemporary societies (Upchurch and Mathers, 2011, p 266). In fact, under the guise of neoliberalism class politics has arguably become more important. Ultimately, trade unions are inherently better at engaging in *collective bargaining* with employers. Trade unions thus have the capacity to connect different workers located in various places across a range of industries, while social movement unionism tends to be good at representing the interests and social identities of a particular locality of workers (Givan, 2007; Taylor and Mathers, 2008).

It is taken as a given, of course, that the exploitative class dynamics at work in capitalist relations of production are refracted through a number of social identities at play at different levels and in different workplaces. Class relations will always be expressed through a variety of social identities – age, disability, race and ethnicity, gender, sexuality and so forth – and this implies that class relations encompass a set of complex dynamics in actual contexts (Moore, 2011, chapter 1). This point can be stated slightly differently by noting that contemporary capitalism is still reliant on the *collective* worker, that is to say, on the necessity for labour to valorise capital through the procurement of surplus value and surplus labour. Capitalists are thus keen to regulate the *collective* identity of the workforce within a particular labour process even when management regulates the *individual* nature of each worker's contribution to workplace relations (Lucio and Stewart, 1997). This is also true in the competent public sphere. For example, the increasing privatisation of the public sector implies that struggles in and around public–private partnerships become battlegrounds over collective and individual strategies by management and unions to control and govern the workplace. Management will attempt to govern the collective behaviour of workers through the likes of hired consultants who construct 'performance targets' for workers. Management will similarly endeavour to govern the individual behaviour of workers through the likes of personalised performance indicators. Unions will attempt to reveal the damaging effects of these management strategies both on the collective workforce and on certain individual workers. For instance, unions continue to campaign against the low wages that result from the privatisation of the public sector and the intensification of working conditions that this brings for individual employees (Smith, 2012).

To be truly 'incompetent' in the public sphere is therefore to be active in the collective power of labour struggling in and against how neoliberal 'competence' fragments and individualises labour. To be effective, this struggle needs to be widened to the rest of society. For localities, this implies using community forums to not only campaign for wider rights in particular localities but also reject the very basis of consensus politics upon which competent workfarism rests. PPPs are a case in point. PPPs often try to build a 'consensus' in communities among different 'partners' about the necessity to engage in productive dialogue about restructuring and regenerating a community. However, they tend to leave unequal power relations outside the sphere of dialogue when 'partners' come together to discuss their different needs and requirements around regeneration. As Purcell (2009, p 157) rightly observes, such consensus-building, across community divides and networks, between public bodies, private business and local residents can and does often legitimise neoliberal capacity building in localities and regions. Incompetent dialogue should therefore criticise this false consensus and demonstrate where possible that it leads to fragmentation and new divisions in communities due to uneven development and increasing inequalities wrought by neoliberalism and workfare policies.

Incompetent debate should also link these issues to the wider issue of democratic rights in society and in the workplace. What we need more than ever in our bizarre, financialised world is a planned economy that overcomes the contradictions of capital. We require, for example, proper tax policies to ensure that we restore major industries and utilities as common property. Taxing the capital assets of such industries and utilities will start to address this issue because the money accumulated can then be restored to the economy through public and community investment banks (Schweickart, 2002, p 47). An elected government could set the rate of this tax and then determine the amount of funds that would be distributed for local public investments (Smith, 2006, p 304).

An incompetent public sphere would further stress the need to overcome the division between workers and managers by allowing workers to democratically control some of the major enterprises and industries in society. This would be a society in which wage labourers would no longer be employed by capital but would instead enjoy citizenship rights at their place of work. Management would be democratically accountable to its own workforce. Of course, this seems highly incompetent to capital because it rejects the idea the wage labour is a commodity like any other commodity. Yet a decent and humane society insists that 'labour is the residual claimant' (Schweickart, 2002, p 49), to the extent that labour receives the profits once other factors like an asset tax have been paid.

Being incompetent is thus to declare that planning and design in communities must be to the overall benefit of labour. Demanding an integrated approach that brings together physical, economic and social planning, the incompetent public sphere, or what I have called elsewhere a proletarian public sphere (Roberts, 2009), would try to convince people that an improved society that benefits all is one in which industrial capacity is not destroyed by private finance; that public investment in public services is a good in itself; that private businesses should be able to utilise the resources of a reinvigorated public sector; that new training opportunities emerge through increased profitability; that democracy is extended to the workplace; that communities have a genuine greater say in local redevelopments; that public housing is increased; that national health services receive better funding; that business interests and private property are properly taxed; and that inequalities are tackled (Eisenschitz, 2008, pp 143–7). If such a politics can also connect with GSMs and new media, then this would be a politics proper in so far that it brings into being a wide-ranging, class-based socialist public sphere capable of providing a true challenge to the collective financial, neoliberal power of capital. To become incompetent in the public sphere is therefore to speak about the necessity of socialist answers to the ills of neoliberal workfarism. New media has a role to play in helping to stimulate and build this public sphere in order to contribute towards developing a contemporary socialist hegemonic project.

References

Abe, K. (2009) 'The myth of media interactivity: technology, communications and surveillance in Japan', *Theory, Culture and Society*, vol 26, nos 2–3, pp73–88.

Ackerly, B.A. (2006) 'Deliberative democratic theory for building global civil society: designing a virtual community of activists', *Contemporary Political Theory*, vol 5, no 2, pp 113–41.

ACLU (American Civil Liberties Union) (2003) *Freedom under fire: Dissent in post-9/11 America*. Available at: www.aclu.org/FilesPDFs/dissent_report.pdf (accessed 25 October 2007).

Akkar, M. (2005) 'The changing publicness of contemporary public spaces: a case study of the Grey's Monument Area, Newcastle upon Tyne', *Urban Design International*, vol 10, no 2, pp 95–113.

Albo, G., Gindin, S. and Panitch, L. (2010) *In and out of crisis*, Oakland, CA: PM Press.

Albrecht, S. (2006) 'Whose voice is heard in online deliberation? A study of participation and representation in political debates on the internet', *Information, Communication and Society*, vol 9, no 1, pp 62–82.

Albritton, R. (2010) 'Eating the future: capitalism out of joint', in R. Albritton, B. Jessop and R. Westra (eds) *Political economy and global capitalism*, London: Anthem Press, pp 43–66.

Alcock, P. (2012) 'The Big Society: a new policy environment for the third sector?' Third Sector Research Centre, Working Paper no 82, pp 1–13.

Alcock, P. and Kendall, J. (2011) 'Constituting the third sector: processes of decontestation and contention under the UK Labour governments in England', *Voluntas: International Journal of Voluntary and Nonprofit Organizations*, vol 22, no 3, pp 450–69.

Allen, M. (2013) 'What was Web 2.0? Versions as the dominant mode of internet history', *New Media and Society*, vol 15, no 2, pp 260–75.

Alvesson, M. (2004) *Knowledge work and knowledge-intensive firms*, Oxford: Oxford University Press.

Amin, A. and Graham, S. (1997) 'The ordinary city', *Transactions of the Institute of British Geographers*, vol 22, no 4, pp 411–29.

Amin, A. with Thrift, N. (2007) 'Cultural-economy and cities', *Progress in Human Geography*, vol 31, no 2, pp 143–61.

Amoore, L. (2006) 'Biometric borders: governing mobilities in the war on terror', *Political Geography*, vol 25, no 3, pp 336–51.

Amoore, L. and Langley, P. (2004) 'Ambiguities of global civil society', *Review of International Studies*, vol 30, no 1, pp 89–110.

Anderson, A. (2003) 'Risk, terrorism and the internet', *Knowledge, Technology and Policy*, vol 16, no 2, pp 24–33.

Anderson, K.M., Henriksen, H.Z., Medaglia, R., Danziger, J.N., Sannarnes, M.K. and Enemaerke, M. (2010) 'Fads and facts of e-government: a review of impacts of e-government (2003–2009)', *International Journal of Public Administration*, vol 33, no 11, pp 564–79.

Andrejevic, M. (2002) 'The world of being watched: interactive media and the exploitation of self-disclosure', *Critical Studies in Media Communication*, vol 19, no 2, pp 230–48.

Andrejevic, M. (2009a) 'Critical media studies 2.0: an interactive upgrade', *Interactions: Studies in Communication and Culture*, vol 1, no 1, pp 35–50.

Andrejevic, M. (2009b) 'Exploiting YouTube', in P. Vonderau and P. Snickars (eds) *The YouTube reader*, Stockholm: National Library of Sweden, pp 33–51.

Arquilla, J. and Ronfeldt, D. (eds) (2001) *Networks and netwars*, Santa Monica, CA: RAND.

Arvidsson, A. and Colleoni, E. (2012) 'Value in informational capitalism and on the internet', *The Information Society*, vol 28, no 3, pp 135–50.

Asen, R. (2002) 'Imagining in the public sphere', *Philosophy and Rhetoric*, vol 35, no 4, pp 345–67.

Asen, R. and Brouwer, D.C. (eds) (2001) *Counterpublics and the state*, New York: State University of New York.

Åström, J. and Granberg, M.G. (2007) 'Understanding elite support for e-participation', *Journal of Information Technology and Politics*, vol 4, no 2, pp 63–77.

Åström, J. and Grönlund, Å. (2012) 'Online consultations in local government: what works, when, and why?' in S. Coleman and P.M. Shane (eds) *Connecting democracy*, Cambridge, MA: The MIT Press, pp 75–96.

Axford, B. (2001) 'The transformation of politics or anti-politics?' in B. Axford and R. Huggins (eds) *New Media and Politics*, London: Sage, pp 1–29.

Axtmann, R. (2002) 'What's wrong with cosmopolitan democracy?' in N. Dower and J. Williams (eds) *Global citizenship: A critical reader*, Edinburgh: Edinburgh University Press, pp 101–13.

Baines, S. and Hardill, I. (2008) '"At least I can do something": the work of volunteering in a community beset by worklessness', *Social Policy and Society*, vol 7, no 3, pp 307–17.

Bakhtin, M.M. (1981) *The dialogic imagination*, trans C. Emerson and M. Holquist, ed M. Holquist, Austin, TX: University of Texas Press.

Bakhtin, M.M. (1984) *The problems of Dostoevsky's poetics*, ed and trans C. Emerson, Minneapolis: University of Minneapolis Press.

Bakhtin, M.M. and Medvedev, P.N. (1978) *The formal method in literary scholarship*, trans A.J. Wehrle, Baltimore, MD: Johns Hopkins University Press.

Baldwin, J.N., Gauld, R. and Goldfinch, S. (2012) 'What public servants really think of e-government', *Public Management Review*, vol 14, no 1, pp 105–27.

Bambra, C. (2011) 'Work, worklessness and the political economy of health inequalities', *Journal of Epidemiology Community Health*, vol 65, no 9, pp 746–50.

Bang, H. and Esmark, A. (2009) 'Good governance in network society: reconfiguring the political from politics to polity', *Administrative Theory and Praxis*, vol 31, no 1, pp 7–37.

Bannister, F. and Wilson, D. (2011) 'O(ver)government? Emerging technology, citizen autonomy and the regulatory state', *Information Polity*, vol 16, pp 63–79.

Barassi, V. and Treré, E. (2012) 'Does Web 3.0 come after Web 2.0? Deconstructing theoretical assumptions through practice', *New Media and Society*, vol 14, no 8, pp 1269–85.

Barnes, M., Newman, J. and Sullivan, H. (2006) 'Discursive arenas: deliberation and the constitution of identity in public participation at a local level', *Social Movement Studies*, vol 5, no 3, pp 193–207.

Barnett, C., Clarke, N., Cloke, P. and Malpass, A. (2008) 'The elusive subjects of neo- liberalism: beyond the analytics of governmentality', *Cultural Studies*, vol 22, no 5, pp 624–53.

Barney, D. (2000) *Prometheus wired*, Chicago: Chicago University Press.

Barney, D. (2008) 'Politics and emerging media: the revenge of publicity', *Global Media Journal*, vol 1, no 1, pp 89–106.

Barry, A. (2006) 'Technological zones', *European Journal of Social Theory*, vol 9, no 2, pp 239–53.

Beebeejaun, Y. (2006) 'The participation trap: the limitations of participation for ethic and racial groups', *International Planning Studies*, vol 11, no 1, pp 3–18.

Beer, D. (2008) 'Social network(ing) sites ... revisiting the story so far: a response to danah boyd and Nicole Ellison', *Journal of Computer-Mediated Communication*, vol 13, no 2, pp 516–29.

Beer, D. (2009) 'Power through the algorithm? Participatory web cultures and the technological unconscious', *New Media and Society*, vol 11, no 6, pp 985–1002.

Beer, D. and Burrows, R. (2007) 'Sociology and, of and in Web 2.0: some initial considerations', *Sociological Research Online*, vol 12, no 5, available at www.socresonline.org.uk/12/5/17.html.

Beetham, D., Byrne, I., Ngan, P. and Weir, S. (2002) *Democracy under Blair*, London: Politico.

Bell, D. (2007) 'The hospitable city: social relations in commercial spaces', *Progress in Human Geography*, vol 31, no 1, pp 7–22.

Bennett, W.L. (2003) 'Communicating global activism: strengths and vulnerabilities of networked politics', *Information, Communication and Society*, vol 6, no 2, pp 143–68.

Bertot, J.C., Jaeger, P.T. and Grimes, J.M. (2012) 'Promoting transparency and accountability through ICTs, social media, and collaborative e-government', *Transforming Government: People, Process and Policy*, vol 6, no 1, pp 5–12.

Bessant, J. (2014) 'The political in an age of the digital: propositions for empirical investigations', *Politics*, vol 34, no 1, pp 33–44.

Bevir, M. and Rhodes, R.A.W. (2010) *The state as cultural practice*, Oxford: Oxford University Press.

Bhaskar, R. (1993) *Dialectic: the pulse of freedom*, London: Verso.

Biccum, A. (2005) 'The World Social Forum: exploiting the ambivalence of "open" spaces', *ephemera*, vol 5, no 2, pp 116–33.

Biddulph, M. (2011) 'Urban design, regeneration and the entrepreneurial city', *Progress in Planning*, vol 76, no 2, pp 63–103.

Birch, K. and Mykhnenko, V. (2010) 'Introduction: a world turned right way up', in K. Birch and V. Mykhnenko (eds) *The rise and fall of neoliberalism*, London: Zed, pp 1–20.

Blank, G. and Reisdorf, B.C. (2012) 'The participatory web: a user perspective on Web 2.0', *Information, Communication and Society*, vol 15, no 4, pp 537–54.

Blick, A., Choudhury, T. and Weir, S. (2006) *The rules of the game: terrorism, community and human rights*, York: Joseph Rowntree Reform Trust. Available at: www.democraticaudit.com/download/breaking-news/Terrorism-Final.pdf (accessed 5 November 2007).

Bohman, J. (1996) *Public deliberation*, Cambridge, MA: MIT Press.

Bonefeld, W. (1993) *The recomposition of the state during the 1980s*, Aldershot: Dartmouth Publishing.

Bonefeld, W. (2010) 'Abstract labour: against its nature and on its time', *Capital and Class*, vol 34, no 2, pp 257–76.

Bonefeld, W. (2011) 'Debating abstract labour', *Capital and Class*, vol 35, no 3, pp 475–79.

Bonefeld, W. (2012) 'Freedom and the strong state: on German ordoliberalism', *New Political Economy*, vol 17, no 5, pp 633–56.

Bottomley, A. and Moore, N. (2007) 'From walls to membranes: fortress polis and the governance of urban public space in 21st century Britain', *Law Critique*, vol 18, no 2, pp 171–206.

Boulianne, S. (2009) 'Does internet use affect engagement? A meta-analysis of research', *Political Communication*, vol 26, no 2, pp 193–211.

Box, R.C., Marshall, G.S., Reed, B.J. and Reed, C.M. (2001) 'New public management and substantive democracy', *Public Administration Review*, vol 61, no 5, pp 608–19.

boyd, d. and Ellison, N.B. (2007) 'Social network sites: definition, history, and scholarship', *Journal of Computer-Mediated Communication*, vol 13, no 1, pp 210–30.

Boyle, P. and Haggerty, K.D. (2009) 'Spectacular security: mega-events and the security complex', *International Political Sociology*, vol 3, no 3, pp 257–74.

Brabham, D.C. (2012) 'The myth of amateur crowds: a critical discourse analysis of crowdsourcing coverage', *Information, Communication and Society*, vol 15, no 3, pp 394–410.

Breindl, Y. (2010) 'Critique of the democratic potentialities of the internet: a review of current theory and practice', *tripleC*, vol 8, no 1, pp 43–59.

Brownill, S. (2010) 'London Docklands revisited: the dynamics of waterfront regeneration', in G. Desfor, Q. Stevens and D. Schubert (eds) *The fixity and flow of waterfront regeneration*, London: Routledge, pp 121–42.

Bruns, A. (2008) *Blogs, Wikipedia, Second Life and beyond*, New York: Peter Lang.

Bryan, D. (2012) 'The duality of labour and the financial crisis', *The Economic and Labour Relations Review*, vol 20, no 2, pp 49–60.

Bucher, T. (2012) 'Want to be on the top? Algorithmic power and the threat of invisibility on Facebook', *New Media and Society*, vol 14, no 7, pp 1164–80.

Buller, J. and Flinders, M. (2005) 'The domestic origins of depoliticisation in the area of British economic policy', *The British Journal of Politics and International Relations*, vol 7, no 4, pp 526–43.

Burnham, P. (2006) 'Marxism, the state and British politics', *British Politics*, vol 1, no 1, pp 67–83.

Burton-Jones, A. (1999) *Knowledge capitalism*, Oxford: Oxford University Press.

Butler, T. (2007) 'For gentrification?', *Environment and Planning A*, vol 39, no 1, pp 161–81.

Button, M. (2003) 'Private security and the policing of quasi-public space', *International Journal of the Sociology of Law*, vol 31, no 3, pp 227–37.

CABE Space (2004) *The value of public space*. Available at: www.cabe.org.uk/default.aspx?contentitemid=475&field=browse_subject&term=Public%20space&type=2 (accessed 14 June 2007).

Campbell, E.R.A. (2011) 'A critique of the Occupy movement from a black occupier', *The Black Scholar*, vol 41, no 4, pp 42–51.

Capgemini, Rand Europe, IDC, Sogeti and DTI (2009) *Smarter, faster, better eGovernment, 8th Benchmark Measurement for the European Commission*, DG INFSO, November.

Caraway, B. (2011) 'Audience labor in the new media environment: a Marxian revisiting of the audience commodity', *Media, Culture and Society*, vol 33, no 5, pp 693–708.

Carchedi, G. (2011) *Behind the crisis*, Leiden: Brill.

Carducci, V. (2006) 'Culture jamming: a sociological perspective', *Journal of Consumer Culture*, vol 6, no 1, pp 116–38.

Carter, B., Danford, A., Howcroft, D., Richardson, H., Smith, A. and Taylor, P. (2011) 'Lean and mean in the civil service: the case of processing in HMRC', *Public Money and Management*, vol 31, no 2, pp 115–22.

Castells, M. (2000) *The rise of the network society* (new edn), Oxford: Blackwell.

Castells, M. (2001) *The internet galaxy*, Oxford: Oxford University Press.

Castells, M. (2009) *Communication power*, Oxford: Oxford University Press.

Castells, M. (2010) *The power of identity* (2nd edn), London: Wiley-Blackwell.

Castells, M. (2012) *Networks of outrage and hope*, Cambridge: Polity.

Cerny, P. G. (2008) 'Embedding neoliberalism: the evolution of a hegemonic paradigm', *The Journal of International Trade and Diplomacy*, vol 2, no 1, pp 1–46.

Chadwick, A. (2003) 'Bringing e-democracy back in: why it matters for future research on e-governance', *Social Science Computer Review*, vol 21, no 4, pp 443–55.

Chadwick, A. (2009) 'Web 2.0: new challenges for the study of e-democracy in an era of informational exuberance', *I/S: A Journal of Law and Policy for the Information Society*, vol 5, no 1, pp 11–41.

Chadwick, A. (2013) *The hybrid media system*, Oxford: Oxford University Press.

Chakravartty, P. and Schiller, D. (2010) 'Neoliberal newspeak and digital capitalism in crisis', *International Journal of Communication*, vol 4, pp 670–92.

Chambers S. (2003) 'Deliberative democratic theory', *Annual Review of Political Science*, vol 6, no 1, pp 307–26.

Chandler, D. (2004) *Constructing global civil society*, London: Palgrave.

Chesters, G. and Welsh, I. (2006) *Complexity and social movements*, London: Routledge.

Choi, C.G. and Choi, S.O. (2012) 'Collaborative partnerships and crime in disorganized communities', *Public Administration Review*, vol 72, no 2, pp 228–39.

Chorev, N. (2005) 'The institutional project of neo-liberal globalism: the case of the WTO', *Theory and Society*, vol 34, no 3, pp 317–55.

Christensen, C. (2011) 'Discourses of technology and liberation: state aid to net activists in an era of "Twitter Revolutions"', *The Communication Review*, vol 14, no 3, pp 233–53.

Christensen, M. and Christensen, C. (2013) 'The Arab Spring as meta-event and communicative spaces', *Television and New Media*, vol 14, no 4, pp 351–64.

Cina, C.S., Molinero, C.M. and Queiroz, A.B. (2003) 'The measurement of intangible assets in the public sector using scaling techniques', *Journal of Intellectual Capital*, vol 4, no 2, pp 249–75.

Clarke, J. (2010) 'After neo-liberalism? Markets, state and the reinvention of public welfare', *Cultural Studies*, vol 24, no 3, pp 375–94.

Clarke, S. (1988) *Keynesianism, monetarism and the crisis of the state*, Aldershot: Edward Elgar.

Clarke, S. (1990–91) 'The Marxist theory of overaccumulation and crisis', *Science and Society*, vol 54, no 4, pp 442–67.

Clarke, S. (1991) *Marx, marginalism and modern sociology*, London: Macmillan.

Coaffee, J. and Rogers, P. (2008a) 'Reputational risk and resiliency: the branding of security in place-making', *Place Branding and Public Diplomacy*, vol 4, no 3, pp 205–17.

Coaffee, J. and Rogers, P. (2008b) 'Rebordering the city for new security challenges: from counter-terrorism to community resilience', *Space and Polity*, vol 12, no 1, pp 101–18.

Cohen, N.S. (2008) 'The valorization of surveillance: towards a political economy of Facebook', *Democratic Communiqué*, vol 22, no 1, pp 5–22.

Cohen, N.S. (2012) 'Cultural work as a site of struggle: freelancers and exploitation', *tripleC*, vol 10, no 2, pp 141–55.

Cohen, R. and Rai, S. (2000) *Global social movements*, London: Continuum.

Colás, A. (2003) 'The power of representation: democratic politics and global governance', *Review of International Studies*, vol 29, S1, pp 97–118.

Coleman, E.G. and Golub, A. (2008) 'Hacker practice: moral genres and the cultural articulation of liberalism', *Anthropological Theory*, vol 8, no 3, pp 255–77.

Coleman, R. (2003) 'Images from a neoliberal city: the state, surveillance and social control', *Critical Criminology*, vol 12, no 1, pp 21–42.

Coleman, R., Tombs, S. and Whyte, D. (2005) 'Capital, crime control and statecraft in the entrepreneurial city', *Urban Studies*, vol 42, no 13, pp 2511–2530.

Coleman, S. (2004) 'Connecting parliament to the public via the internet: two case studies of online consultations', *Information, Communication and Society*, vol 7, no 1, pp 1–22.

Coleman, S. (2005) 'The lonely citizen: indirect representation in an age of networks', *Political Communication*, vol 22, no 2, pp 197–214.

Coleman, S. and Moss, G. (2012) 'Under construction: the field of online deliberation research', *Journal of Information, Technology and Politics*, vol 9, no 1, pp 1–15.

Collins, D. (2000) *Management fads and buzzwords*, London: Routledge.

Comor, E. (2010) 'Contextualizing and critiquing the fantastic prosumer: power, alienation and hegemony', *Critical Sociology*, vol 37, no 3, pp 309–27.

Conway, H. (1991) *People's parks: The design and development of Victorian parks in Britain*, Cambridge: Cambridge University Press.

Conway, M. (2002) 'Reality bytes: cyberterrorism and the "use" of the internet', *First Monday*, vol 7, no 11, available at: http://ojphi.org/ojs/index.php/fm/article/view/1001/922 (accessed 29 December 2013).

Cook, I.R. and Whowell, M. (2011) 'Visibility and the policing of public space', *Geography Compass*, vol 5, no 8, pp 610–22.

Cordella, A. (2007) 'E-government: towards the e-bureaucratic form?' *Journal of Information Technology*, vol 22, pp 265–74.

Corrigan, P., Ramsay, H. and Sayer, D. (1980) 'The state as a relation of production', in P. Corrigan (ed) *Capitalism, state formation and Marxist theory*, London: Quartet Books, pp 1–25.

Costanza-Chock, S. (2012) 'Mic check! Media cultures and the Occupy movement', *Social Movement Studies*, vol 11, nos. 3–5, pp 375–85.

Coté, M. and Pybus, J. (2007) 'Learning to immaterial labour 2.0: MySpace and social networks', *ephemera*, vol 7, no 1, pp 88–106.

Cottle, S. (2011) 'Media and the Arab uprisings of 2011: research notes', *Journalism*, vol 12, no 5, pp 647–59.

Couldry, N. and Littler, J. (2011) 'Work, power and performance: analysing the "reality" game of *The Apprentice*', *Cultural Sociology*, vol 5, no 2, pp 263–79.

Coursey, D. and Norris, D.F. (2008) 'Models of e-government: are they correct? An empirical assessment', *Public Administration Review*, May–June, pp 523–36.

Coutard, O. (2008) 'Placing splintering urbanism: an introduction', *Geoforum*, vol 39, no 6, pp 1815–20.

Coutard, O. and Guy, S. (2007) 'STS and the city: politics and the practice of hope', *Science, Technology and Human Values*, vol 32, no 6, pp 713–34.

Cover, R. (2004) 'New media theory: electronic games, democracy and reconfiguring the author–audience relationship', *Social Semiotics*, vol 14, no 2, pp 173–91.

Cramer, C. (2002) '*Homo Economicus* goes to war: methodological individualism, rational choice and the political economy of war', *World Development*, vol 30, no 11, pp 1845–64.

Crang, M. (2000) 'Public space, urban space and electronic space: would the real city please stand up?' *Urban Studies*, vol 37, no 2, pp 301–17.

Crawford, L., Costello, K., Pollack, J. and Bentley, L. (2003) 'Managing soft change projects in the public sector', *International Journal of Project Management*, vol 21, pp 443–8.

Crick, M. (2012) 'Social media use in the Bronx: new research and innovations in the study of YouTube's digital neighbourhood', *Journal of Technology in Human Services*, vol 39, pp 262–98.

Crompton, J.L. (2005) 'The impact of parks on property values: empirical evidence from the past two decades in the United States', *Managing Leisure*, vol 10, October, pp 203–18.

Daguerre, A. (2004) 'Importing workfare: policy transfer of social and labour market policies from the USA to Britain under New Labour', *Social Policy and Administration*, vol 38, no 1, pp 41–6.

Dahlberg, L. (2001) 'The internet and democratic discourse', *Information, Communication and Society*, vol 4, no 4, pp 615–33.

Dahlberg, L. (2011) 'Re-constructing digital democracy: an outline of four "positions"', *New Media and Society*, vol 13, no 6, pp 855–72.

Daly, S. (2011) 'Philanthropy, the Big Society and emerging philanthropic relationships in the UK', *Public Management Review*, vol 13, no 8, pp 1077–94.

Daniels, P.W. (2012) 'Service industries at a crossroads: some fragile assumptions and future challenges', *The Service Industries Journal*, vol 32, no 4, pp 619–39.

Davenport, E. (2002) 'Mundane knowledge management and microlevel organizational learning: an ethological approach', *Journal of the American Society for Information Science and Technology*, vol 53, no 12, pp 1038–46.

Davidson, M. (2007) 'Gentrification as global habitat: a process of class formation or corporate creation?' *Transactions of the Institute of British Geographers*, vol 32, no 4, pp 490–506.

Davidson, R. (2012) 'The emergence of popular personal finance magazines and the risk shift in American society', *Media, Culture and Society*, vol 34, no 1, pp 3–20.

Davies, J.S. (2011) *Challenging governance theory*, Bristol: Policy Press.

Davies, S. (2011) 'Outsourcing, public sector reform and the changed character of the UK state–voluntary sector relationship', *International Journal of Public Sector Management*, vol 24, no 7, pp 641–49.

Davis, A. (2010) 'New media and fat democracy: the paradox of online participation', *New Media and Society*, vol 12, no 5, pp 745–61.

Dawley, S., Pike, A. and Tomaney, J. (2010) 'Towards the resilient region?' *Local Economy*, vol 25, no 8, pp 650–67.

Day, R.E. (2001) 'Totality and representation: a history of knowledge management through European documentation, critical modernity, and post-Fordism', *Journal of the American Society for Information Science and Technology*, vol 52, no 9, pp 725–35.

Debatin, B., Lovejoy, J.P., Horn, A.-K. and Hughes, B.N. (2009) 'Facebook and online privacy: attitudes, behaviors, and unintended consequences', *Journal of Computer-Mediated Communication*, vol 15, no 1, pp 83–108.

de Brunhoff, S. (1978) *The state, capital and economic policy*, trans M. Sonenscher, London: Pluto.

de Certeau, M. (1984) *The practice of everyday life*, trans S. Rendall, Berkeley, CA: University of California Press.

De Cock, C., Baker, M. and Volkmann, C. (2011) 'Financial phantasmagoria: corporate image-work in times of crisis', *Organization*, vol 18, no 2, pp 153–72.

Deleuze, G. (1988) *Foucault*, trans and ed S. Hand, London: Althone.

Deleuze, G. (1990) 'Postscript on control societies', in G. Deleuze, *Negotiations: 1972–1990*, New York: Columbia University Press, pp 177–82.

Deleuze, G. and Guattari, F. (1988) *A thousand plateaus*, trans Brian Massumi, London: Althone Press.

Delicath, J.W. and Deluca, K.M. (2003) 'Image events, the public sphere, and argumentative practice: the case of radical environmental groups', *Argumentation*, vol 17, no 3, pp 315–33.

DeLuca, K. and Peeples, J. (2002) 'From public sphere to public screen: democracy, activism, and the "violence" of Seattle', *Critical Studies in Media Communication*, vol 19, no 2, pp 125–51.

DeLuca, K., Lawson, S. and Sun, Y. (2012) 'Occupy Wall Street on the public screens of social media: the many framings of the birth of a protest movement', *Communication, Culture and Critique*, vol 5, no 4, pp 483–509.

De Magalhães, C. (2010) 'Public space and the contracting-out of publicness: a framework for analysis', *Journal of Urban Design*, vol 15, no 4, pp 559–74.

Deuze, M. (2007) *Media work*, London: Polity.

Diamond, L. (2010) 'Liberation technology', *Journal of Democracy*, vol 21, no 3, pp 69–83.

Dodge, M. and Kitchen, R. (2005) 'Codes of life: identification and the machine-readable world', *Environment and Planning D: Society and Space*, vol 23, no 6, pp 851–81.

Doogan, K. (2009) *New capitalism? The transformation of work*, Cambridge: Polity.

Dorling, D. (2012) *The no-nonsense guide to equality*, Oxford: New Internationalist Publications.

Dube, A. and Kaplan, E. (2012) 'Occupy Wall Street and the political economy of inequality', *The Economists' Voice*, vol 9, no 3, pp 1–7.

Dunleavy, P., Margetts, H., Bastow, S. and Tinkler, J. (2005) 'New public management is dead – long live digital-era governance', *Journal of Public Administration Research and Theory*, vol 16, pp 467–94.

Dunn, C. (2005) 'Balancing the right to protest in the aftermath of September 11', *Harvard Civil Rights–Civil Liberties Law Review*, vol 40, pp 327–57.

Dutil, P.A., Howard, C., Langford, J. and Roy, J. (2007) Rethinking government–public relationships in a digital world: customers, clients, or citizens?', *Journal of Information Technology & Politics*, vol 4, no 1, pp 77–90.

Earl, J. and Schussman, A. (2003) 'The new site of activism: on-line organizations, movement entrepreneurs, and the changing location of social movement decision making', *Research in Social Movements, Conflicts and Change*, vol 24, pp 155–87.

Earl, M. (2001) 'Knowledge management strategies: towards a taxonomy', *Journal of Management Information Systems*, vol 18, no 1, pp 215–33.

Eisenschitz, A. (2008) 'Town planning, planning theory and social reform', *International Planning Studies*, vol 13, no 2, pp 133–49.

Ellis, C. (2012) 'Letting it slip: the Labour Party and the "mystical halo" of nationalization, 1951–1964', *Contemporary British History*, vol 26, no 1, pp 47–71.

Ellison, N. and Burrows, R. (2007) 'New spaces of (dis)engagement? Social politics, urban technologies and the rezoning of the city', *Housing Studies*, vol 22, no 3, pp 295–312.

Ellström, P.-E. and Kock, H. (2008) 'Competence development in the workplace: concepts, strategies and effects', *Asia Pacific Education Review*, vol 9, no 1, pp 5–20.

Elwood, S. (2002) 'Neighbourhood revitalization through "collaboration": assessing the implications of neoliberal urban policy at the grassroots', *GeoJournal*, vol 58, nos 2–3, pp 121–30.

Engelen, E., Ertürk, I., Froud, J., Johal, S., Leaver, A., Moran, M. and Williams, K. (2012) 'Misrule of experts? The financial crisis as elite debacle', *Economy and Society*, vol 41, no 3, pp 360–82.

Epstein, K. (2013) 'Total surveillance', *Counterpunch*, available at: www.counterpunch.org/2013/06/28/total-surveillance (accessed 6 August 2013).

Evans-Cowley, J.S. (2010) 'Planning in the age of Facebook: the role of social networking in planning processes', *Geojournal*, vol 75, pp 407–20.

Evans-Cowley, J.S. and Hollander, J. (2010) 'The new generation of public participation: internet-based participation tools', *Planning Practice and Research*, vol 25, no 3, pp 397–408.

Ewing, K.D. (2010) *Bonfire of the liberties: New Labour, human rights and the rule of law*, Oxford: Oxford University Press.

Fainstein, S.S. (2005) 'Planning theory and the city', *Journal of Planning, Education and Research* vol 25, no 2, pp 121–30.

Farman, J. (2012) *Mobile interface theory*, London: Routledge.

Farnsworth, K. (2006) 'Globalisation, business and British public policy', *Contemporary Politics*, vol 12, no 1, pp 79–93.

Feenberg, A. (1999) *Questioning technology*, London: Routledge.

Fenton, N. and Barassi, V. (2011) 'Alternative media and social networking sites: the politics of individuation and political participation', *The Communication Review*, vol 14, no 3, pp 179–96.

Field, A. (2009) 'The "new terrorism": revolution or evolution?' *Political Studies Review*, vol 7, no 2, pp 195–207.

Fine, B. (2010) 'Locating financialisation', *Historical Materialism*, vol 18, no 2, pp 97–116.

Fine, J. (2005) 'Community unions and the revival of the American labor movement', *Politics and Society*, vol 33, no 1, pp 153–99.

Finn, M. (1993) *After Chartism: class and nation in English radical politics, 1848–1874*, Cambridge: Cambridge University Press.

Finnegan, C.A. and Kang, J. (2004) '"Sighting" the public: iconoclasm and public sphere theory', *Quarterly Journal of Speech*, vol 90, no 4, pp 377–402.

Finney, N. and Simpson, L. (2009) '"*Sleepwalking to segregation*"? *Challenging myths about race and migration*, Bristol: Policy Press.

Fisher, E. (2010) *Media and new capitalism in the digital age*, London: Palgrave.

Fisher, E. (2012) 'How less alienation creates more exploitation? Audience labor on social network sites', *triple*, vol 10, no 12, pp 171–83.

Fiske, J. (1994) *Media matters*, Minnesota: University of Minnesota Press.

Fitzpatrick, T. (2001) 'New agendas for social policy and criminology: globalization, urbanism and the emerging post-social security state', *Social Policy and Administration*, vol 35, no 2, pp 212–29.

Flew, T. (2008) *New media: An introduction*, Oxford: Oxford University Press.

Flinders, M. (2005) 'The politics of public-private partnerships', *British Journal of Politics and International Relations*, vol 7, no 2, pp 215–39.

Flinders, M. and Skelcher, C. (2012) 'Shrinking the quango state: five challenges in reforming quangos', *Public Money & Management*, vol 32, no 5, pp 327–34.

Florida, R. (2002) *The rise of the creative class*, New York: Basic Books.

Foster, J.B. and McChesney, R.W. (2012) *The endless crisis*, New York: Monthly Review Press.

Francoli, M. and Ward, S. (2008) '21st century soapboxes? MPs and their blogs', *Information Polity*, vol 13, pp 21–39.

Fraser, N. (1992) 'Rethinking the public sphere: a contribution to the critique of actually existing democracy', in C. Calhoun (ed) *Habermas and the public sphere*, Cambridge, MA: The MIT Press, pp 109–42.

Freelon, D.G. (2010) 'Analyzing online political discussion using three models of democratic communication', *New Media and Society*, vol 12, no 7, pp 1172–90.

Freeman, A. (2012) 'The profit rate in the presence of financial markets: a necessary correction', *Journal of Australian Political Economy*, vol 70, pp 167–92.

Froud, J., Sukhdev, J. and Williams, K. (2002) 'Financialisation and the coupon pool', *Capital and Class*, no 78, Autumn, pp 119–51.

Fuchs, C. (2010) 'Labor in informational capitalism and on the internet', *The Information Society* vol 26, no 3, pp 179–96.

Fudge, S. and Williams, S. (2006) 'Beyond left and right: can the Third Way deliver a reinvigorated social democracy?' *Critical Sociology*, vol 32, no 4, pp 583–602.

Funnell, W., Jupe, R. and Andrew, J. (2009) *In government we trust*, London: Pluto.

Fussey, P. (2008) 'Beyond liberty, beyond security: the politics of public surveillance', *British Politics*, vol 3, no 1, pp 120–35.

Fyfe, N.R. and Milligan, C. (2003) 'Out of the shadows: exploring contemporary geographies of voluntarism', *Progress in Human Geography*, vol 27, no 4, pp 397–413.

Gaby, S. and Caren, N. (2012) 'Occupy online: how cute old men and Malcom X recruited 400,000 US users to OWS on Facebook', *Social Movement Studies*, vol 11, nos. 3–4, pp 367–74.

Garavan, T.N. and McGuire, D. (2001) 'Competencies and workplace learning: some reflections on the rhetoric and reality', *Journal of Workplace Learning*, vol 13, no 4, pp 144–63.

Garrett, P.M. (2005) 'Social work's "electronic turn": notes on the deployment of information and communication technologies in social work with children and families', *Critical Social Policy*, vol 25, no 4, pp 529–53.

Garrett, R.K. (2006) 'Protest in an information society: a review of literature on social movements and new ICTs', *Information, Communication and Society*, vol 9, no 2, pp 202–24.

Gates, B. (2009) 'A new approach to capitalism', in M. Kinsley (ed), *Creative capitalism*, London: Simon and Schuster, pp 7–16.

Galloway, A.R. (2004) *Protocol*, Cambridge, MA: The MIT Press.

Galloway, A.R. and Thacker, E. (2004) 'Protocol, control and networks', *Grey Room*, vol 17, Fall, pp 6–29.

Gauld, R. (2009) '"E-government": is it the next big public sector trend?' in S.F. Goldfinch and J.L. Wallis (eds), *International handbook of public management reform*, Cheltenham: Edward Elgar Publishing, pp 105–20.

Gearty, C. (2003) 'Reflections on civil liberties in an age of counterterrorism', *Osgoode Hall Law Journal*, vol 41, no 2–3, pp 185–208.

Gearty, C. (2005) 11 September 2001, counter-terrorism, and the Human Rights Act', *Journal of Law and Society*, vol 32, no 1, pp 18–33.

Gearty, C. (2013) *Liberty and security*, Cambridge: Polity.

Gibson, R.K. (2009) 'New media and the revitalization of politics', *Representation*, vol 45, no 3, pp 289–99.

Gibson, T.A. (2005) 'Selling city living: urban branding campaigns, class power and the civic good', *International Journal of Cultural Studies*, vol 8, no 3, pp 259–80.

Gillespie, T. (2010) 'The politics of "platforms"', *New Media and Society*, vol 12, no 3, pp 347–64.

Gilley, S. (1973) 'The Garibaldi riots of 1862', *The Historical Journal*, vol 16, no 4, pp 697–732.

Givan, R.K. (2007) 'Side by side we battle onward? Representing workers in contemporary America', *British Journal of Industrial Relations*, vol 45, no 4, pp 829–55.

Glinavos, I. (2008) 'Neoliberal law: unintended consequences of market-friendly law reforms', *Third World Quarterly*, vol 29, no 6, pp 1087–99.

Godin, B. (2006) 'The knowledge-based economy: conceptual framework or buzzword?' *Journal of Technology Transfer*, vol 31, no 1, pp 17–30.

Goheen, P.G. (1998) 'Public space and the geography of the modern city', *Progress in Human Geography*, vol 22, no 4, pp 479–96.

Gold, J.R. and Revill, G. (2003) 'Exploring landscapes of fear: marginality, spectacle and surveillance', *Capital and Class*, no 80, Summer, pp 27–50.

Goode, L. (2005) *Jürgen Habermas: Democracy and the Public Sphere*, London: Pluto.

Goodhart, M. (2005) 'Civil society and the problem of global democracy', *Democratization*, vol 12, no 1, pp 1–21.

Google (2012) *Google Annual Report 2012*, accessed at, http://investor.google.com/pdf/20121231_google_10K.pdf.

Gough, J. (2002) 'Neoliberalism and socialisation in the contemporary city: opposites, complements and instabilities', *Antipode*, vol 34, no 3, pp 405–26.

Gough, J. (2003) *Work, locality and the rhythms of capital*, London: Continuum.

Gough, J., Eisenschitz, A. and McCulloch, A. (2006) *Spaces of social exclusion*, London: Routledge.

Graham, S. (2010) *Cities under siege*, London: Verso.

Graham, S. (2012) 'When life itself is war: on the urbanization of military and security doctrine', *International Journal of Urban and Regional Research*, vol 36, no 1, pp 136–55.

Graham, S. and Marvin, S. (2001) *Splintering urbanism*, London: Routledge.

Graham, T. (2010) 'Talking politics online within spaces of popular culture: the case of the Big Brother forum', *Javnost – The Public*, vol 17, no 4, pp 25–42.

Gramsci, A. (1986) *Selections from prison notebooks*, London: Lawrence and Wishart.

Grant, G. and Chau, D. (2006) 'Developing a generic framework for e-government', in G. Hunter and F. Tan (eds), *Advanced topics in global information management, Vol 5*, London: Idea Group Publishing, pp 72–101.

Green, F. (2006) *Demanding work*, Princeton, NJ: Princeton University Press.

Grimes, S. (2006) 'Online multiplayer games: a virtual space for intellectual property debates?' *New Media and Society*, vol 18, no 6, pp 969–90.

Grimmelmann, J. (2009) 'Saving Facebook', *Iowa Law Review*, vol 94, pp 1137–206.

Groot, T. and Budding, T. (2008) 'New public management's current issues and future prospects', *Financial Accountability and Management*, vol 24, no 1, pp 1–13.

Gustafsson, U. and Driver, S. (2005) 'Parents, power and public participation: Sure Start, an experiment in New Labour governance', *Social Policy and Administration*, vol 39, no 5, pp 528–43.

Gutmann, A. and Thompson, D. (2004) *Why deliberative democracy?* Princeton, NJ: Princeton University Press.

Habermas, J. (1987) *A theory of communicative action*, vol 2, trans T. McCarthy, Cambridge: Polity.

Habermas, J. (1996) *Between facts and norms*, trans W. Rehg, Cambridge: Polity.

Haggerty, K.D. and Ericson, R.V. (2000) 'The surveillant assemblage', *The British Journal of Sociology*, vol 51, no 4, pp 605–22.

Hague, B.N. and Loader, B.A. (1999) 'Digital democracy: an introduction', in B.N. Hague and B.D. Loader (eds) *Digital democracy*, London: Routledge, pp 3–22.

Hambrick, M.C. (2012) 'A case study of democratic celebrity dissent rhetoric', *Journal of Social Justice*, vol 2, pp 1–16.

Hands, J. (2011) *@ is for activism*, London: Pluto.

Hannam, K., Sheller, M. and Urry, J. (2006) 'Editorial: mobilities, immobilities and moorings' *Mobilities*, vol 1, no 1, pp 1–22.

Hansen, S., Berente, N. and Lyytinen, K. (2009) 'Wikipedia, critical social theory, and the possibility of rational discourse', *The Information Society*, vol 25, no 1, pp 38–59.

Hänska-Ahy, M.T. and Shapour, R. (2013) 'Who's reporting the protests? Converging practices of citizen journalists and two BBC World Service newsrooms, from Iran's election protests to the Arab uprisings', *Journalism Studies*, vol 14, no 1, pp 29–45.

Haque, M.S. (2007) 'Revisiting the new public management', *Public Administration Review*, vol 7, no 1, pp 179–82.

Hardt, M. and Negri, A. (2000) *Empire*, Cambridge, MA: Harvard University Press.

Hardt, M. and Negri, A. (2004) *Multitude*, New York: Penguin.

Harmes, A. (2006) 'Neoliberalism and multinational governance', *Review of International Political Economy*, vol 13, no 5, pp 725–49.

Harvey, D. (1989) *The condition of postmodernity*, Oxford: Blackwell.

Harvey, D. (1996) *Justice, nature and the geography of difference*, Oxford: Blackwell.

Harvey, D. (2006) 'Neoliberalism as creative destruction', *Geografiska Annaler: Series B, Human Geography*, vol 88, no 2, pp 145–58.

Hassan, R. (2011) 'The speed of collapse: the space-time dimensions of capitalism's first great crisis of the 21st century', *Critical Sociology*, vol 37, no 4, pp 385–402.

Hatem, M.F. (2012) 'The Arab Spring meets the Occupy Wall Street movement: examples of changing definitions of citizenship in a global world', *Journal of Civil Society*, vol 8, no 4, pp 401–15.

Heinrich, M. (2004) *An introduction to the three volumes of Marx's Capital*, New York: Monthly Review Press.

Hempel, L. and Töpfer, E. (2009) 'The surveillance consensus: reviewing the politics of CCTV in three European countries', *European Journal of Criminology*, vol 6, no 2, pp 157–77.

Herman, A., Coombe, R.J. and Kaye, L. (2006) 'Your Second Life? Goodwill and the performativity of intellectual property in online digital gaming', *Cultural Studies*, vol 20, no 2–3, pp 184–210.

Hier, S.P. (2004) 'Risky spaces and dangerous faces: urban surveillance, social disorder and CCTV', *Social and Legal Studies*, vol 13, no 4, pp 541–54.

Hirsch, J. (2003) 'The state's new clothes: NGOs and the internationalization of states', *Rethinking Marxism*, vol 15, no 2, pp 237–62.

Hodkinson, S. (2011) 'The Private Finance Initiative in English council housing regeneration: a privatisation too far?' *Housing Studies*, vol 26, no 6, pp 911–32.

Hodkinson, S. and Chatterton, P. (2006) 'Autonomy in the city? Reflections on the social centres movement in the UK', *City*, vol 10, no 3, pp 305–15.

Hollander, J.A. and Einwohner, R.L. (2004) 'Conceptualizing resistance', *Sociological Forum*, vol 19, no 4 pp 533–54.

Holloway, J. (1995) 'Global capital and the national state', in W. Bonefeld and J. Holloway (eds), *Global capital, national state and the politics of money*, London: Macmillan, pp 116–40.

Hood, C. (1991) 'A public management for all seasons?', *Public Administration*, vol 69, Spring, pp 3–19.

Horton, S. (2000) 'Introduction – the competency movement: its origins and impact on the public sector', *The International Journal of Public Sector Management*, vol 13, no 4, pp 306–18.

Howell, P. (1993) 'Public space and the public sphere: political theory and the historical geography of modernity', *Environment and Planning D: Society and Space*, vol 11, no 3, pp 303–22.

Howkins, J. (2007) *The creative economy*, London: Penguin.

Huczynski, A. (2006) *Management gurus* (revised edn), London: Routledge.

Hudson, J. (2003) 'E-galitarianism? The information society and New Labour's repositioning of welfare', *Critical Social Policy*, vol 23, no 2, pp 268–90.

Hughes, M. (2011) 'The challenges of informed citizen participation in change', *Transforming Government: People, Process and Policy*, vol 5, no 1, pp 68–80.

Hussain, M.M. and Howard, P.N. (2013) 'What best explains successful protest cascades? ICTs and the fuzzy causes of the Arab Spring', *International Studies Review*, vol 15, no 1, pp 48–66.

Hyman, R. (2001) *Understanding European trade unionism*, London: Sage.

Ivanova, M.N. (2011) 'Money, housing and world market: the dialectic of globalised production', *Cambridge Journal of Economics*, vol 35, no 5, pp 853–71.

Jackson, N. and Lilleker, D. (2011) 'Microblogging, constituency service and impression management: UK MPs and the use of Twitter', *The Journal of Legislative Studies*, vol 17, no 1, pp 86–105.

Jaeger, P.T. and Bertot, J.C. (2010) 'Transparency and technological change: ensuring equal and sustained public access to government information', *Government Information Quarterly*, vol 27, pp 371–6.

James, Z. (2006) 'Policing space: managing new travellers in England', *British Journal of Criminology*, vol 46, no 3, pp 470–85.

Jenkins, H. (2006) *Convergence culture*, New York: New York University Press.

Jessop, B. (2000) 'The state and the contradictions of the knowledge-driven economy', in J. Bryson, P.W. Daniels, N. Henry and J. Pollard (eds) *Knowledge, space, economy*, London: Routledge, pp 63–78.

Jessop, B. (2002) *The future of the capitalist state*, Cambridge: Polity.

Jessop, B. (2003) From Thatcherism to New Labour: neo-liberalism, workfarism, and labour market regulation', in H. Overbeek (ed) *The political economy of European employment*, London: Routledge, pp 137–53.

Jessop, B. (2010) 'From hegemony to crisis? The continuing ecological dominance of neoliberalism', in K. Birch and V. Mykhnenko (eds) *The rise and fall of neoliberalism*, London: Zed, pp 171–87.

Jessop, B. (2012) 'Narratives of crisis and crisis response: perspectives from North and South', in P. Utting, S. Razavi and R. V. Buchholz (eds) *The global crisis and transformative change*, London: Macmillan, pp 23–42.

Jessop, B. (2013) 'Revisiting the regulation approach: critical reflections on the contradictions, dilemmas, fixes and crisis dynamics of growth regimes', *Capital and Class*, vol 37, no 1, pp 5–24.

John, N.A. (2012) 'Sharing and Web 2.0: the emergence of a keyword', *New Media and Society*, vol 15, no 2, pp 167–82.

Johnson, R. (2007) 'Post-hegemony? I don't think so', *Theory, Culture and Society*, vol 24, no 3, pp 95–110.

Jones, T. and Newburn, T. (2002) 'Policy convergence and crime control in the USA and the UK: streams of influence and levels of impact', *Criminal Justice*, vol 2, no 2, pp 173–203.

Jordan, T. (1999) *Cyberpower*, London: Routledge.

Joseph, J. (2012) *The social in the global*, Cambridge: Cambridge University Press.

Juris, J.J. (2012) 'Reflections on the #Occupy Everywhere', *American Ethnologist*, vol 39, no 2, pp 259–79.

Kang, H. and McAllister, M.P. (2011) 'Selling you and your clicks: examining the audience commodification of Google', *tripleC*, vol 9, no 2, pp 141–53.

Kavaratzis, M. (2007) 'City marketing: the past, the present and some unresolved issues', *Geography Compass*, vol 1, no 3, pp 695–712.

Kay, G. (1979) 'Why labour is the starting point of capital', in D. Elson (ed), *Value: The representation of labour in capitalism*, London: CSE Books, pp 46–66.

Keenan, A. and Shiri, A. (2009) 'Sociability and social interaction on social networking websites', *Library Review*, vol 58, no 6, pp 438–50.

Khiabany, G. and Sreberny, A. (2007) 'The politics of/in blogging in Iran', *Comparative Studies of South Asia, Africa and the Middle East*, vol 27, no 3, pp 363–79.

Kiely, R. (2005) *The clash of globalisations*, Leiden: Brill.

Kim, J. (2012) 'The institutionalization of YouTube: from user-generated content to professionally generated content', *Media, Culture and Society*, vol 34, no 1, pp 53–67.

King, M. (2013) 'Disruption is not permitted: the policing and social control of Occupy Oakland', *Critical Criminology*, vol 21, no 4, pp 463–75.

Knight, J. and Johnson, J. (1999) 'What sort of equality does deliberative democracy require?' in J. Bohman and W. Rehg (eds), *Deliberative democracy: Essays on reason and politics*, Cambridge, MA: MIT Press.

Kohn, M. (2004) *Brave new neighborhoods*, London: Routledge.

Kolsaker, A. (2006) 'Reconceptualising egovernment as a tool of governance: the UK case', *Electronic Government*, vol 3, no 4, pp 347–55.

Kolsaker, A. and Lee-Kelley, L. (2008) 'Citizens' attitudes towards e-government and e-governance: a UK study', *International Journal of Public Sector Management*, vol 21, no 7, pp 723–38.

Korf, B. (2006) 'Cargo cult science, armchair empiricism and the idea of violent conflict', *Third World Quarterly*, vol 27, no 3, pp 459–76.

Kornberger, M. (2012) 'Governing the city: from planning to urban strategy', *Theory, Culture and Society*, vol 29, no 2, pp 84–106.

Kotamraju, N.P. and van der Geest, T.M. (2012) 'The tension between user-centred design and e-government services', *Behaviour and Information Technology*, vol 31, no 3, pp 261–73.

Kreiss, D. (2011) 'Open source as practice and ideology: the origin of Howard Dean's innovations in electoral politics', *Journal of Information Technology and Politics*, vol 8, no 3, pp 367–82.

Kreiss, D., Finn, M. and Turner, F. (2011) 'The limits of peer production: some reminders from Max Weber for the network society', *New Media and Society*, vol 13, no 2, pp 243–59.

Kurtulus, E.N. (2011) 'The "new terrorism" and its critics', *Studies in Conflict and Terrorism*, vol 34, no 6, pp 476–500.

Lacher, H. (2003) 'Putting the state in its place: the critique of state-centrism and its limits', *Review of International Studies*, vol 29, no 4, pp 521–41.

Laguerre, M.S. (2004) 'Virtual time: the processuality of the cyberweek', *Information, Communication and Society*, vol 7, no 2, pp 223–47.

Lam, S.K. and Riedl, J. (2011) 'The past, present and future of Wikipedia', *Social Computing*, vol 44, no 3, pp 87–90.

Lang, A.S. and Lang/Levitsky, D. (2012) *Dreaming in public: Building the occupation movement*, Oxford: New Internationalist Publications.

Lange, P.G. (2007) 'Publicly private and privately public: social networking on YouTube', *Journal of Computer-Mediated Communication*, vol 13, no 1, pp 361–80.

Langley, P. (2008) *The everyday life of global finance*, Oxford: Oxford University Press.

Langman, L. (2005) 'From virtual public spheres to global justice: a critical theory of internetworked social movements', *Sociological Theory*, vol 23, no 1, pp 42–74.

Lansley, S. (2012) *The cost of inequality*, London: Gibson Square Books.

Lapavitsas, C. (2011) 'Theorizing financialization', *Work, Employment and Society*, vol 25, no 4, pp 611–26.

Lapsley, I. (2008) 'The NPM agenda: back to the future', *Financial Accountability and Management*, vol 24, no 1, pp 77–96.

Larner, W. and Walters, W. (2004) Globalization and governmentality', *Alternatives*, vol 29, no 5, pp 495–514.

Larrain, J. (1983) *Marxism and ideology*, London: Macmillan.

Larsson, A.O. and Moe, H. (2011) 'Studying political microblogging: Twitter users in the 2010 Swedish election campaign', *New Media and Society*, vol 14, no 5, pp 729–47.

Lash, S. (2002) *Critique of information*, London: Sage.

Lash, S. (2007) 'Power after hegemony: cultural studies in mutation', *Theory, Culture and Society*, vol 24, no 3, pp 55–78.

Lash, S. and Urry, J. (1987) *The end of organized capitalism*, London: Polity.

Lash, S. and Urry, J. (1994) *Economies of signs and space*, London: Sage.

Latour, B. (2005) *Reassembling the social*, Oxford: Oxford University Press.

Lavin, M. and Whysall, P. (2004) 'From enterprise to empowerment: the evolution of an Anglo-American approach to strategic urban economic regeneration', *Strategic Change*, vol 13, no 4, pp 219–29.

Lefebvre, H. (1991) *The production of space*, trans D. Nicholson-Smith, Oxford: Blackwell.

Leicht, K.T., Walter, T., Sainsaulieu, I. and Davies, S. (2009) 'New public management and new professionalism across nations and contexts', *Current Sociology*, vol 57, no 4, pp 581–605.

Levine, A. (1988) *Arguing for socialism* (revised edn), London: Verso.

Lewis, J. (2001) *Constructing public opinion*, New York: Columbia University Press.

Leydesdorff, L. (2006) *The knowledge-based economy*, Boca Raton, FL: Universal Publications.

Leys, C. and Player, S. (2011) *The plot against the NHS*, London: Merlin Press.

Liberty (2005) *Newsletter* (Summer). Available at: www.liberty-human-rights.org.uk/publications/2-newsletter/summer-05.pdf (accessed 14 June 2007).

Lindsay, C., McQuaid, R.W. and Dutton, M. (2008) 'Inter-agency cooperation and new approaches to employability', *Social Policy and Administration*, vol 42, no 7, pp 715–32.

Lippert, R. (2012) '"Clean and safe" passage: Business Improvement Districts, urban security modes, and knowledge brokers', *European Urban and Regional Studies*, vol 19, no 2, pp 167–80.

Lips, M. (2010) 'Rethinking citizen–government relationships in the age of digital identity: insights from research', *Information Polity*, vol 15, no 4, pp 273–89.

Lips, M., Taylor, J.A. and Organ, J. (2009) 'Managing citizen identity information in e- government service relationships in the UK', *Public Management Review*, vol 11, no 6, pp 833–56.

Lister, R. (2004) 'The Third Way's social investment state', in J. Lewis and R. Surender (eds) *Welfare state change: Towards a third way?* Oxford: Oxford University Press, pp 157–81.

Little, A. (2007) 'Between disagreement and consensus: unravelling the democratic paradox', *Australian Journal of Political Science*, vol 42, no 1, pp 143–59.

Livingstone, R. (2011) 'Better at life stuff: consumption, identity, and class in Apple's "Get a Mac" campaign', *Journal of Communication Inquiry*, vol 35, no 3, pp 210–34.

Livingstone, S. and Lunt, P. (2007) 'Representing citizens and consumers in media and communications regulation', *The ANNALS of the American Academy of Political and Social Science*, vol 611, no 1, pp 51–65.

Lodge, M. and Gill, D. (2011) 'Toward a new era of administrative reform? The myth of post-NPM in New Zealand', *Governance*, 24, no 1, pp 141–66.

Lodge, M. and Hood, C. (2005) 'Symposium introduction: competency and higher civil servants', *Public Administration*, vol 83, no 4, pp 779–87.

Lovering, J. (2010) 'Will the recession prove to be a turning point in planning and urban development thinking?', *International Planning Studies*, vol 15, no 3, pp 227–43.

Lowndes, V. and Squires, S. (2012) 'Cuts, collaboration and creativity', *Public Money and Management*, vol 32, no 6, pp 401–8.

Lucio, M.M. and Stewart, P. (1997) 'The paradox of contemporary labour process theory: the rediscovery of labour and the disappearance of collectivism', *Capital and Class* Summer, no 62, pp 49–77.

Lundborg, T. and Vaughan-Williams, N. (2011) 'Resilience, critical infrastructure, and molecular security: the excess of "life" in biopolitics', *International Political Sociology*, vol 5, no 4, pp 367–83.

Lynch, M. (2011) 'After Egypt: the limits and promise of online challenges to the authoritarian Arab state', *Perspectives on Politics*, vol 9, no 2, pp 301–10.

Lyon, D. (2004) 'Globalizing surveillance: comparative and sociological perspectives', *International Sociology*, vol 19, no 2, pp 135–49.

Macauley, M. and Lawton, A. (2006) 'From virtue to competence: changing the principle of public service', *Public Administration Review*, vol 66, no 5, pp 702–10.

McCarthy, J.D. and McPhail, C. (2006) 'Places of protest: the public forum in principle and practice', *Mobilization*, vol 11, no 2, pp 229–47.

McChesney, R.W. (2013) *Digital disconnect*, New York: The New Press.

McCulloch, A., Mohan, J. and Smith, J.P. (2012) 'Patterns of social capital, voluntary activity, and area deprivation in England', *Environment and Planning A*, vol 44, no 5, pp 1130–47.

Mace, R. (1976) *Trafalgar Square: emblem of an empire*, London: Lawrence and Wishart.

McGuinness, F., Cracknell, R., Davies, M. and Taylor, M. (2012) 'UK election statistics: 1918–2012', *House of Commons Library Research Paper 12/43*, August, pp 1–57.

McInroy, N. (2000) 'Urban regeneration and public space: the story of an urban park', *Space and Polity*, vol 4, no 1, pp 23–40.

Mackenzie, A. and Vurdubakis, T. (2011) 'Codes and codings in crisis: signification, performativity, and excess', *Theory, Culture and Society*, vol 28, no 6, pp 3–23.

McKeown, P. (2009) *Information technology and the networked economy* (2nd edn), Boston, MA: Thomson Course Technology Publishing.

McKnight, A. (2005) 'Employment: tackling poverty through "work for those who can"', in J. Hills and K. Stewart (eds) *A more equal society? New Labour, poverty, inequality and exclusion*, Bristol: Policy Press, pp 23–46.

McLaughlin, C. and Vitak, J. (2011) 'Norm evolution and violation on Facebook', *New Media and Society*, vol 4, no 2, pp 299–315.

McLaughlin, E. and Baker, J. (2007) 'Equality, social justice and social welfare: a road map to the new egalitarianisms', *Social Policy and Society*, vol 6, no 1, pp 53–68.

McLaughlin, L. and Pickard, V. (2005) 'What is bottom-up about global internet governance?' *Global Media and Communication*, vol 1, no 3, pp 357–73.

MacLeod, G. (2011) 'Urban politics reconsidered: growth machine to post-democratic city?' *Urban Studies*, vol 48, no 12, pp 2629–60.

MacLeod, G. and Ward, K. (2002) 'Spaces of utopia and dystopia: landscaping the contemporary city', *Geografiska Annaler*, vol 84, no 3–4, pp 153–70.

Macmillan, R. (2011) '"Supporting" the voluntary sector in an age of austerity: the UK coalition government's consultation on improving support for frontline civil society organisations in England', *Voluntary Sector Review*, vol 2, no 1, pp 115–24.

McNally, D. (1993) *Against the market*, London: Verso.

McNeal, R., Hale, K. and Dotterweich, L. (2008) 'Citizen–government interaction and the internet: expectations and accomplishments in contact, quality, and trust', *Journal of Information Technology & Politics*, vol 5, no 2, pp 213–29.

Maeckelbergh, M. (2012) 'Horizontal democracy now: from alterglobalization to occupation', *Interface: A Journal For and about Social Movements*, vol 4, no 1, pp 207–34.

Magro, M.J. (2012) 'A review of social media use in e-government', *Administrative Science*, vol 2, no 2, pp 148–61.

Manilov, M. (2013) 'Occupy at one year: growing the roots of a movement', *The Sociological Quarterly*, vol 54, no 2, pp 206–13.

Mansour, E. (2012) 'The role of social networking sites (SNSs) in the January 25th revolution in Egypt', *Library Review* vol 61, no 2, pp 128–59.

Marazzi, C. (2008) *Capital and language*, trans G. Conti, Los Angeles, CA: Semiotext(e).

Marazzi, C. (2011) *Capital and affects*, trans G. Mecchia, Los Angeles, CA: Semiotext(e).

Marcuse, P. (2005) '"The City" as perverse metaphor', *City*, vol 9, no 2, pp 247–54.

Marden, P. (2011) 'The digitised public sphere: re-defining democratic cultures or phantasmagoria?' *Javnost – The Public*, vol 18, no 1, pp 5–20.

Marsh, D. (2011) 'Late modernity and the changing nature of politics: two cheers for Henrik Bang', *Critical Policy Studies*, vol 5, no 1, pp 73–89.

Marston, G. (2006) 'Employment services in an age of e-government', *Information, Communication and Society*, vol 9, no 1, pp 83–103.

Marx, G.T. (2007) 'Personal information, borders, and the new surveillance studies', *Annual Review of Law and Social Science*, vol 3, pp 375–95.

Marx, K. (1988) *Capital*, vol 1, London: Pelican.

Marx, K. and Engels, F. (1994) *The German ideology*, ed C.J. Arthur, London: Lawrence and Wishart.

Mayer, M. (2013) 'First world urban activism: beyond austerity urbanism and creative city politics', *City*, vol 17, no 1, pp 5–19.

Migone, A. (2007) 'Hedonistic consumerism: patterns of consumption in contemporary capitalism', *Review of Radical Political Economics*, vol 39, no 2, pp 173–200.

Milbourne, L. and Cushman, M. (2013) 'From the third sector to the Big Society: how changing UK government policies have eroded third sector trust', *Voluntas*, vol 24, no 2, pp.485–508.

Min, S.-J. (2007) 'Online vs. face-to-face deliberation: effects on civic engagement', *Journal of Computer-Mediated Communication*, vol 12, no 4, pp 1369–87.

Mitchell, D. (1995) 'The end of public space? People's park, definitions of the public, and democracy', *Annals of the Association of American Geographers*, vol 85, no 1, pp 108–33.

Mitchell, D. and Staeheli, L.A. (2005) 'Permitting protest: parsing the fine geography of dissent in America', *Journal of Urban and Regional Research*, vol 29, no 4, pp 796–813.

Moore, D.R., Cheng, M.-I. and Dainty, A.R.J. (2002) 'Competence, competency and competencies: performance assessment in organisation', *Work Study*, vol 51, no 6, pp 314–19.

Moore, S. (2011) *New trade union activism*, London: Palgrave.

Moran, J. (2005) 'State power in the war on terror: a comparative analysis of the UK and USA', *Crime, Law and Social Change*, vol 44, no 4–5, pp 335–59.

Moran, J. (2007) 'Generating more heat than light? Debates on civil liberties in the UK', *Policing*, vol 1, no 1, pp 80–93.

Morris, M. (2001) *Rethinking the communicative turn*, New York: SUNY.

Mosco, V. (2009) *The political economy of communication*, London: Sage.

Moshe, M. (2012) 'Media time squeezing: the privatization of media time sphere', *Television and New Media*, vol 13, no 1, pp 68–88.

Mouffe, C. (2000) *The democratic paradox*, London: Verso.

Mouffe, C. (2005) *On the political*, London: Routledge.

Mulqueen, T. and Tataryn, A. (2012) 'Don't occupy this movement: thinking law in social movement', *Law Critique*, vol 23, no 3, pp 283–98.

Munck, R. (2002) 'Global civil society: myths and prospects', *Voluntas: International Journal of Voluntary and Nonprofit Organizations*, vol 13, no 4, pp 349–61.

Murphy, E.C. (2009) 'Theorizing ICTs in the Arab world: informational capitalism and the public sphere', *International Studies Quarterly*, vol 53, no 4, pp 1131–53.

Nanabhay, M. and Farmanfarmaian, R. (2011) 'From spectacle to spectacular: how physical space, social media and mainstream broadcast amplified the public sphere in Egypt's "Revolution"', *Journal of North African Studies*, vol 16, no 4, pp 573–603.

Newman, I. (2011) 'Work as a route out of poverty: a critical evaluation of the UK welfare to work policy', *Policy Studies*, vol 32, no 2, pp 91–108.

Newman, J. and Clarke, J. (2009) *Publics, politics and power*, London: Sage.

Nielsen, L.B. (2004) *License to harass*, Princeton, NJ: Princeton University Press.

Noakes, J.A., Klocke, B.V. and Gillham, P.F. (2005) 'Whose streets? Police and protestor struggles over space in Washington, DC, 29–30 September 2001', *Policing and Society*, vol 15, no3, pp 235–54.

Noordegraaf, M. (2000) 'Professional sense-makers: managerial competencies amidst ambiguity', *The International Journal of Public Sector Management*, vol 13, no 4, pp 319–32.

Noordegraaf, M. and Newman, J. (2011) 'Managing in disorderly times', *Public Management Review*, vol 13, no 4, pp 513–38.

Norris, C., McCahill, M. and Wood, D. (2004) 'The growth of CCTV: a global perspective on the international diffusion of video surveillance in publicly accessible space', *Surveillance and Society*, vol 2, no 2–3, pp 110–35.

O'Connor, J. (2010) 'Marxism and the three movements of neoliberalism', *Critical Sociology*, vol 36, no 5, pp 691–715.

O'Leary, D. (2008) 'Wikis: from each according to his knowledge', *Computer*, vol 41, no 2, pp 34–41.

Olesen, T. (2004) 'The transnational Zapatista solidarity network: an infrastructure analysis', *Global Networks*, vol 4, no 1, pp 89–107.

Olesen, T. (2005) 'Transnational publics: new spaces of social movement activism and the problem of long-sightedness', *Current Sociology*, vol 53, no 3, pp 419–40.

O'Malley, P. (2010) 'Resilient subjects: uncertainty, warfare and liberalism', *Economy and Society*, vol 39, no 4, pp 488–09.

Orhangazi, Ö. (2011) '"Financial" vs. "real": an overview of the contradictory role of finance', *Research in Political Economy*, vol 27, pp 112–48.

Örnebring, H. (2008) 'The consumer as producer – of what? User-generated tabloid content in *The Sun* (UK) and *Aftonbladet* (Sweden)', *Journalism Studies*, vol 9, no 5, pp 771–85.

Osborne, S. and Brown, L. (2011) 'Innovation, public policy and public services delivery in the UK: the word that would be king?', *Public Administration*, vol 89, no 4, pp 1335–50.

Otero, G. (2004) 'Global economy, local politics: indigenous struggles, civil society and democracy', *Canadian Journal of Political Science*, vol 37, no 2, pp 325–46.

Pan, S.L. and Leidner, D.E. (2003) 'Bridging communities of practices with information technology in pursuit of global knowledge sharing', *Journal of Strategic Information Systems*, vol 12, no 1, pp 71–88.

Panagiotopoulos, P., Sams, S., Elliman, T. and Fitzgerald, G. (2011) 'Do social networking groups support online petitions?' *Transforming Government: People, Process and Policy*, vol 5, no 1, pp 20–31.

Pantazis, C. and Pemberton, S. (2012) 'Reconfiguring security and liberty: political discourses and public opinion in the new century', *British Journal of Criminology*, vol 52, no 3, pp 651–67.

Papacharissi, Z. (2011) 'A networked self', in Z. Papacharissi (ed), *A networked self: Identity, community, and culture on social network sites*, London: Routledge, pp 304–18.

Papke, L.E. (1993) 'What do we know about Enterprise Zones?' in J.M. Poterba (ed) *Tax policy and the economy*, Cambridge, MA: The MIT Press, pp 37–72.

Pateman, C. (1970) *Participation and democratic theory*, Cambridge: Cambridge University Press.

Patrick, A. (2013) 'Regulating surveillance, respecting private life', in J. Killock, P. Bradwell, and B. Zevenbergen (eds), *Digital surveillance*, London: Open Rights Group, pp 17–29.

Pearce, J. (2013) 'Power and the twenty-first century activist: from the neighbourhood to the square', *Development and Change*, vol 44, no 3, pp 639–63.

Peck, J. (1995) 'Moving and shaking: business elites, state localism and urban privatism', *Progress in Human Geography*, vol 19, no 1, pp 16–46.

Peck, J. and Tickell, A. (2002) 'Neoliberalizing space', *Antipode*, vol 34, no 3, pp 380–404.

Penney, J. and Dadas, C. (2013) '(Re)tweeting in the service of protest: digital composition and circulation in the Occupy Wall Street movement', *New Media and Society*, vol 16, no 1, pp 74–90.

Perez, C. (2009) 'The double bubble at the turn of the century: technological roots and structural implications', *Cambridge Journal of Economics*, vol 33, no 4, pp 779–805.

Picciotto, S. (1991) 'The internationalisation of the state', *Capital and Class*, no 43, Spring, pp 43–63.

Pickard, V.W. (2006) 'United yet autonomous: Indymedia and the struggle to sustain a radical democratic network', *Media, Culture and Society*, vol 28, no 3, pp 315–36.

Pickerill, J. (2006) 'Radical politics on the net', *Parliamentary Affairs*, vol 59, no 2, pp 266–82.

Pickerill, J. and Chatterton, P. (2006) 'Notes towards autonomous geographies: creation, resistance and self-management as survival tactics', *Progress in Human Geography*, vol 30, no 6, pp 730–46.

Pierre, J. and Stoker, G. (2002) 'Toward multi-level governance', in P. Dunleavy, A. Gamble, I. Holliday and G. Peele (eds) *Developments in British politics 6*, London: Macmillan, pp 29–46.

Pike, A., Dawley, S. and Tomaney, J. (2010) 'Resilience, adaptation and adaptability', *Cambridge Journal of Regions, Economy and Society*, vol 3, no 1, pp 59–70.

Platen, S. and Deuze, M. (2003) 'Indymedia journalism: a radical way of making, selecting and sharing news?' *Journalism*, vol 4, no 3, pp 336–55.

Pleace, N. (2007) 'Workless people and surveillant mashups: social policy and data sharing in the UK', *Information, Communication and Society*, vol 10, no 6, pp 943–60.

Polleta, F., Chen, P.C.B. and Anderson, C. (2009) 'Is information good for deliberation? Link-posting in an online forum', *Public Deliberation*, vol 5, no 1, pp 1–20.

Pollitt, C. (2011) 'Mainstreaming technological change in the study of public management', *Public Policy and Administration*, vol 26, no 4, pp 377–97.

Pollock, V.L. and Sharp, J. (2012) 'Real participation or the tyranny of participatory practice? Public art and community involvement in the regeneration of the Raploch, Scotland', *Urban Studies*, vol 49, no 14, pp 3063–79.

Porter, M. (1985) *Competitive advantage*, New York: Free Press.

Postigo, H. (2011) 'Questioning the Web 2.0 discourse: social roles, production, values, and the case of the human rights portal', *The Information Society*, vol 27, no 3, pp 181–93.

Postone, M. (1996) *Time, labor and social domination*, Cambridge: Cambridge University Press.

Potts, J., Cunningham, S., Hartley, J. and Ormerod, P. (2008) 'Social network markets: a new definition of the creative industries', *Journal of Cultural Economy*, vol 32, no 3, pp 166–85.

Poulantzas, N. (2000) *State, power, socialism* (new edn), trans P. Camiller, London: Verso.

Prainsack, B. and Toom, V. (2010) 'The Prüm regime: situated dis/empowerment in transnational DNA profile exchange', *British Journal of Criminology*, vol 50, no 6, pp 1117–35.

Prahalad, C.K. and Hamel, G. (1990) 'The core competence of the corporation', *Harvard Business Review*, May–June, pp 79–90.

Price, V. and Cappella, J.N. (2002) 'Online deliberation and its influence: the electronic dialogue project in Campaign 2000', *IT and Society*, vol 1, no.1, pp 303–29.

Purcell, M. (2009) 'Resisting neoliberalization: communicative planning or counter- hegemonic movements?' *Planning Theory*, vol 8, no 2, pp 140–65.

Raco, M. and Street, E. (2012) 'Resilience planning, economic change and the politics of post-recession development in London and Hong Kong', *Urban Studies*, vol 49, no 5, pp 1065–87.

Rainie, L. and Wellman, B. (2012) *Networked: The new social operating system*, Cambridge, MA: MIT Press.

Reddick, C.G. (2011) 'Citizen interaction and e-government: evidence for the managerial, consultative, and participatory models', *Transforming Government: People, Process and Policy*, vol 5, no 2, pp 167–84.

Rehmann, J. (2013) 'Occupy Wall Street and the question of hegemony: a Gramscian analysis', *Socialism and Democracy*, vol 27, no 1, pp 1–18.

Richter, D.C. (1981) *Riotous Victorians*, Athens and London: Ohio University Press.

Ridderstråle, J. and Nordström, K. (2008) *Funky business forever: How to enjoy capitalism* (3rd edn), London: Prentice Hall & Financial Times.

Roberts, A. (2012) 'Why the Occupy movement failed', *Public Administration Review*, vol 72, no 5, pp 754–62.

Roberts, J.M. (2004) 'What's social about social capital?' *British Journal of Politics and International Relations*, vol 6, pp 471–93.

Roberts, J.M. (2009) *The competent public sphere*, London: Palgrave.

Roberts, J.M. and Crossley, N. (2004) 'Introduction', in N. Crossley and J.M. Roberts (eds) *After Habermas: New perspectives on the public sphere*, Oxford: Blackwell, pp 1–27.

Roberts, J.M. and Devine, F. (2004) 'Some everyday experiences of voluntarism: social capital, pleasure, and the contingency of participation', *Social Politics*, vol 11, no 2, pp 280–96.

Rose, M. (2002) 'The seductions of resistance: power, politics, and a performative style of systems', *Environment and Planning D: Society and Space*, vol 20, no 4, pp 383–400.

Rose, N. (1999) *Powers of freedom*, Cambridge: Cambridge University Press.

Ross, D. (2013) 'The place of free and open source software in the social apparatus of accumulation', *Science & Society*, vol 77, no 2, pp 202–26.

Saad-Filho, A. (1997) 'Concrete and abstract labour in Marx's theory of value', *Review of Political Economy*, vol 9, no 4, pp 457–77.

Saad-Filho, A. (2002) *The value of Marx*, London: Routledge.

Saccarelli, E. (2004) 'Empire, Rifondazione Comunista, and the politics of spontaneity', *New Political Science*, vol 26, no 4, pp 569–91.

Sager, T. (2011) 'Neo-liberal urban planning policies: A literature survey 1990–2010', *Progress in Planning*, vol 76, no 4, pp 147–99.

Sakr, N. (2002) 'Arab satellite channels between state and private ownership: current and future implications', *TBS Archives*, no 9, Autumn. Available at: www.tbsjournal.com/Archives/Fall02/Sakr_paper.html (accessed 27 June 2013).

Salskov-Iversen, D., Hansen, H.K. and Bislev, S. (2000) 'Governmentality, globalization, and local practice: transformations of a hegemonic discourse', *Alternatives*, vol 25, no 2, pp 183–222.

Salter, L. (2005) 'Colonization tendencies in the development of the World Wide Web', *New Media and Society*, vol 7, no 3, pp 291–309.

Sassen, S. (2002) 'Towards a sociology of information technology', *Current Sociology*, vol 50, no 3, pp 365–88.

Savat, D. (2013) *Uncoding the digital*, London: Palgrave.

Schweickart, D. (2002) *After capitalism*, Oxford: Rowman and Littlefield.

Scott, A. (1990) *Ideology and the new social movements*, London: Unwin Hyman.

Segell, G.M. (2007) 'Reform and transformation: the UK's Serious Organized Crime Agency', *International Journal of Intelligence and Counter Intelligence*, vol 20, no 2, pp 217–39.

Sennett, R. (2006) *The culture of the new capitalism*, New Haven, CT: Yale University Press.

Shapely, P. (2011) 'The entrepreneurial city: the role of local government and city-centre redevelopment in post-war industrial English cities', *Twentieth Century British History*, vol 22, no 4, pp 498–520.

Shaw, K. (2012) 'The rise of the resilient local authority?' *Local Government Studies*, vol 38, no 3, pp 281–300.

Sheller, M. (2004) 'Mobile publics: beyond the network perspective', *Environment and Planning D: Society and Space*, vol 22, no 1, pp 39–52.

Shepard, B.H. (2012) 'Labor and Occupy Wall Street: common causes and uneasy alliances', *WorkingUSA*, vol 15, March, pp 121–34.

Silver, H., Scott, A. and Yurikazepov, Y. (2010) 'Participation in urban contention and deliberation', *International Journal of Urban and Regional Research*, vol 34, no 3, pp 453–77.

Sinekopova, G.V. (2006) 'Building the public sphere: bases and biases', *Journal of Communication*, vol 56, no 3, pp 505–22.

Sites, W., Chaskin, R.J. and Parks, V. (2007) 'Framing community practice for the 21st century: multiple traditions, multiple challenges', *Journal of Urban Affairs*, vol 29, no 5, pp 519–41.

Sitrin, M. (2012) 'Horizontalism and the Occupy Movements', *Dissent*, Spring, pp 74–5.

Slater, T. (2008) '"A literal necessity to be re-placed": a rejoinder to the gentrification debate', *International Journal of Urban and Regional Research*, vol 32, no 1, pp 212–23.

Smith, A. (2012) '"Monday will never be the same again": the transformation of employment and work in a public-private partnership', *Employment, Work and Society*, vol 26, no 1, pp 95–110.

Smith, M.E.G. (2010) *Global capitalism in crisis*, Halifax and Winnipeg: Fernwood Publishing.

Smith, T. (2006) *Globalisation: A systematic Marxian account*, Leiden: Brill.

Sparks, C. (2005) 'Media and the global public sphere: an evaluative approach', in W. de Jong, M. Shaw and N. Stammers (eds) *Global activism, global media*, London: Pluto, pp 34–49.

Sparks, C. (2006) 'Contradictions in capitalist media practices', in L. Artz, S. Macek and D.L. Cloud (eds) *Marxism and communication studies*, New York: Peter Lang, pp 111–32.

Spencer, A. (2011) 'Sic[k] of the "new terrorism" debate? A response to our critics', *Critical Studies on Terrorism*, vol 4, no 3, pp 459–67.

Staeheli, L.A. and Mitchell, D. (2006) 'USA's destiny? Regulating space and creating community in American shopping malls', *Urban Studies*, vol 43, no 5–6, pp 977–92.

Steijn, B., Klijn, E.-H. and Edelenbos, J. (2011) 'Public-private partnerships: added value by organizational form or management?' *Public Administration*, vol 89, no 4, pp1235–52.

Stevenson, N. (2003) 'Cultural citizenship in the "cultural" society: a cosmopolitan approach', *Citizenship Studies*, vol 7, no 3, pp 331–48.

Stewart, P., McBride, J., Greenwood, I., Stirling, J., Holgate, J., Tattersall, A., Stephenson, C. and Wray, D. (2009) 'Introduction', in J. McBride and I. Greenwood (eds) *Community unionism*, London: Palgrave, pp 3–20.

Stromer-Galley, J. (2003) 'Voting and the public sphere: conversations on internet voting', *PS*, October, pp 727–31.

Stromer-Galley, J., Webb, N. and Muhlberger, P. (2012) 'Deliberative e-rulemaking project: challenges to enacting real world deliberation', *Journal of Information, Technology and Politics*, vol 9, pp 82–96.

Szerszynski, B. and Urry, J. (2006) 'Visuality, mobility and the cosmopolitan: inhabiting the world from afar', *The British Journal of Sociology*, vol 57, no 1, pp 113–31.

Tabb, W.K. (2005) 'Capital, class and the state in the global political economy', *Globalizations*, vol 2, no 1, pp 47–60.

Tapscott, D. and Williams, A.D. (2008) *Wikinomics* (revised edn), London: Atlantic Books.

Tarafdar, M. and Gordon, S.R. (2007) 'Understanding the influence of information systems competencies on process innovation: a resource-based view', *Journal of Strategic Information Systems*, vol 16, no 4, pp 353–92.

Tatarchevskiy, T. (2011) 'The "popular" culture of internet activism', *New Media and Society*, vol 13, no 2, pp 297–313.

Taylor, G. and Mathers, A. (2008) 'Organising unions, organising communities? Trades union councils and community union politics in England and Wales', Centre for Employment Studies Research, Working Paper 10, Bristol Business School, University of the West of England.

Taylor, M. (2007) 'Community participation in the real world: opportunities and pitfalls in new governance spaces', *Urban Studies*, vol 44, no 2, pp 297–317.

Taylor, P.A. (2005) 'From hackers to hacktivists: speed bumps on the global information superhighway?' *New Media and Society*, vol 7, no 5, pp 625–46.

Teicher, J., Hughes, O. and Dow, N. (2002) 'E-government: a new route to public sector quality', *Managing Service Quality*, vol 12, no 6, pp 384–93.

Terranova, T. (2004) *Network culture*, London: Pluto.

Terry, L.D. (2005) 'The thinning of administrative institutions in the hollow state', *Administration and Society*, vol 37, no 4, pp 426–44.

Tewksbury, D. (2013) 'Online-offline knowledge sharing in the Occupy movement: Howtooccupy.org and discursive communities of practice', *American Communication Journal*, vol 15, no 1, pp 11–23.

Theocharis, Y. (2012) 'Cuts, tweets, solidarity, and mobilisation: how the internet shaped the student occupations', *Parliamentary Affairs*, vol 65, no 1, pp 162–94.

Theodore, N. and Peck, J. (2011) 'Framing neoliberal urbanism: translating "commonsense" urban policy across the OECD zone', *European Urban and Regional Studies*, vol 19, no 1, pp 20–41.

Thiel, S. van (2012) 'Debate: from trendsetter to laggard? Quango reform in the UK', *Public Money and Management*, vol 32, no 5, pp 399–400.

Thompson, J.B. (2005) 'The new visibility', *Theory, Culture and Society*, vol 22, no 6, pp 31–51.

Thorson, K., Driscoll, K., Ekdale, B., Edgerly, S., Thompson, L.G., Schrock, A., Swartz, L., Vraga, E.K. and Wells, C. (2013) 'YouTube, Twitter and the Occupy movement: connecting content and circulation practices', *Information, Communication and Society*, vol 16, no 3, pp 421–51.

Thrift, N. and French, S. (2002) 'The automatic production of space', *Transactions of the Institute of British Geographers* (New Series) vol 27, no 3, pp 309–35.

Tkacz, N. (2010) 'Wikipedia and the politics of mass collaboration', *PLATFORM: Journal of Media and Communication*, vol 2, no 2, pp 40–53.

Tormey, S. (2006) '"Not in my name": Deleuze, Zapatismo and the critique of representation', *Parliamentary Affairs*, vol 59, no 1, pp 1–17.

Tufekci, Z. (2008) 'Grooming, gossip, Facebook and MySpace', *Information, Communication and Society*, vol 11, no 4, pp 544–64.

Tufekci, Z. and Wilson, C. (2012) 'Social media and the decision to participate in political protest: observations from Tahrir Square', *Journal of Communication*, vol 62, no 2, pp 363–79.

Turner, B.S. (2007) 'The enclave society: towards a sociology of immobility', *European Journal of Social Theory*, vol 10, no 2, pp 287–304.

Turner, G. (2009) *No way to run an economy*, London: Pluto.

Ugarteche, O. (2007) 'Transnationalizing the public sphere: a critique of Fraser', *Theory, Culture and Society*, vol 24, no 4, pp 65–9.

UNCSTD (1997) 'Elements of the resolution of UNCSTD adopted at its 12–16 May 1997 session', cited in R. Mansell and U. Wehn (eds) *Knowledge societies: Information technology for sustainable development*, Oxford: Oxford University Press, pp 266–71.

Upchurch, M. and Mathers, A. (2011) 'Neoliberal globalization and trade unionism: toward radical political unionism?' *Critical Sociology*, vol 38, no 2, pp 265–80.

van den Broek, D. (2010) 'From Terranova to terra firma: a critique of the role of free labour and the digital economy', *Economic and Labour Relations Review*, vol 20, no 2, pp 123–34.

van Deusen Jr, R. (2002) 'Public space design as class warfare: urban design, the "right to the city" and the production of Clinton Square, Syracuse, NY', *GeoJournal*, vol 58, nos 2–3, pp 149–58.

van Dijck, J. (2009) 'Users like you? Theorizing agency in user-generated content', *Media, Culture and Society*, vol 31, no 1, pp 41–58.

van Dijck, J. and Nieborg, D. (2009) 'Wikinomics and its discontents: a critical analysis of Web 2.0 business manifestos', *New Media and Society*, vol 11, no 5, pp 855–74.

Virtanen, T. (2000) 'Changing competencies of public managers: tensions in commitment', *The International Journal of Public Sector Management*, vol 13, no 4, pp 333–41.

Vitale, A.S. (2005) 'From negotiated management to command and control: how the New York Police Department polices protest', *Policing and Society*, vol 15, no 3, pp 283–304.

Voloshinov, V.N. (1973) *Marxism and the philosophy of language*, trans L. Matejka and I.R. Titunik, New York: Seminar Press.

Voyce, M. (2006) 'Shopping malls in Australia: the end of public space and the rise of "consumerist citizenship"?' *Journal of Sociology*, vol 42, no 3, pp 269–86.

Waddington, P.A.J. (1994) 'Coercion and accommodation: policing public order after the Public Order Act', *British Journal of Sociology*, vol 45, no 3, pp 367–85.

Wahl, A. (2011) *The rise and fall of the welfare state*, London: Pluto.

Waiton, S. (2010) 'The politics of surveillance: Big Brother on prozac', *Surveillance and Society*, vol 8, no 1, pp 61–84.

Walterova, I. and Tveit, L. (2012) 'Digital local agenda: bridging the digital divide', *Transforming Government: People, Process and Policy*, vol 6, no 4, pp 345–57.

Walters, W. (2002) 'Social capital and political sociology: re-imagining politics?' *Sociology*, vol 36, no 2, pp 377–97.

Warhurst, C. (2008) 'The knowledge economy, skills and government labour market intervention', *Policy Studies*, vol 29, no 1, pp 71–86.

Warner, M. (2002) *Publics and counterpublics*, New York: Zone Books.

Watson, S. (2006) '"England expects": Nelson as a symbol of local and national identity within the museum', *Museum and Society*, vol 4, no 3, pp 129–51.

Wayne, M. (2003) *Marxism and media studies*, London: Pluto.

Webster, W. (2009) 'CCTV policy in the UK', *Surveillance and Society*, vol 6, no 1, pp 10–22.

Weintraub, J. (1997) 'The theory and politics of the public/private distinction', in J. Weintraub and K. Kumar (eds) *Public and private in thought and practice*, Chicago, IL: The University of Chicago Press, pp 1–42.

Welch, M. (2003) 'Trampling human rights on the war on terror: implications to the sociology of denial', *Critical Criminology*, vol 12, no 1, pp 1–20.

Welsh, I. (2007) 'In defence of civilisation: terrorism and environmental politics in the 21st century', *Environmental Politics*, vol 16, no 2, pp 356–75.

Wettergren, A. (2009) 'Fun and laughter: culture jamming and the emotional regime of late capitalism', *Social Movement Studies*, vol 8, no 1, pp 1–15.

Whitfield, D. (2012) *In place of austerity*, Nottingham: Spokesman.

Wikland, H. (2005) 'A Habermasian analysis of the deliberative democratic potential of ICT-enabled services in Swedish municipalities', *New Media and Society*, vol 7, no 2, pp 247–70.

Wilhelm, A.G. (1999) 'Virtual sounding boards: how deliberative is online political discussion?' in B.N. Hague and B.D. Loader (eds) *Digital democracy*, London: Routledge, pp 154–78.

Wilhelm, A.G. (2004) *Digital nation*, Cambridge, MA: The MIT Press.

Wilkin, P. (2000) 'Solidarity in a global age – Seattle and beyond', *Journal of World-Systems Research*, vol 11, no 1, pp 19–64.

Williamson, O.E. (1999) 'Strategy research: governance and competence perspectives', *Strategic Management Journal*, vol 20, no 12, pp 1087–108.

Wills, J. (2012) 'The geography of community and political organisation in London today', *Political Geography*, vol 31, no 2, pp 114–26.

Wills, J. and Simms, M. (2003) 'Building reciprocal community unionism in the UK', *Capital and Class*, no 82, Spring, pp 59–84.

Willse, G. (2008) '"Universal data elements", or the biopolitical life of homeless populations', *Surveillance and Society*, vol 5, no 3, pp 227–51.

Wilson, J. and Musick, M. (1997) 'Who cares? Toward an integrated theory of volunteer work', *American Sociological Review*, vol 62, no 5, pp 694–713.

Wolfsfeld, G., Segev, E. and Sheafer, T. (2013) 'Social media and the Arab Spring: politics comes first', *The International Journal of Press/Politics*, vol 18, no 2, pp 115–37.

Wood, E.M. (1989) 'Rational choice Marxism: is the game worth the candle?' *New Left Review*, no 177, September–October, pp 41–88.

Woodiwiss, A. (2001) *The visual in social theory*, London: Althone.

Woolthuis, R.K., Hillebrand, B. and Nooteboom, B. (2005) 'Trust, contract and relationship of development', *Organization Studies*, vol 26, no 6, pp 813–40.

Worth, O. and Abbott, J.P. (2006) 'Land of false hope? The contradictions of British opposition to globalization', *Globalizations*, vol 3, no 1, pp 49–63.

Wright, S. (2006) 'Government-run online discussion fora: moderation, censorship and the shadow of control', *British Journal of Politics and International Relations*, vol 8, no 4, pp 550–68.

Wright, S. (2012) 'Welfare-to-work, agency and personal responsibility', *Journal of Social Policy*, vol 41, no 2, pp 309–28.

Wright, S. and Street, J. (2007) 'Democracy, deliberation and design: the case of online discussion forums', *New Media and Society*, vol 9, no 5, pp 849–69.

Yesil, B. (2006) 'Watching ourselves: video surveillance, urban space and self- responsibilization', *Cultural Studies*, vol 20, nos 4–5, pp 400–16.

Yiä-Anttila, T. (2005) 'The world social forum and the globalization of social movements and public sphere', *ephemera*, vol 5, no 2, pp 423–42.

Yildiz, M. (2007) 'E-government research: reviewing the literature, limitations, and ways forward', *Government Information Quarterly*, vol 24, no 3, pp 646–65.

Youmans, W.L. and York, J.C. (2012) 'Social media and the activist toolkit: user agreements, corporate interests, and the information infrastructure of modern social movements', *Journal of Communication*, vol 62, no 2, pp 315–29.

Zedner, L. (2003) 'Too much security?', *International Journal of the Sociology of Law*, vol 31, no 3, pp 155–84.

Zick, T. (2006a) 'Place, space and speech: the expressive topography', *The George Washington Law Review*, vol 74, no 3, pp 1701–76.

Zick, T. (2006b) 'Speech and spatial tactics', *Texas Law Review*, vol 84, no 3, pp 581–651.

Index

Page references for notes are followed by n